CHICAGO PUBLIC LIBRARY

D0819288

Prosperity in the Information Age

DISCARD

To Mr. Jack Fuller
with compliments from

Prosperity

in the

Information Age

Creating Value with Technology
From Mailrooms to Boardrooms

James K. Ho

INFOTOMICS
Wilmette, Illinois

HC 79 .I55 H61 1994
Ho, James K. K.
Prosperity in the
 information age

INFOTOMICS
Wilmette, IL 60091-8028

PROSPERITY IN THE INFORMATION AGE
COPYRIGHT © 1994 BY JAMES K. HO

All rights reserved. No part of this publication may be reproduced, stored in a retrieval system, or transmitted in any form by any means, electronic, mechanical, photocopy, recording, multimedia, or otherwise, without the prior written consent of the publisher, except for the inclusion of brief quotations in a review.

International Standard Book Number: 1-885058-08-X

Library of Congress Catalog Card Number: 93-080630

Printed on acid free paper in the United States of America

See Appendix B for ordering information

94 95 96 97 98 99 10 9 8 7 6 5 4 3 2 1

Clip Art from HyperCard Stacks © Apple Computer, Inc.
Used with permission

RO3107 78925

To Anna

Contents

Preface

Ever since the first time I learned to use a computer twenty seven years ago, I have been wondering how this technology is going to change the way we work and live. Along the way, there were many revelations, enlightenments as well as trepidations and even disillusions. Gradually, they built up a perspective that, every now and then, seemed insightful enough to inspire a book on what it would take to make the best of technological advancement. Such a project never materialized, mainly due to personal priorities and circumstances. In retrospect, what appeared as missed opportunities turned out to be premature celebrations or false alarms after all. They reminded me of a Chinese parable known as "The Frontiersman's Lost Horse." There was a man who settled near the border of the old kingdom. One day, his prized stallion ran away. All his friends offered sympathy, but the man did not seem overly saddened. A week later, the stallion wandered back—with a beautiful, wild filly in tow. While his friends toasted his luck, the man remained nonchalant. A year went by. His friends were overcome by the news that his youngest son was crippled after being thrown by the filly. The man was stoic, as usual. Soon after, war broke out. All the young sons of his friends were drafted. Many never returned. So, who could tell whether losing a horse is a misfortune? Similarly, when is the right time to say whether living with new technology is indeed a blessing? Perhaps we can never know for sure. However, it is irrefutable that most barriers in time and distance are being eliminated by information technology. As an all-connecting and interactive cyberspace becomes our next frontier, it dawns on me that there is renewed urgency to face the future with the proper perspective. In particular, the days of minding one's own business as an innocent bystander are over. Henceforth, one is either part of a solution or part of a problem. Though it may sound ominous, this assumption actually presents unprecedented opportunities and optimism. This is how I know that it is time to tell about my view. But why a book? If I pretend to be forward looking, shouldn't this be done in digital multimedia? The fact that you are reading is one main reason—which also illustrates the theme throughout: What matters is a *balance* between how things get done and how technology can help.

While the book is composed entirely on my electronic desktop—in fact quite a few desktops on three continents at one point or another—it has benefited from observations of and discussions with colleagues, students, business associates, and friends. Too numerous to list, I thank them one and all. Especially encouraging is the seemingly pervasive reaction that regardless of personal opinion, everyone can immediately think of at least a dozen people who should be reading such a book.

I am particularly grateful to Joanne Gailar, Sylvia Khong-Terpstra, and Nelia Santana for helpful editorial suggestions; Apple Computer for permission to use its art bits in the illustrations; and Stephen Roach for permission to use his data on productivity.

Introduction

As we witness historical events live on television, and feel the pulse of the nation in virtually instantaneous opinion polls, there is little question that we have entered the Information Age. Knowledge capital and intellectual resources have become at least as important as their physical counterparts in the creation of economic value and the distribution of wealth. By ever expanding the access to information, technology is liberating the customer from the mass market, and the power of knowledge from the traditional gatekeepers. What does it all mean? Are we going to be better off? Judging from the global economic outlook as we approach a new millennium, the answer is not obvious. In this book, we take a common sense approach to sorting things out. Our point of view is that of someone who looks forward to an enjoyable life through rewarding work and meaningful social interactions.

While the book is addressed to a broad audience, its linear—line by line—format makes it impossible to customize the content to individual reader's interests and needs. To maximize its value, several tracks are suggested. The cover-to-cover track is for those with a stake in the future development of business in general, and management in particular. A self-improvement or career-development track is for those concerned with jobs and careers, and how to prepare for the workplace of tomorrow. Observers of the impact of technology on society can follow a third track. A fourth can be used as a nontechnical chronicle of current developments in social and economic affairs. A guide to these tracks is diagramed on the following page.

HOW TO USE THIS BOOK

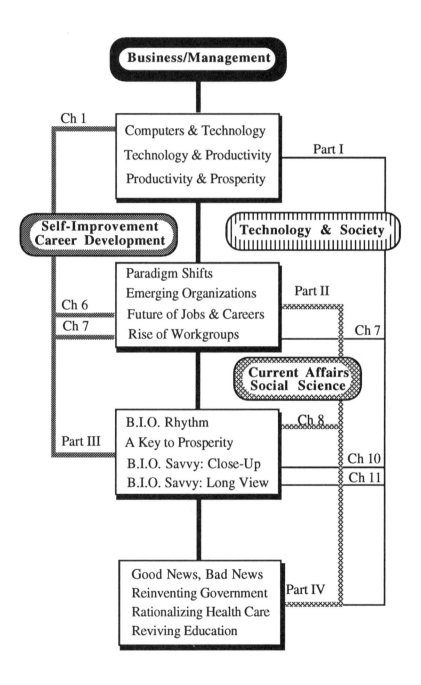

THE MOVEMENTS

While the four parts of the book follow a logical progression, each part can also be read on its own. In Part I, we take up a few most often asked questions regarding how we might work and live in the future. Do we all need to program computers to do well? Is there more to information technology than computers? Does this technology really improve our productivity? Does increased productivity automatically lead to prosperity for the work force? In the absence of clear-cut answers, several myths have taken hold. I shall attempt to debunk them so that we can focus on the real issues.

Much of the confusion is due to rapid changes that are taking place around us. We know that. But what are the two most significant changes that are reshaping the world of business? Why are they upsetting the status quo? In Part II, I will point out that even the status quo may not be well understood. There is much talk about our moving from an Industrial Age into an Information Age. It turned out that what happened between the two can be used to explain much of our predicament. With this knowledge, we can envision the next stages in the evolution of business enterprises. We will gain insight into the future of jobs and careers. What do employee loyalty and job security mean in the new age? What are going to be the building blocks for the economy? What are the new job opportunities? What are the scenarios for a prosperous society?

There is no denying that information technology is here to stay. However, what you see is often not what you get. Do fax machines and desktop publishing really change the way people work? Why is home banking so slow to catch on while ATMs flourish? Why do retailers get suppliers to manage their inventory? I show a way to explain these and other recent developments in the world of business. It is not a theory. It is not a prescription. It is an observation that there is a winning mind-set. I call it B.I.O. Rhythm. The initials stand for Business Information and Operations. The rhythm is a continually improving balance of technology and work. After explaining why it is the key to prosperity at all levels of a business enterprise, I discuss how we might get hold of it. Essentially, we need to cultivate an awareness of how things get done, and how technology can help. From this perspective, we take a close-up look at many contemporary technological issues. This is followed by a longer view of several topics with farther-reaching impacts. Many of the buzzwords may already sound familiar. What you can expect to get out of Part III is a way to make good sense out of them. The subtitle of the book: Creating value with technology—from mailrooms to boardrooms, is obviously put there to catch your attention. By the end of this third part, I can leave you to imagine what the future mailrooms and boardrooms will be like.

In Part IV, we look beyond business to see whether our insight can throw some light on other pressing social issues: government, health care, and education. The main problem, as we may find it somewhat shocking to discover, is that none of these sectors has entered the Information Age. Why? In any case, we see that the logical extension of B.I.O. Rhythm from a business mind-set to a social culture can show the way to a better society. However, we also get to recognize how formidable the obstacles are. And what they really are. The challenge is ours. Each of us must become part of a solution. My own humble bid is to share some hopes with you in the following pages.

Part I

Debunking the Myths

- Does everyone need to program computers in the workplace of tomorrow?

- Is there more to information technology than computers?

- What is the significance of the information infrastructure?

- How is white-collar productivity measured?

- Does information technology increase productivity in the workplace?

- Does increased productivity automatically lead to prosperity for the work force?

1

Computer and Technology

THE TORTOISE AND THE HARE

Natural evolution is a very slow process. Decades, even centuries are all but indiscernible on its scale of time. Yet, the human species, with its intelligence, has managed to accelerate the technological evolution of its own inventions to a mind-boggling pace. The centerpiece of this study in contrasts is the computer. As a machine, its capability has grown by leaps and bounds while its size shrank from room-filling to palm-fitting in just a matter of a few decades. Such progress is indeed impressive and perhaps overwhelming, especially in light of the role computers are playing in all modern forms of human activities that have become information intensive. It is only natural for many of us to equate the computer with information technology, and the lack of total confidence in commanding such machines with a symptom of falling behind the times. According to a poll conducted in 1994 by the Associated Press, more than half of the adult population feel this way. The discomfort can range from mild anxiety to acute "technophobia." As the bells and whistles multiply with what seems to be exponential growth of the power of microprocessors, the gap will only widen. Can one ever catch up? Even if one can handle a task on hand, the feeling of not being able to fully control the computer at will leaves much to be desired. It also seems to signify a power shift to those who can dictate their wishes on the smart machines. This feeling that one needs to be able to program computers to prosper in the Information Age is a myth.

One reason is that as computing technology matures, its intelligent use will be further removed from any of its technical details in both software and hardware. Another reason is that while information technology is indeed becoming critical to all economic activities involved in the production of goods and services, the computer will be just one of its several components. Therefore, it will be a significant waste of human resources if too many of us dabble in a narrowly focused topic that ultimately may not add value to our collective endeavors. This is not to undermine the importance of computer programming, but rather to emphasize that it is best left to those with particular interest and talent to specialize as professionals.

SHAKESPEARE AND SPREADSHEETS

There is no dispute that everyone should be at least computer literate. What does it mean in the current state of technology? For literacy in a written language, there can be functional guidelines for proficiency at various levels such as filling out a job application or reading a newspaper. The ability to comprehend and enjoy Shakespeare is probably beyond any basic definition of literacy. The situation is similar with computers. The current threshold, especially in the business environment, revolves around the familiarity with several so-called productivity tools: word processors, spreadsheets, and databases. However, no matter how much experience one has gained with the manipulation of such tools, it can still be a far cry from serious computer programming. Still, the myth persists: To be truly literate, one must know how to program.

How did this myth come about? A brief history may help unravel some of the mystiques surrounding our computing machines. Like other major inventions that changed our lives, such as the steam engine and the electric motor, computers were not originally conceived with popular use in mind. They were created by engineers and scientists for engineers and scientists to solve complex problems that would require endless person-years of tedious hand computation. It turns out that most mathematical methods for solving such problems are highly structured. Typically, they start with some initial guess at the solution, which can be way off the answer sought. Next, they make some changes by well spelled-out rules to improve on this first guess. Then they keep repeating the same process of improvement at every step until some conditions signaling a solution are met. This is the essence of algorithms: the organized, step-by-step procedures to solve numerical problems. While the actual sequence of operations required by algorithms to solve the problem can become very complicated, their iterative structure should still be relatively easy to describe. Therefore, it is ideal for machinery that can be organized to take care of the nitty-gritty details. To get started, we need to be able to represent any problem in a way that can be interpreted physically by machines. Our wealth of mathematics has already helped us express problems in terms of numbers. Naturally, we are most accustomed to the decimal number system, which uses the ten distinct elements of 0 to 9, perhaps because our hands have ten fingers. However, it takes only routine translation to convert to other number systems with any kind of basic elements. The simplest one has only two: 0 and 1. As usual, they are used for zero and one, respectively. To count to two, we already run out of basic elements. Unlike the decimal system, we do not have the use of 2 here, and so must proceed to use 10. The number three is represented by 11, and four by 100, and so on. This is known as the binary system. Few people can translate between the decimal and the binary systems on sight. And there is no need to. All we need to know is that it can be done routinely once we understand the correspondence. Now, the binary system is much more natural to express physically. There are many things that can take on one of two states at a time: electric currents can be on or off; magnetic poles can be positive or negative. Once we can establish such a correspondence between some physical state of matter and the binary numbers of 0 and 1, we are on the way to designing computers. The major task, by no means trivial, is to build logical switches that can turn the thing on when some conditions are met, and leave it off otherwise. By using appropriate combinations of logical switches, all the basic operations to compare conditions, to do simple arithmetic, and to store and retrieve individual items of information can be constructed. They all boil down to a sort of filling and emptying buckets. The isolated actions are rather mundane, but collectively they can accomplish truly marvelous feats.

SMALL IS BEAUTIFUL

By putting together a suitable collection of logical switches and memory registers (the buckets), we have the CPU (central processing unit). This is the "brain" of the computer. The first generation of such machines, dating back to the 1940s, had switches made of vacuum tubes, each roughly the size of a light bulb. Roomfuls of them were required to build a machine that did little more than what a credit card-size pocket calculator can do today. The ENIAC, which is commonly referred to as the first general purpose computer, had 18,000 vacuum tubes (consuming 150,000 watts of power!) and performed about 5,000 instructions per second. With the invention of transistors in 1947, the second generation of switching circuitry went solid state and became more compact. In the late 1950s, another breakthrough using semiconductors led to the third generation: integrated circuits (IC). These allowed an entire processor with about 100 components to be etched on a silicon chip. The fourth generation has progressively more components packed on a single chip. These computers on a chip are commonly known as microprocessors, microchips, or simply chips. The bench mark today is on the scale of ultra-large-scale integration (ULSI), which means around 3 million transistors capable of over 100 million instructions per second (MIPS). It is all on a chip of the size shown here on the left that consumes less than 10 watts of power. Intel's Pentium and Motorola's PowerPC microprocessors are examples of this class. Although absolute limits are imposed by the laws of physics, the trend of miniaturization is expected to continue for some time.

WATCH YOUR LANGUAGE

The electronic and logical nature of the machinery leads us to the first impression about computers: They speak in arcane languages and are very difficult to work with. This is definitely true at the level of dealing directly with the machines. All the logical switches that make up the instructions—for simple arithmetic, storing and retrieving data, and checking logical conditions—have to be strung together carefully to make anything work. To expedite communication with the hardware, these instructions are coded in extremely terse symbols and with little or no syntax. The approach is called programming in a machine language. The analogy is giving detailed instructions to an automobile as to exactly how much fuel to inject, and when to fire a particular cylinder: something we would not dream of doing while driving. At this level, even the seemingly trivial task of, say, sorting a bunch of numbers into ascending order will entail a sequence of undecipherable commands. As the demand for computer programming grew, higher-level languages were developed to ease the task. The level of sophistication is broadly chronicled by generations—the current being the fourth—that roughly correspond to the development of CPUs. Hence we see 4GL, which stands for fourth generation languages. Progressively, these languages are either more natural (i.e., English like) to the programmer, or have more powerful commands, or both. What make this possible are other programs that do the job of translators (actually known as compilers) or act as building blocks. They provide the shells within which a programmer can work without dealing directly with the primitive controls and instructions used to drive the hardware.

Before microprocessor chips were mass-produced in the early 1970s at relatively low costs, computers came mostly as large, expensive units called mainframes (e.g., the IBM 360 series) or slightly smaller and less expensive ones called minis (e.g., the DEC PDP series). They remained in the domain of engineers and scientists as well as data processing centers for large business or government organizations. The early microcomputers were mainly made for hobbyists. It was not until the introduction of VisiCalc, the first electronic spreadsheet application, that personal computing really caught on. Nowadays, word processors, spreadsheets, databases, and network communication are considered the standard productivity tools for computer users and the reference points for computer literacy.

As personal computers become more powerful with each generation of microchips, the software applications that run on them have also been improved so that they are more easy to use. User-friendliness is the operational catch phrase to reassure the insecure. Is it true that computers are now so easy to program that one can construct any custom-tailored application without undue hardship? Unfortunately, that is not the case. The reason is that while the user interface—what one sees and does to interact with the machine—has become more appealing, the need for perfect logic remains exactly as before. With the use of a graphical user interface (GUI), which may include menus, icons, and familiar metaphors such as file folders and desktops, the control functions can be quite intuitive. Consider the spreadsheet, for example. There is the grid of cells standing by, all ready to accept data or formulas through simple pointing and typing. If a spreadsheet model is already in place, say, for the 1040 income tax form, then using it may indeed be easy. However, the setting up of the model is bona fide programming. Although it is greatly facilitated by the spreadsheet environment, the logical process is no less rigorous than any other form of computer programming: past, present, and future. Just ask the question: "How do you know that it is 100% correct?"

BETTER PAVED ROADS, BUT NO SHORTCUTS

Designed for ease of use, popular software applications are providing computer users with a programming environment that features myriad development tools. When you access a spreadsheet package, it starts out with a blank sheet. To figure out your income tax, you will need either a ready-made template for the 1040 form, or to build one on your own. If you buy one off the shelf (or more likely

Figure 1.1   Who needs to program computers?

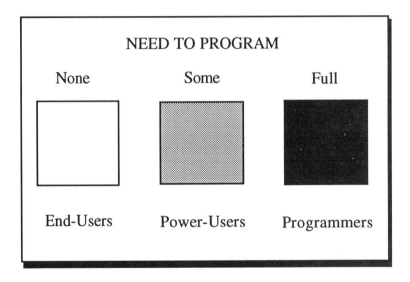

over the phone nowadays), you are an end-user. Apart from following instructions to enter the necessary data, there is no need to do any programming. Should you choose to program the tax form, you are an advanced or so-called power-user. This form of programming is also known as end-user computing. How far you get into serious programming depends of course on the complexity of the task involved. Adding up quarterly sales to find the annual total is simple enough. Coding a tax form with all the conditional rules and formulas will take more. In Figure 1.1, we depict this need to program as some shade of gray between the extremes for a pure end-user and a full-fledged programmer. Meanwhile, computer programming itself remains as complex and challenging as it has always been. With every enhancement to ease development, there will be more lofty goals to achieve. It is as exacting as any scientific endeavor. Any oversight, any lapse in logic, or simply a typographical error constitutes a "bug." A program will not work at all, or it will not work properly as long as there is a single bug left undetected. Even with the availability of highly sophisticated software design and development tools, the process of debugging programs remains as much an art as a science. It is usually impractical to test out all possible scenarios that the program can encounter. When a malfunction is observed, it is evident that a bug exists. By tracing the steps, sufficient clues may be discovered to pinpoint the culprit. However, when everything seems to work well, it may still be premature to guarantee that the program is completely bug free. A single bug in millions of lines of computer code had caused nationwide telephone networks to grind to a halt; another flipped a jet fighter over when it crossed the equator.

Software development has evolved as a craft. Most projects start from scratch with much effort spent on duplicating previous work. The industry is currently striving to adopt a manufacturing orientation, with products that can be engineered and assembled from standardized parts and component modules. In any case, computers themselves have not necessarily become easier to work with directly. What have become easier, or more user-friendly, are application programs such as word processors and spreadsheets. The important thing for the end-user is to focus on the application, evaluate how well it serves his or her purpose, and judge how easy or convenient it is to use. As we shall see below, there are many more aspects to information technology besides the computer. There is no need to insist on programming computers to benefit from the power of technology in the future.

THE SUM AND THE PARTS

Beginning with the 1990s, a new type of retail outlet emerges for consumer electronic products. These are the so-called superstores that carry all kinds of audio, video, phone, facsimile, and computer equipment under one roof.

Figure 1.2   The Converging Information Technologies

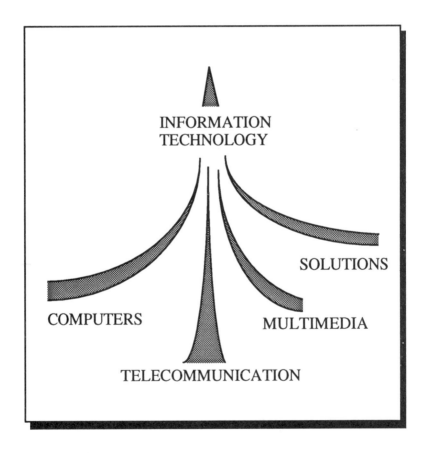

While the products are still grouped into clearly marked departments, such one-stop shopping is symbolic of things to come. They are all component parts to serve our needs to assess, process, and exchange information. Because of the way the different aspects of information processing have developed historically, we tend to keep them as distinct functions in our minds. We turn on the radio or television for news and entertainment, pick up the phone to talk to someone, drop a letter in the mail, and figure out income taxes on a personal computer. Already, many of these functions are being merged. With a fax machine, a letter can be transmitted over the phone line. Using a modem, the income tax return can be filed electronically. This is just the beginning. The convergence of information technologies is likely to shape the way we conduct business and enjoy our leisure as we enter the third millennium. To appreciate its full potential, it is important to identify its major components. In Figure 1.2 we depict the coming together of the computer, telecommunication, multimedia and solution technologies into what we shall henceforth refer to as *Information Technology* (IT).

THE VEHICLE

Computers, being the most visible and exemplary of electronic advancement, are often heralded as IT itself. In fact, they provide mainly the hardware and software environment in which information can be manipulated. We happen to be at a stage where such environments still require an ostensible presence of the hardware. So we sit in front of monitors, type on keyboards, insert diskettes into their drives, and perform assorted rituals of using computers. As further progress is made in the development of such environments, the physical aspects of the machinery will recede more and more into the background. Just as one can call home from anywhere to retrieve messages left on a recorder, eventually there is no need to be where the hardware is to process information.

THE ROAD

To accomplish what technologists envision as "ubiquitous information processing," telecommunication has to play a major role. Already, phone, fax, and data transmissions are commonplace. The major advances to come involve significant improvements in speed and bandwidth (which is analogous to the number of lanes on a highway) provided by networks of optical fibers or wireless microwaves. For a perspective of various transmission rates, we note that it takes about eight seconds to fax a page over conventional phone lines that operate at 2,400 bps (bits per second). At this rate, it will take over 1,900 years to transmit the entire textual content of the Library of Congress. With fiber-optic cables that are rated at 1.7 Gbps (Giga, or billion bits per second), this can be done in under 24 hours! Even without any call for downloading the Library of Congress, the capacity provided by fiber optics is necessary to carry high volumes of data-intensive messages such as full-motion video. It is also essential if we wish to connect all potential users to information suppliers eventually. Each single fiber is thinner than a human hair. It can deliver three episodes of a half-hour TV show per second. While cables with 20 to 40 strands of optical fibers have been in use, a half-inch cable can accommodate up to 130 strands. This is the basis of having a network of electronic super-highways as the infrastructure for our communication needs in the future. Actually, both the technology and a significant portion of the networking are already in place. By the end of 1992, there are over two hundred thousand miles of optical networks installed by local telephone and cable-TV companies, with another hundred thousand miles laid by long-distance companies. Questions remain as to who has control and how to police the superhighway; whether it should be left to free-market, competitive commercialization, or government-regulated, universal service; and what we can really get out of such unprecedented level of connectivity.

THE FUEL

This brings us naturally to the third component part of IT: multimedia. It includes all kinds of purveyors of information and entertainment in formats that can be served by telecommunication. For this reason, "infotainment" has also been used as an alternative neologism. Conventional television and the cable networks are obvious players. On-line information services that supply news briefs, stock quotes, home shopping, and travel reservations have also been around for years. Both federal and local governments are beginning to provide access to demographic and economic databases. Soon, movies can be ordered and viewed on demand; newspapers, magazines, museum tours can likewise be downloaded electronically. Teachers can design multimedia presentations drawing on material in remote libraries and research centers. The possibilities are endless. The scurry of deal making among phone companies, cable networks, and Hollywood that began in earnest in 1993 is evidence of the commercial potential of multimedia technology. Skeptics wonder whether the public will ever need a thousand movie channels. We shall see later on that the more challenging question to ask is whether we can tap the technology to solve some of society's problems and to improve the way we live.

With the volume and speed of data transmission, one can easily suffer from information overload. Critics are worried that following the trend set by conventional television, commercialization of the electronic superhighway will further turn us into a nation of couch potatoes. There is no dispute that the profit motive can sniff out the path of least resistance in the market culture. The injection of seemingly excessive doses of sex and violence by the entertainment industry is definitely less a conspiracy against society's moral fabric than simply pitching what sells best. This time around, there is a major difference though. TV has been a one-way street. Except for the choice of turning it (or any channel) on or off, the viewer is totally passive. Multimedia over the information superhighway will be interactive, allowing the user on the receiving end much more control. Potentially, this can change our whole mind-set toward information and entertainment. Instead of seeing what is on, and probably settling for whatever has been programmed, one can afford to be much more demanding in satisfying specific needs. One can begin to ask questions and look for answers. These can be as frivolous or as intellectual as one wishes. If analyzing the Brandenburg concerti sounds too serious, perhaps chatting electronically about an episode of a soap opera with a network of fellow devotees would be more fun. In any case, multimedia will be thought provoking and that may be our best hope of truly benefiting from the technology.

THE MAP

Once we start looking for answers, a fourth component of information technology comes into play. We shall call it the solution technology—solve-tech for short. Depending on the nature of the questions posed, this can span the gamut from simple database queries to the most sophisticated behavioral modeling and problem-solving methodologies. Since this is perhaps the least familiar aspect of IT, we will take a closer look in a later chapter. For the time being, we can get a good idea of its significance by imagining the following scenarios. It is after a long day of work. Things have been particularly hectic. A major project you are in charge of may have to miss its deadline. After a late super, you know it is best to take work off your mind a bit. How about a movie? Even the idea of having to pick one out of the thousands of available titles seems bothersome. Instead, you go to your computer, and quickly check off a list to summarize the mood you are in. In a second, a movie whose title you have never even heard of starts to show on the TV screen. Before you realize it, you are totally engrossed. When it is over, you feel relaxed and ready for a good night's sleep. Before retiring to bed, you remember to enter a brief comment on how much you liked the movie into the computer. Back in the office the next day, you set up a teleconference with the other key people involved in the project. Although they are all at different locations, you can discuss with them "face to face" through video windows on your computer screen. Gathering all the input each of them can provide, you pose the following questions. How much can be accomplished by the deadline with the current budget? Where is the bottleneck that is holding you back from doing better? What is the least additional budget you need to beat the deadline? The answers come out of the solution technology built into the IT systems you have access to. Armed with such information, you proceed to map out the best strategy with your colleagues. Is this science fiction? Not exactly. Most of the technological components have been around for years, if not decades. However, their convergence to a point that they become a seamless agent of information has yet to come. In anticipation, an awareness of the prospective benefits of converging IT will be crucial in our quest for prosperity in the Information Age.

Figure 1.3   An Extended Highway Analogy for IT

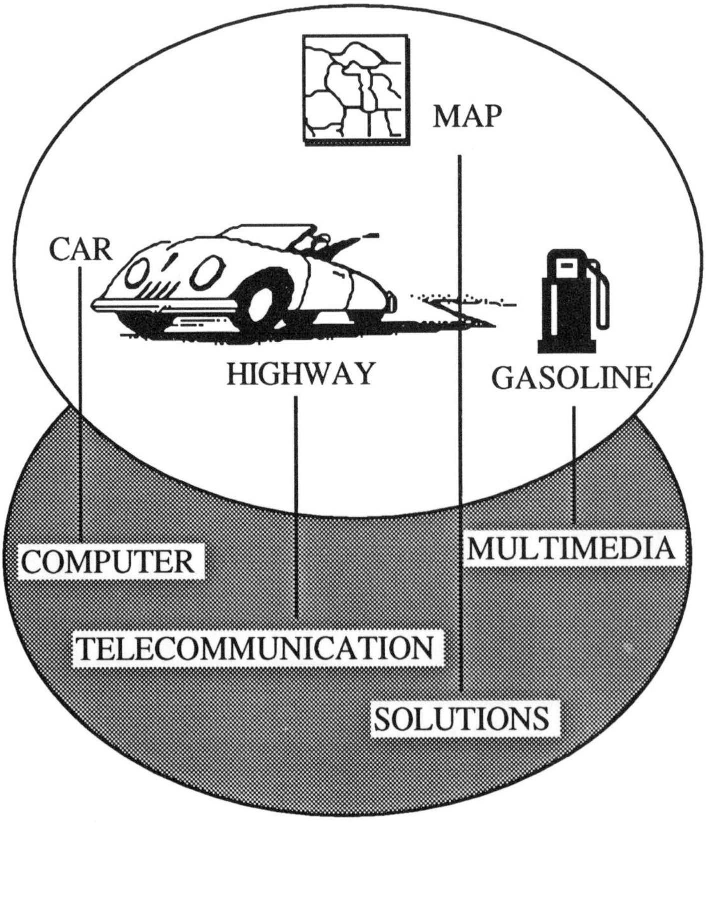

THE BIG PICTURE

Finally, it may help fix ideas to complete the picture of the electronic infrastructure as the information superhighway. If the telecommunication networks of fiber optics are the roadways, then computers are the cars that move us from place to place. Multimedia is the gasoline that fuels this transportation. Solution technology is the map that helps find the way. There is an important point to this extended analogy. We must remember that the road, the car, the gas, and the map are all only means to an end. If the travel is purposeful, there must be a destination. We want to get somewhere. How far or how fanciful that destination is may vary. Together, the four means get us there. Similarly, none of computer, telecommunication, multimedia, and solve-tech is an end to itself. We must have a destination for every trip on the information superhighway. It may be for the simple purpose of amusement, or economic gains, or more challenging goals of knowledge and skill, or even more noble ambitions of contributing to the common good. In this context, thinking of multimedia as a fuel—food for thought if you will—rather than an end product to be consumed is particularly apt. It may also hold the key to the eventual success or failure of the new infrastructure. Even though the technological means are ripe and Big Business (with the help of Big Government) is hungry to push the idea, there is no guarantee that it will fly. To be sure, if all it can do is to get us to watch endless movies and play interactive games, there is serious doubt that we can be productive enough to pay for what it will all cost.

Returning to the first myth that we are trying to debunk, we now see that information technology has indeed the potential to be a great enabler, and computers are just a part of it. Computer programming is akin to automobile maintenance in our highway analogy. It is a highly useful skill if you like it and have a knack for it. Other than that, there is no reason for it to be in the way of getting to where you wish to go. With that in mind, we want to see if IT can indeed help us become more productive at work.

2

Technology and Productivity

THE PARADOX

What is known as the *productivity paradox* has received considerable coverage in the popular press as well as more serious economic analysis. Essentially, it is the observation that the productivity growth in the nonmanufacturing sectors of the economy has been flat in the decades of the 1970s and 1980s. Meanwhile, close to a trillion dollars have been invested in information technology that is supposed to facilitate every task in the workplace and increase overall output per person-hour. Conclusion? Information technology does not lead to productivity gains and the investment in it has not paid off. This came from very influential economists and became part of the folklore of white-collar productivity. How true is it? As we shall see, for a combination of reasons, we may never know for sure. With hindsight, the apparent causes of the paradox can, however, be explained. In any case, it does not matter much anymore as we entered the 1990s, as there is convincing evidence that the investment in information technology is indeed paying off.

Let us review the productivity paradox in the 1970s and 1980s. The first issues to address are naturally: what to measure, and how to measure. With all the statistics on frequent display in the media, we might expect some clear-cut, logical answers. Amazingly, that is not the case. In essence, productivity is an indicator of how well we do turning input into output. The input can be human labor, raw material, capital, energy, etc. The output can be farmed or manufactured products, construction work, or services delivered, just to name a few. In the United States, most statistics related to estimates of productivity are based on measurements prepared by the Bureau of Labor Statistics (BLS) of the Department of Labor. It is therefore important to get at least an overview of how such statistics come about. BLS measures both input and output in terms of units, for example, the number of automobiles made, and not in terms of costs or prices. This is adopted to keep the results independent of inflation. Otherwise, changes in costs or prices can influence the productivity measurement even though the process of production remains the same. Depending on available data, it can happen that the only measurement of certain inputs and outputs are in dollar values. What is usually done in this case is to adjust for the effects of inflation by converting the current dollar values to "constant dollar" values of some given base year. For instance, suppose the price of an automobile is $10,500 in year 2 compared to $10,000 in year 1, and that this price increase is due to inflation. Then a sales volume of $105 million in year 2 (10,000 cars) is equivalent to a sales volume of $100 million in year 1 (also 10,000 cars). We can report the sales volume in year 2 as $100 million in constant year 1 dollars. This is consistent with the fact that although the dollar volume has increased from year 1 to year 2, the number of cars sold (10,000 in each case) has not changed.

Ideally, productivity should be measured by dividing the outputs by all inputs. It is difficult to imagine any product that does not involve a multitude of ingredients and production factors. However, it is often quite impossible to track and record all relevant factors. That is why we seldom see exact formulas expressing the output in terms of input. Instead, many different productivity measurements are in use by the BLS. The situation is not unlike the blind men trying to figure out an elephant. Collectively, all these measurements can indeed provide useful information. However, one must be aware of their limitations, especially when they are studied individually.

MEASURES OF OUTPUT

The total annual output for the entire country is commonly known as the Gross National Product (GNP). It accounts for all the goods and services produced by us as a nation, expressed in terms of inflation adjusted constant dollars for some base year. This measure of national productivity —actually just the output rather than output divided by input—is the charge of the Department of Commerce. As it is often of interest to focus on domestic activities, another common measure is the Gross Domestic Product (GDP), which is GNP minus all imports and exports. Now, it is easy to say: "Let's tally up all the goods and services produced in a year as the national output." However, in many cases it is not obvious at all how such contributions to GDP can be evaluated. When the output is a tangible product with a price tag, it seems that we can use the value of total sales. For example, the fee paid for any government subsidized service constitutes a revenue from the sale of such service. However, it certainly does not reflect the amount of productive work involved in providing the service. It turns out that in all cases where sales values cannot be used meaningfully, the Department of Commerce uses instead the cost of producing the output as the value of the output. In other words, output is equated to input. This implies that

Figure 2.1   Components of the Gross National Product

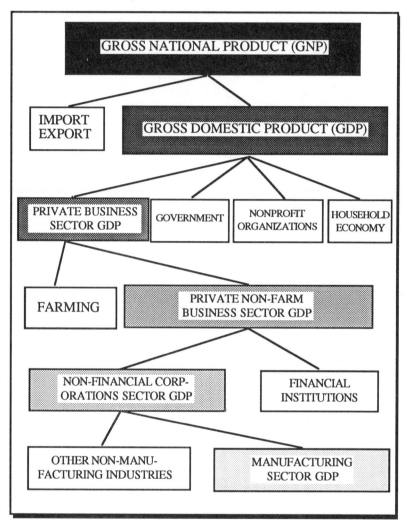

productivity will always remain at 100%. If the cost of production goes up, the value of the output goes up by the same amount. This way, we will never see an increase, or decrease, in productivity. Needless to say, this solution will not be too useful in any serious attempt to track productivity growth. Being aware of such shortcomings, BLS successively excludes sectors of the economy where it encounters difficulties with measurement so that the remainder can be more meaningful. This is illustrated in Fig. 2.1 in which the progressively narrower focuses are given in the shaded boxes. These are known as aggregate sectors of the economy. At each level, the white boxes represent subsectors that are either problematic or subject of separate accounting, and so have been isolated from the rest of the GDP.

Let us go down the tree, starting from the GDP. For Government and Nonprofit Organizations, as we have already seen, it is not clear what the output is and how it can be measured. Household economy, based on the labor of the domestically self-employed, is productive work but also defies accurate accounting. Leaving these three out, the aggregate remainder is broadly classified as the Private Business Sector. By its unique nature and historical significance, the Farming sector is treated separately. Within Non-Farm Private Business, output from financial institutions also lacks precise definition. This leaves Non-Farm, Non-Finance Private Business, which includes the Service and Manufacturing sectors. How does one measure the output of, say, the health-care industry? Again, BLS resorts to using the total cost of health care. The last remaining aggregate sector is Manufacturing, where the measurement of output is relatively more straight forward, as we can count the number of automobiles produced, for example.

MEASURES OF PRODUCTIVITY

To measure the productivity of an economic activity, we need to track both its input and output. We now see that in many sectors of the economy, it is quite difficult to identify and define the output precisely. The convention used by the Department of Commerce, in the accounting of the GNP and the GDP, is to equate input with output. This simply precludes meaningful discussion of productivity. For such reasons, the Bureau of Labor Statistics reports productivity measures for specific aggregate sectors of the economy. Several measures are used. The best known is the output per hour, which is given by the units of output divided by the number of work hours spent on their production. Note that this measure of productivity carries the assumption that labor is at least the primary component of the input. Another popular and related measure is the output per worker. It is perhaps intuitive for a business organization to consider its gross revenue divided by the number of workers as at least a rough indicator of their productivity. Similarly, output per worker should be useful for aggregate sectors of the economy. We therefore see economic output figures like $41,200/worker in the manufacturing sector compared to $28,700/worker in the service sector for the year 1985 as recorded in the 1987 Economic Report of the President of the U.S.A. Once again, we need to keep in mind that in large portions of the service sector, output is equated to input. Consequently, the numerator of the dollar per worker ratio may represent the cost rather than the value added. Even the denominator can be problematic. The number of workers employed at any time, as reflected by the number of jobs tracked by BLS, may not be known to any accuracy. In June 1992, BLS overestimated the number of jobs created in the economic expansion of the late 1980s by over half a million. Using that estimate, it reported that the recession, which lasted officially from June 1990 through March 1991, had cost that many more jobs than it really did. Such a margin of error had perhaps nontrivial consequences in the economic issues involved in the presidential election of that year. How can the government statistics be off by that much? It turns out that BLS relies in part on payroll and tax data provided by some six million U.S. companies to the Internal Revenue Service and state tax agencies. In the 1980s, many companies "outsourced" such data processing to contractors who counted payroll checks instead of employees. This way, any worker with a regular paycheck, an overtime check, and a bonus check was counted as three jobholders instead of one. This problem went unnoticed until a form was introduced in 1990 to count employees. As the new form was adopted into computer programs used by the data processing contractors, the sudden drop in the job count revealed the existence of the imaginary jobs. Rather than making light of such glaring discrepancies, we should simply be mindful of the many fundamental difficulties in getting a meaningful handle on what seems to be a straightforward notion of productivity. Nonetheless, based on government statistics, industry data as well as private research, many accounts of productivity growth for the U.S. economy are available. An example is given in Figure 2.2. This shows that while investment in information technology has been growing steadily, white-collar productivity is not keeping pace over the period from 1963 to 1989.

WHERE IS THE TECHNOLOGY PAYOFF?

Regardless of how productivity is measured, there is no dispute that the U.S. economy was rather stagnant in the decades of the 1970s and 1980s. As this coincided with the intensive introduction of information technology in the workplace, many influential critics questioned the wisdom

Figure 2.2   White-Collar Productivity through the 1980s lags Investment in IT

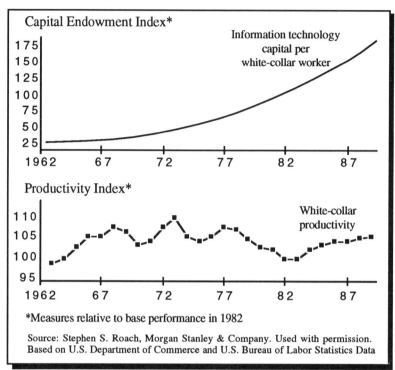

*Measures relative to base performance in 1982

Source: Stephen S. Roach, Morgan Stanley & Company. Used with permission. Based on U.S. Department of Commerce and U.S. Bureau of Labor Statistics Data

of such investments. Robert Solow from The Massachusetts Institute of Technology (MIT), a winner of the Nobel Memorial Prize in Economic Science, was quoted to say:

> "We see computers everywhere but in the productivity statistics."

Gary Loveman, an economist at Harvard University, reported at the 1991 Stewart Alsop computer conference:

> "...we simply can't find evidence that there has been a substantial productivity increase—and in some cases any productivity increase—from the substantial growth in information technology."

Stephen S. Roach, chief economist at Morgan Stanley & Company, wrote in the financial firm's *Economic Perspective*:

> "I dispute the idea that we need ever-increasing computational power to get work done by white-collar workers in the service sector. American business managers are hooked on technology."—July 1988.

> "The service sector owns more than 85% of installed base of information technology and its productivity increase is the lowest (average of 0.8%/year since 1982)."—January 1991.

According to various industry watch groups, the total investment in information technology amounted to anywhere from 800 billion to one trillion dollars since 1980. Just in terms of personal computer purchases alone, we see figures of 57 million units valued at some $90 billion during the 1980s. That is enough to put $10,000's worth of computing power on the desktop of each and every white-collar worker in the work force. Yet, there is no evidence of positive return to these investments. Such critical observations apparently have fueled skepticism in corporate suites as to the wisdom of following the high-tech trend. Meanwhile, more sympathetic and perhaps more far-sighted analysts offered various explanations for the phenomenon. These clues to the paradox all revolve around the word "change."

Change takes time:

It was observed that all the previous major technological innovations that seemed to have changed our lives overnight actually took time. Examples include the steam engine and the electric motor. Thirty years are not unusual for a new technology to take hold. By this yardstick, information technology is still on schedule, even if its own rapid development would lead one to expect a shorter gestation period.

Change calls for different measures:

As long as we take the output-divided-by-input view of productivity, and assume that the whole process remains stable, we are talking primarily about the efficiency of work. Suppose a customer service department handles 100 calls per day. If this number can be increased to 120 a day by using new technology, then we are quite ready to credit an increase of productivity to this change. However, with the help of information technology, the customer service agents can provide better service on each call because of more accurate on-line information. By eliminating the need for some repeated calls, the total number of calls may decrease. This effectively lowers the output. Depending on subsequent changes in the number of agents, the new system may or may not show an increase in productivity by our traditional measurements. Nonetheless, there is little doubt that the quality of service has improved.

Not enough of the right change:

It is obvious that doing the same wasteful things faster is not likely to lead to improvement. Unfortunately, that is the approach taken by many initial efforts to automate existing work processes. Data is collected in databases on computers; documents are digitized and sent over communication networks. However, most steps in the work sequences ended up in the same kind of bottleneck as before, when paper documents sat in people's in-bins most of the time. Eventually, it became clear that fundamental changes in the design of work processes are necessary to take full advantage of all the new capabilities afforded by ever-advancing technology. This typically goes under the catchword of "reengineering," which we will take up in more detail in a later chapter.

The above arguments suggest that with the proper mind-set and perhaps some patience, we can expect to see suitable payoff from information technology. Nevertheless, the influence of the critics has apparently been quite substantial and led many corporations to rein in their spending on information systems. According to a survey by the International Data Corporation, a research and consulting firm for information technology, less than half of major American companies approved increased budgets for technology in 1992—bucking a trend that lasted for over a decade. The economic recession in the preceding years must have been part of the reason. The uncertainty of positive pay-back, as promulgated in the productivity paradox, was also seen as a major factor.

IT IS HERE AT LAST

Just as the paradox is becoming part of the folklore for business and economic observers, new studies based on more up-to-date and more accurate data are claiming to have debunked its myth. Specifically, a report released in 1993 by Erik Brynjolfsson and Lorin Hitt of the Sloan School of Management at MIT tracked spending on centralized information systems at 400 of the Fortune 500 companies between 1987 and 1991. It sought to isolate the effect of computer purchases from other capital inputs on a company's output as measured by revenue. The results showed an average return on investment (ROI) of 54% in manufacturing companies, and 68% for manufacturing and services combined. The authors pointed out that their work focused on recent data, in contrast to previous studies that used data from the late 1970s and early 1980s. Moreover, the data was at the level of individual firms, which should provide better insight than those from industry averages. Critics were quick to remark that focusing only on centralized information systems and ignoring the impact of personal computing cannot produce a complete clarification of this complex issue. While the debate is bound to continue, we can nevertheless expect this and similar studies to provide the basis for a positive outlook regarding the impact of technology on productivity. A report by McKinsey & Company in 1992 indicated that American workers in many industries are more productive than their European counterparts in large measure due to spending on information technology in the 1980s. Along the same lines, Morgan Stanley's Stephen Roach wrote in 1993, "The U.S. economy is now entering its first productivity-driven recovery since the 1980s, courtesy of efficiency gains being realized through intensified use of information technology."

That there is finally evidence of the technology payoff in the productivity statistics reported by government and industry is certainly encouraging. Even though we must still take most of the actual measures and figures with a grain of salt, we can be confident that collectively they do signal a positive trend in the benefits of IT. The reasons behind such a turn-around are again due to the change process. First, companies have by now gone through the "growing pain" portion of the learning curve in harnessing technology. As a result, they have learned that simply

**Figure 2.3   Conventional Work Process for
Insurance/Loan Application**

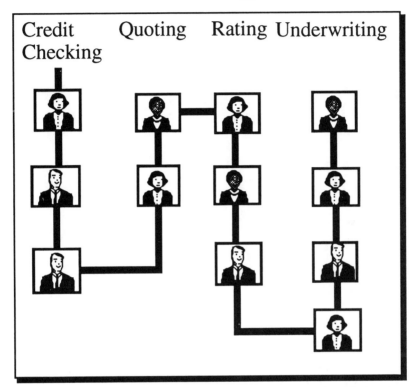

automating existing work processes does not usually lead to improvement in productivity. To make the technology payoff, more and more companies are remaking themselves and incorporating entirely new and more streamlined methods of doing business. Perhaps the most striking examples come from the financial-service companies where the return to a continuous wave of investment in cutting-edge technology had been most disappointing. Aetna Life and Casualty Company, for instance, was no newcomer to computerization. Yet, up to 1992, it still took up to 15 days to issue a basic policy through 22 business centers with a staff of 3,000. Since as many as 60 different employees were

Figure 2.4   Computerization of Conventional Work Process

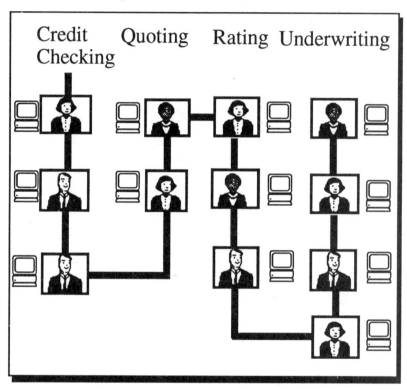

involved in handling an application, much of the total processing time was spent in people's in-baskets. Therefore, computerization of the individual steps of the process did not save much time. By changing the entire process, Aetna can now get a policy issued within 5 days. This is done by having a single case manager process an entire application. He or she can access all the necessary actuarial information using a personal computer connected to a network of companywide databases. Furthermore, it takes only 4 business centers with 700 employees. This example of rethinking work to take real advantage of technology is depicted schematically in Figures 2.3-2.5.

Another example is the Federal National Mortgage

Association, the largest buyer of home mortgages in the U.S., and known affectionately as Fannie Mae. It has long relied on a centralized approach to information management, deploying some of the most powerful mainframe computers. As its business grew in both volume and complexity, it became apparent that processing information in this manner would not allow the company to keep up. To meet the challenge, it adopted the approach of using teams that comprise all the necessary business functions—such as finance, accounting, and marketing—to work on any particular assignment. The teams are connected through a network of over 2,000 personal computers. With this strategy, Fannie Mae was able to handle close to a doubling of its business volume from 1991 to 1992 with only a 3% increase of its work force of about 3,000. Profits jumped 13% and the $10 million investment in the decentralized information network was said to have paid for itself within a year.

Figure 2.5 Technology Payoff through Reengineered Work Process

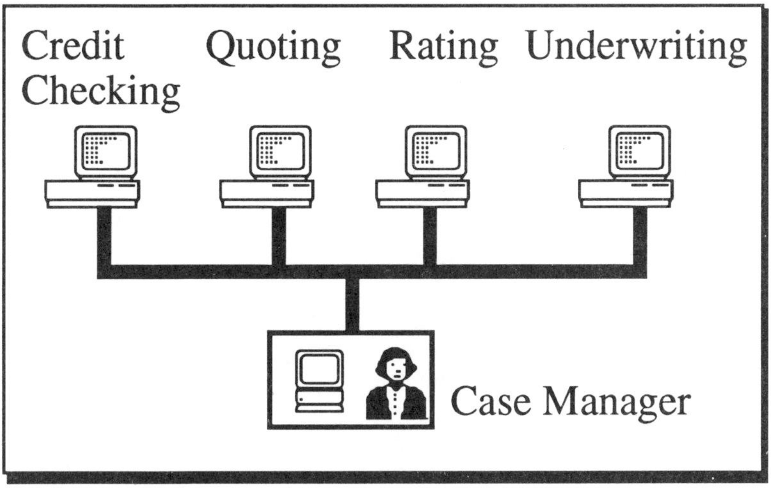

3

Productivity and Prosperity

Whether we count from the days when the first mainframe computer was installed in the corporate world some forty years ago, or when the first personal computer (PC) was introduced commercially in 1971, the time lag in adapting to the new technology for significant gain in white-collar productivity appeared to have come to past. The business press is now ebullient with reports on the technology payoff. It also points out that since the U.S. appears to be ahead in this regard, we might be able to regain some of the competitive advantages lost over the last few decades to Europe and Asia. Even the garment industry is said to have hopes of a revival by tapping into information technology. The latter allows manufacturers to produce clothing that has actually been ordered rather than stockpiling parts for garments with highly uncertain demands due to the vagaries of fashion.

Should we conclude that we have finally caught the wave, and that we can expect our economy to prosper from continuing gains in productivity? Should the strategy for Corporate America be based on an extrapolation of this payoff? If we can indeed learn from history, this may very well be another myth in the making. In that case, we would be better off debunking it before it takes hold. My contention is that productivity is necessary but not sufficient for prosperity. Just like quality, it will become a prerequisite for survival in business but not the key to growth and advancement.

There are a number of issues involved here. First and foremost is the question of sustainable success. In the industrial era, products and markets changed relatively slowly

41

and predictably. By now the blunder made by the U.S. automobile industry in failing to recognize the demand for fuel-efficient small cars seems obvious. One may think that we will be smart enough in the future not to see history repeat itself. Then how about IBM's failure to recognize the fading dominance of mainframe computers? For a given product with a constant demand, high quality can certainly help with the market share; productivity gains can raise the profit margin. With technological advances, products and market demand can change overnight. Once digital recording on compact discs caught on, the fate of the phonograph record is sealed regardless of how well or how efficiently they can be manufactured. Being able to do more with less means higher productivity, but it counts only if we are doing the right thing.

THE MARKETING OF VALUE

In the heyday of mass production, economy of scale allowed large conglomerates to influence market forces, cultural taste, and even social values. This has given rise to strategic marketing. You have got to have it if you are "hip," "cool," "with-it," or whatever the current lingo for the consumer as conformist happens to be. The approach worked quite well with the mind-set of conspicuous consumption in the baby-boomer generation of the 1980s. With stagnating growth in the global economy, consumers are a lot more value conscious. High quality at reasonable cost to meet customized demand becomes the slogan for value marketing. Not only does it have to be good, it also helps to be demonstrably differentiable from one's competition. In this light, the plight of the ailing airline industry seems almost self-evident. They all fly more or less the same

planes, serve the same not so appetizing food, and go to
about the same places at about the same time. Only the
colors of the paint job or carpeting tell the airlines apart
—and of course the languages if you consider the industry
worldwide. Why do airlines have such a hard time differ-
entiating their services? Productivity is the reason. I am
sure you agree that the most enjoyable flights are more
than half empty. One can stretch out and breathe relatively
clean air while being offered the option of keeping the
entire can of soda. The problem is the more satisfied customers like that, the sooner for that airline to go out of
business. So, productivity means squeezing as many seats as
possible into the body of the plane, and using the latest
yield-management technology to try to pack every flight.
Similarly, all automobiles become looking more or less the
same. Given the amount of room desired in a design, the
required quality and performance, the target costs, etc.,
there are just not that many "optimal" solutions.

All this does not say that it is impossible, just hard to
compete when customers are value rather than trend or
fashion conscious. At least in the case of the automobile,
consumers have over the years been accustomed to relatively constant value standards. The price of the average
car actually remains remarkably stable after adjusting for
inflation. The Ford Mustang was introduced in 1964 at a
base price of $2,368. Assuming an average inflation rate of
5.5% per year, this amount would be about $13,372 in
1994. This is amazingly close to the $13,365 base price for
the all-new model introduced that year. Obviously, one gets
significantly more advanced features for performance,
safety, and comfort in 1994 for the same money. This is
again a definite form of productivity gain that does not
show up in econometric statistics. In any case, consumers

know somehow what to expect from a $14,000 car. It is not difficult to envision the costs of research and development, labor, raw material, production, distribution, marketing, etc., as a tangible framework to evaluate the worth of such a product.

TROUBLE IN THE SKIES

This is not the case with airfare. With economy of scale and improved productivity, air travel is indeed getting less expensive in terms of cost per passenger-mile. However, it is much more difficult to gauge the value of the service provided by an airline to fly us from Chicago to San Francisco. Casually, we may recall that it cost a few hundred dollars in 1974, and it costs a few hundred dollars in 1994. Even more vividly, what stuck in our minds are probably those super-low, $99 round-trip fares that are the results of occasional and perhaps even periodical fare wars among the competing airlines. This has the unfortunate effect of giving customers the impression that $99 is what the trip is really worth. Any higher fare must represent a comfortable profit margin. Since the airlines keep losing money—the magnitude of continual losses is indeed mind-boggling: $10 billion in 1990-1992 for the industry—they must be doing something wrong. Among the perceived problems is paying their top executives what many consider to be inordinately high salaries and benefits. This view is obviously naïve, but if it is the perspective of the customers, caveat vendor!

While we are on the subject, let us examine the customer's point of view even further. It is safe to assume that for any traveler, a trip starts from one's residence, office, or a hotel at the originating city and ends also at one such location in the destination city. It does not just go from one airport to another. In fact, the amount of time it takes, and the cost of local transportation to and from the airport are usually nontrivial. Especially for a stranger in town, it can also be the part of the trip that causes the most anxiety. Yet, the airline industry apparently never gave much thought to this door-to-door rather than airport-to-airport perspective of a passenger. A few airlines do operate "city terminals" in some major cities where passengers can check in their luggage in town, and take a shuttle bus to the airport. While these exceptions are few and far in between, they are at least in the right direction of catering to the basic need of the customer. Seen in this light, perhaps some notion of door-to-door service may not be so far-fetched and can provide new and revitalizing opportunities for competition. After all, the major airlines have already begun to shed off their less profitable regional routes to smaller carriers who can operate at lower overhead costs. Partnerships are formed to expedite flight connections and baggage transfers to minimize inconvenience to passengers heading to a small-town destination. It is therefore quite conceivable that alliances can be struck with local ground transportation services to provide a seamless door-to-door package for any particular voyage. Another assumption is that no one really goes on a flight for the meal service. Nevertheless, it is what I perceive as what over 90% of the in-flight service is about—with flight attendants contorting in tight quarters to perform the elaborate routines. Typically, we get what amounts to a child's portion of a meal that may cost us between $5 to $10 at a diner. I am sure it costs the airlines more for the production, and of course it shows up in the fare. Given that a flight covers meal time, and that the typical passenger spends at least half an hour waiting at the gate, I wonder if it would be more cost-effective to serve a meal at a cafeteria near the gates.

While these ideas may or may not be practicable, they do serve as examples of new kinds of value judgment by the customers. To prosper in the future, businesses will have to learn to be flexible and responsive to such changes. By contrast, even sophisticated approaches to improving productivity along conventional lines can seem tangential. Let us take a look at yield management. This is a dynamic planning tool that airlines have been developing and using to maximize revenue from their fleet and crew capacities. For various reasons, many passengers book flights and never show up. If airlines book only up to capacity, chances are even fully booked flights will leave with empty seats. Therefore, it pays for airlines to routinely overbook in the hope of getting just the right number of passengers. The downside is of course when too many people do show up. The penalty then is in the form of loss of good will, and extra costs to accommodate or transfer those who are booked on the nonexistent capacity. With such tradeoffs, what is the appropriate amount to overbook? It turns out that the problem is amenable to statistical decision analysis, and powerful mathematical models have been implemented to guide the reservation systems. A closely related problem is that of allocating seats to the many different fare classes. Obviously, it would be ideal to sell every seat at full fare. Knowing that this is not likely, airlines entice customers with myriad discount fares. The discounts come with varying restrictions on advance purchase, minimum stay, flight changes, and cancellation to help lock in more plan-ahead sales. This should be done insofar as not having to turn away passengers ready to pay full fare. Again, given sufficient data—on past demands for the flight, patterns of customer behavior, and the fare differentials—optimal allocations can be computed. By linking such yield-management systems to the reservation systems, the fare allocations can be revised dynamically, perhaps on a daily basis, relying on the latest information on actual bookings. According to the airlines, the practice of yield management has become a very significant factor in their continuing efforts to increase productivity. This is very encouraging, but it should be remarked that so far, such efforts are based on established values that may be changing. Unless airlines can anticipate and be responsive to new customer needs, productivity figures may not lead to sustainable prosperity. What kind of changes are conceivable? The assumption has been that business travelers can afford full fare and need the flexibility of little or no restrictions. Leisure or budget-conscious travelers, on the other hand, can plan ahead and forgo flexibility in return for substantial savings. A couple of random observations recently made me wonder whether such trends will soon be bucked. First, on certain routes, I was surprised how difficulty it is to book even well in advance. An example is from Chicago to Vancouver, B.C. in the summer. It turns out that Alaskan cruises leaving from the Canadian port have become quite popular. Unlike typical land-based vacations, the cruise schedules are rather rigidly planned. Therefore, travelers need to lock into the appropriate flights, with or without the incentive of fare discount. In the economics parlance of "shadow pricing," airlines are perhaps undercharging for such flights. Meanwhile, a seat on a flight is a perishable good. Once the plane takes off, the value of the empty seat disappears forever. With information technology allowing easy access to what is available on any flight, it may be just a matter of time that some airline will start "auctioning" off remaining seats with fares dropping as flight time approaches. Again, far-fetched ideas for the moment, but no one knows for sure. With business striving to cut costs and the advent of video conferencing reducing the need for conventional business travel, nothing should be ruled out.

THE TECHNOLOGY TRADEOFF

The second issue in linking productivity directly to prosperity is more social than individual in nature. It stamps from the fact that the emerging technology payoff in productivity is accompanied by significant job losses. Economists and politicians steeped in the boom-and-bust precept of the business cycle may be optimistic about an upturn sometime soon. Even if information technology does displace white-collar workers, they are confident that new jobs will be created just like our previous transitions, first from farming, and later with factory automation. The difference is that this time around, the job loss is not simply the result of a weak economy in recession. When many of the Fortune 500 companies—including General Motors, IBM, Proctor & Gamble, and Sears Roebuck—restructure with massive layoffs, many of the jobs are gone forever. Most are positions in middle management that became redundant with more information being processed by fewer employees using computers and communication networks. In 1993, Procter & Gamble announced the elimination of 13,000 jobs and the closing of 147 manufacturing plants over three years. CEO Edwin Artzt predicted that by 1996, the restructuring will lead to fewer layers of management and a simplified approach to running the business. The emerging management dogma is to focus on what adds value to the business. Everything else that does not, be it paperwork, outdated products, even entire branches and departments, can be trimmed off as excess fat.

What we witness are fundamental changes in how business gets done. It is no inadvertent release of the genie out of the bottle. Intensifying global competition within a stagnating international economy called for such changes. With information technology shrinking time and distances, a credo for business in the 1990s can very well be: If you are not doing it well, someone else will do it somewhere else. Even IBM, which for decades prided itself in a no-layoff policy, must succumb to market forces and down-size. The rippling effect through the economy amplifies the impact of restructuring by major corporations. It is esti-mated that half a million people may be put out of work with General Motors' layoff of 74,000 planned in 1992.

The changes are structural and not cyclical, and hence are not amenable to conventional intervention by the gov-ernment through its fiscal and monetary policies to stimu-late the economy. If we subscribe to the perpetuity of the business cycle, 1993 fits the bill for a recovery from the recession that officially ended in March 1991. Both interest rates and inflation are at record lows. Consumers are expected to take advantage of low-interest financing for big-ticket items such as homes, cars, and appliances. Spurred by the increased demand, businesses will borrow money to expand production and operations, which in turn should stimulate growth in the supporting service and tech-nology industries. A surge of hiring should accompany the increase in output. Then, as demand for loans and products have increased enough to drive up interest rates and inflate prices, consumer spending and borrowing will decline. Businesses curtail production and lay off workers, drop-ping prices to reduce inventory. So the cycle repeats itself.

The National Bureau of Economic Research, a private group that is the official caller of the blips and dips, identified 30 complete cycles between 1834 and 1958, each averaging about four years in length. To stimulate the economy, government used to rely on its fiscal and monetary tools: easing the money supply, allowing more investment tax credits, or increasing spending. However, the national debt is already approaching $4 trillion by 1994, requiring well over $200 billion a year to service interest payments alone. Further massive government spending and borrowing can only accelerate the decline. Also, pump-priming the money supply to fine tune the economy no longer works as well as before. This is because much of the output is now generated by newer, smaller firms that are not even tied to the financial system controlled by the federal government.

In any case, what we see by mid-1993 is a persistent reluctance of Corporate America to hire. Most businesses have come to realize that they need to further boost productivity to stay competitive in the global market. That means higher output per worker. With ever-escalating costs of health care and benefits, labor has become even more expensive. In contrast, prices for information technology keep falling. It is therefore only natural to keep payrolls lean while taking advantage of the technology payoff for improved productivity. The wholesale trade, and the insurance and commercial banking industry, both of which are investing heavily in information technology, shed 53,000 and 33,000 jobs in 1992, respectively. The linkage between employment and business output has been severed. As a result, we are likely to see increased profits from business, higher output for the economy, and yet a net decline in living standards—hardly an equation tying productivity to prosperity.

THE PROSPERITY DILEMMA

For the nation to prosper, regardless of the productivity of existing business enterprises, it will be crucial for new jobs to be created. Indeed, President Bill Clinton declared job creation as the key indicator of success for his presidency. It is worth noting that over the past 15 years, the Fortune 1000 companies have collectively cut 3 million jobs instead of contributing to any net increase. Nonetheless, the economy generated 36 million new jobs, most of which are in small and medium-size businesses. Initially, small companies would not expect information technology to be cost-effective for them. The relatively simple paperwork typically could not justify the investment, maintenance, and training involved in computerization. Hence they became creators of the many new jobs. This time around, things have changed. Even the little guys found that it is more productive for them to use technology rather than people. Also, they increasingly find technology to be a prerequisite for dealing with their larger partners. So the recovery cannot count on small and medium-size businesses to make up for the downsizing trend in larger firms that is likely to continue during the 1990s. What kind of new jobs will there be? Is our work force prepared for them? These are important questions that we shall discuss in more detail later.

Now that we have seemingly resolved the *productivity paradox*—that after more than a decade of tinkering we have finally learned how to make information technology payoff—we are faced with what amounts to a *prosperity dilemma*. As we increase productivity through technology, fewer people are needed to do the work. Visions of the future have companies striving to constantly "reinvent" themselves to stay competitive. The industrial-military complex that sustained the economy during the Cold War must now transform itself into nimble and responsive players in the global market. For workers, jobs are at once more challenging and less secure. Gone are lifelong skills and lifelong employment. "Lifelong learning" are new buzzwords being bounced around corridors in corporate human resource departments as well as classrooms in business schools. In the old economic order, most jobs are never done. In the fast-paced Information Age, it seems a job well done is a job done away with. That is ultimate productivity. How should people be motivated? What will be the driving force toward prosperity?

FROM BOOM TO BUST

It used to be the American dream that equated working hard to getting ahead, economically and socially. Stability and security played a major role. Each generation worked for and actually attained better living standards than their parents'. This may no longer be feasible for the 75 million Americans under 30 years of age. They will be the first not to be able to live as well as their parents. Indeed, the median income of households headed by a person under 30 years of age has declined 13% compared to that of 1973, after adjusting for inflation. The 38-odd million born from 1965 to 1975 are referred to as the "baby busters," reflecting the drop in birth rate after the post-World War II baby boom that lasted roughly from 1946 to 1964. The youngest of the baby-bust generation are graduating from high school. The oldest are still under 30. They are the new blood of our work force. A whopping 40% of them are children of divorce. Many grew up as "latchkey" kids

—children with working parents—who came home from school to empty houses. Most are educated in deteriorating public school systems. Mindful of the bleak economic outlook worldwide, and the violence and destitute of the urban plight, this generation is taking on its own attitude toward work. In contrast to the "baby boomers," who are often stereotyped as greedy, pampered, and money-driven yuppies, the "busters" as a group are not inclined to climb the corporate ladder. According to polls conducted by the Roper Organization as well as by USA TODAY/CNN, the majority of them feel that a job is just a job, if one can be found. Unless we can come up with a good way to motivate this generation of workers, we might as well forget about the race for prosperity. I believe it can be done, as I shall attempt to establish the case in the rest of the book.

TRIANGLE OF POWER

Before we can offer hope and paint a more rosy picture for the future, we must dwell a bit more on some root causes of our economic malaise. As we have already indicated, doing things efficiently and improving on productivity can help an organization prosper only if its activities, goals, and directions are aligned with the needs of its customers. The organization must also be responsive to their changing needs and ever more sophisticated demands. This is somewhat easier with smaller, more flexible businesses where managers are owners, and most workers deal more or less directly with customers. In large, complex corporations, it is often difficult, if not impossible, to establish and maintain an effective sense of purpose and direction among diverse groups. This is especially difficult with groups engaged in work that may seem far removed from the customers. Sure enough, top executives have put much emphasis on mission statements and strategic plans. Is that going to work? Perhaps a closer look at the reality of corporate governance will help us appreciate the inherent difficulties. As Michael T. Jacobs explained in *Short-Term America*, there are three parts to the triangle of power in any business enterprise: investors, managers, and workers. Ideally, all three groups should share the common goal of prosperity for the company. If the company does well, all of them benefit. Investors gain from the return on investment, managers from the power and perks for executives, and workers from job security and attractive wages. In practice, it is never possible to determine objectively some universally acceptable standards for equitable distribution of such benefits. Promoting and protecting the interests of the individual groups became familiar scenarios of power struggle in the chronicle of business enterprises. For much of the first half of the twentieth century, the conflict had been between management and workers, as the interests of investors and managers were quite well aligned in their position of economic power. Labor unions were created to enable labor in collective bargaining for improved job conditions, compensations, and other protection from forces of exploitation. Management made every effort to allow for as few concessions as possible. Frequent conflicts resulted in crippling strikes, declining productivity, and antagonistic mind-sets that destroyed morale and team spirit. As unions became a major political force, their demands turned rigid, undermining the competitiveness of the enterprises of which they are an integral part. The do-it-by-the-book mentality espoused doing no more and no less than what is spelled out in a job description. It was not compatible with the culture of quality and continuous improvement that emerged as a key to survival in business in the latter half of the century. Keep in mind that the major reason Detroit fell behind Japan in automobile manufacturing is not cheap labor, but rather the number of hours required to produce similar cars and the number of defects per car. (According to a survey by the International Motor Vehicle Program at MIT, the average figures in 1989 were 16.8 hours/vehicle and 52.1 defects/100 vehicles for Japanese-owned plants in Japan, versus 24.9 hours/vehicle and 78.4 defects/100 vehicles for American-owned plants in North America.) By now, American management and labor are quite aware of the need for better teamwork to keep their companies afloat, not to mention getting ahead. In the mid-1980s General Motors' Saturn project pioneered a new working relationship with the United Auto Workers (UAW) union. Workers participate in management decisions and have their compensation tied to the quality of the products. Significant investments in extensive and continuing training are also made to further improve on the responsiveness of management and the flexibility of labor in adapting to constant changes in the global market. This and other similar efforts to empower workers as part of the process of Total Quality Management seem to be helping many companies boost their competitive advantage.

That is the good news. The bad news is that we are witnessing history repeat itself. Only this time, it is between investors and management. It goes back to the question of ownership and governance. Given that a company has some generic business goals, which necessarily include its economic prosperity and staying power, who should determine its major directions and strategies? For a small company, whose owner and manager are either one and the same, or at least closely allied in the sense that the owner can always fire the manager, the answer is quite obvious. It is up to the owner. With publicly held companies, the issue has become tricky and problematic. In the early days of share-holding capitalism, people bought shares in a company as an investment in that company. Apart from aspiring to partake in its profits, there was at least a sense of acquiescence in what the company stood for: its mission, culture, and even its style of conducting business. In no matter how limited an extent, it was a partnership—a pooling of resources to create value and accumulate wealth. So, investors bought pieces of the IBMs and AT&Ts of American enterprises, along with both rights and responsibility of ownership. Nowadays, these same companies, along with most others, are little more than the numbered slots on the roulette table in a casino. They are largely instruments of a gambling game of high-tech finance. Computerized trading programs issue buy and sell orders based on complex mathematical models of the stock market, rather than on any fundamental reasons reflecting the true value of particular companies. Many investors, whether individual or institutional, such as pension funds, often hold stocks through index funds that treat shares in any company only as part of a bundle of securities. Arbitrageurs have figured out how pieces of many companies can be worth more when sold off than kept in business. They engineer takeover bids that turn shareholders into simple-minded profit seekers who are willing accomplices at the right price. As new owners, their interest is often in milking the organization for what it is worth, rather than truly long-term commitment to foster its business activities. Some observers credit such games on Wall Street for keeping management on its toes, arguing that corporations that are efficiently run are less natural targets of hostile

Figure 3.1   Constituencies of a Modern Business

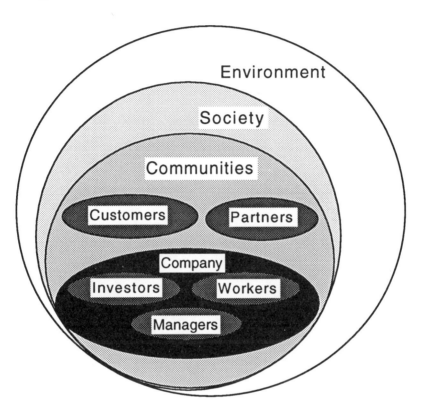

takeovers. Nonetheless, abrupt changes in ownership are generally considered to be counterproductive. To protect itself, management has devised barriers, including changes in corporate laws in most state legislatures, to insulate companies from their owners. This disengagement of ownership raises many issues regarding the accountability of enterprises to their many constituencies. As depicted in Figure 3.1, these include the welfare of society and concerns for the environment. In this context, productivity is only one factor in the equation for prosperity.

Part II

A New Driving Force

- What happened between the Industrial Era and the Information Age?

- What are the two most significant changes that are reshaping the world of business?

- How are organizations adapting?

- Where are the new jobs and what kind of career paths will they bring?

- What do employee loyalty and job security mean in the new age?

- What are going to be the building blocks for the economy of the future?

- What are the scenarios for a prosperous society?

4

Paradigm Shifts

RULES OF THE GAME

All games have rules. The challenge is to play by the rules and win. Within the rules, there must be enough options and variety of uncertain outcomes to make the game interesting. From experience, players learn to favor certain options under various situations. In time, these may become obligatory lessons for the novice and conventional wisdom for the expert, as if they were unwritten rules. How one shoots a basketball, swings a golf club, or holds a tennis racket are all very much part of the cultural foundation of the games. They are the basics, and as such are deemed indispensable for anyone serious in becoming a good player. All the rules, written or unwritten, set the boundaries for the player's actions. It is the player's perception that to win the game, one must operate within such boundaries. We call these perceived boundaries a *paradigm.*

Ironically, only a novice might be naïve enough to question an established paradigm. Why does one hit the ball this way? Once initiated, a player is entrenched in excelling within the boundaries, perhaps concentrating on hitting the ball harder. It is only rarely that someone decides to hit the ball a different way—or with something else—and discovers that its works better. This can change the game without bending the rules. A paradigm shift has occurred. High jumping has relatively simple rules: from a running start, jump and clear a horizontal bar. At the competitive level, all jumpers need to "roll" their bodies over the bar, just barely clearing it. The preferred way was the Western roll: kicking the outside leg (relative to the bar) up and rolling over face down. That was the paradigm for the game until 1968, when Richard Fosbury astounded spectators, judges, fellow competitors and their coaches alike at the Olympic Games in Mexico City. He won the event by "flopping" over backward and clearing the bar with the face up. This was a paradigm shift brought on by an innovative player. By 1980, 13 of the 16 finalists at the Olympic Games were doing the Fosbury flop. A different example is the pole vault. The rules do not specify the length of the pole or the material it is made of. Going from wooden to metallic, and then to fiberglass poles represented major paradigm shifts due to technological advances. The game is changed forever. To compete, a player must adapt to the new boundaries.

NEW MARKET PARADIGM

Business is also full of paradigms. They manifest themselves in many forms, including corporate culture, organizational structure, management styles, and marketing strategies. The assembly line and the mass market for consumer goods defined the major paradigm for the Industrial Age. Making them fast and making them cheap was the formula for success. If there were problems and defects, the customers should not mind bringing the product back to be fixed or replaced as long as a warranty was given. In any case, the consumers, not used to having much choice, were content with what they could get. This worked fine until some competitive players showed that it really did not cost more to do it right the first time. In this regard, the credit usually went to the Japanese automobile manufacturers. As

Figure 4.1 Old Market Paradigm

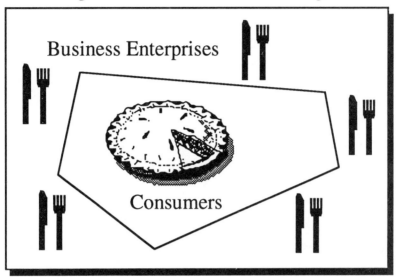

Figure 4.2 New Market Paradigm

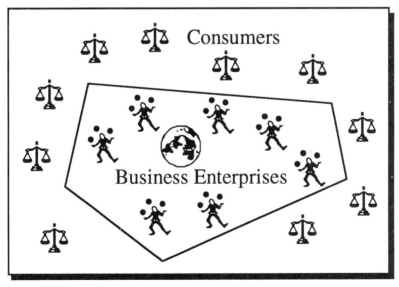

we entered the Information Age, consumers could readily avail themselves to vast amounts of detailed information on competing products from around the world. It did not take long for them to catch on to demanding quality and satisfaction for their money. While "Quality" has been the buzzword—and keyword in quite a few clichés by now—it is only the catalyst for a truly significant paradigm shift in the control of the consumer market: It went from business enterprises to their customers. From Henry Ford's fabled "any color you want as long as it is black," we now have images of a work crew at General Motors' Saturn plant. They are assembling a custom order for a third-grade teacher, passing her picture and hand-written letter down the line so everyone who is building the car can see whom it is for. As we shall see, this paradigm shift has many implications on how business is done from now on.

It may be helpful to visualize this shift metaphorically. In Figure 4.1, the old paradigm for the consumer market is depicted as a scrumptious pie, ready to be cut up by booming business enterprises symbolized by the knives and forks. This was a natural consequence of the tremendous growth in the mass market of the post-World War II era. Opportunities to meet consumer needs abound. Low cost and high output were the main factors for success. With limited information and distribution channels, business had control over what consumers knew about the market. The now defunct Sears Catalog was synonymous with "shopping" in rural America for many decades. Even with increasing competition for more sophisticated customers, American business had stuck with the same paradigm, and continued to treat consumers as objects of persuasion. This led to aggressive techniques in strategic marketing to convince people that "they've got to have it."

Eventually, certain competitors—primarily Japanese and some European—began to attend to customers' wants ahead of their own short-term financial goals. At the same time, information on every conceivable product proliferated, from comprehensive consumer reports to specialty magazines on single brands. Mail-ordering with overnight delivery essentially eliminated any time and distance factors in the marketplace. We now have the picture in Figure 4.2 where competing businesses from around the world are juggling for the attention and value judgment of the consumers symbolized by the metaphorical balances. This liberation of the mass market is not some futurist's vision or alarmist's cry of "Wolf!" It is every bit here and now. Businesses that ignore the new paradigm or fail to adjust to compete within its boundaries are doomed to dropping out of the game.

KEY SUCCESS FACTORS

Let us examine what the shift in control of the market means in terms of key factors of competitiveness. We talked about moving from the Industrial Age to the Information Age. It turns out that there is yet another era in between. This may be called the Financial Age. The Industrial Age was marked by great advances in turning natural resources: energy and raw material, into products at prices that the mass market could afford. The key success factors were volume and speed. Business goals in this era could be summarized as fortune making by satisfying consumers' generic needs. Limitation on variety of products and lack of options to accommodate individual taste were acceptable tradeoffs for cost efficiency, rather than outright disregard for the customer. Production processes and service operations were managed under this philosophy until the 1950s when management by the numbers began to take over. The key success factor in the Financial Age was meeting the bottom line. This approach had top executives set financial goals for the business based on financial and accounting information on costs, profits, and return on investment. These in turn were used to drive production and services, which, as a result, were typically manipulated to suit accounting numbers rather than customer needs. Products deemed profitable were promoted. The assumption was that with sufficient efforts in marketing, consumers could always be persuaded to buy. This phenomenon was epitomized by subliminal advertising in which suggestive messages were sneaked into background music, TV, or movies to induce subconscious urges for certain products. Consumers became no more than lab mice whose behavior could be controlled by applying the suitable stimuli. A less extreme example can be found in the attempt by a major supplier of electrical equipment to forecast sales. Impressive databases of accounting data were sieved to plan for inventory and sales targets. All along, a wealth of qualitative information was available with the regional sales force. This was based on personal contacts with the customers —including news on their prospective projects, and what it would take to win a new contract. However, by nature of this information and the top-down system of management, none of this knowledge figured in the supplier's operations. Top management had detached itself entirely from the customers. Through accounting and financial directives, it was also making managers of its business operations serve the numbers rather than the customers. The most succinct underscore of the Financial Age is perhaps the quotation of Roger B. Smith, former chairman of General Motors: "I look at the bottom line. It tells me what to do."

How critical this remote control is in impairing competitiveness in the new market paradigm depends on one's point of view. The authors H. Thomas Johnson and Robert S. Kaplan called this period from the 1950s through the 1980s the "dark age of relevance lost." Meanwhile, American business schools continue to churn out MBAs with the "Have spreadsheet; will travel" mind-set toward business management. The most prestigious institutions are especially proud of their output of the all-purpose managers that can fit in any business. As long as they know how to manage by the numbers, intimate knowledge and dedication to the specific business and its customers seem irrelevant. This is still very much the status quo as we enter the Information Age of the 1990s. Keeping the bottom-line focus in the new market paradigm has interesting consequences. For example, it explains why many recent attempts by American businesses at Total Quality Management (TQM)—a commitment to quality, customer satisfaction, and continuing improvement—came out looking awkward and contrived. While TQM has been promoted as a culture, efforts to implement it typically take on religious fervor. To many, the major distinction between culture and religion is dogma. Religions are dogmatic. They pertain to feeling righteous, for which there is need to tell good from evil. The rewards are in spiritual fulfillment. Cultures are dogma free. They pertain to feeling right, for which there is no need to exercise moral judgment. The payoffs are in social fulfillment. In a business environment where workers feel that they are in control of the work process, that they are empowered to pursue the tenets of quality, customer satisfaction, and continuing improvement—TQM can indeed be a viable culture. By contrast, where the work processes are bottom line driven, workers' economic instinct will prevail. To be rewarded, one has to serve the numbers. In this setting, TQM becomes dogmatic and by all indications, it does not make a very good religion. This is why so many inspired attempts in Corporate America fizzled after the initial drum beating subsided. In a survey by Arthur D. Little, Inc. in 1992, only 33 percent of 500 companies reported TQM to have significant impact on improving their competitiveness. For the same reasons, TQM always seems more natural in Japan where businesses tend to be more customer-focused than in this country. Now we see that it is not so much due to innate differences in the ethnic cultures, but whether top-down managerial control by financial numbers is the real driving force of the business operation.

With consumers in control of the market, it is obvious that responsiveness to customer needs and wants will be a key success factor for business enterprises. It is important to realize that such responsiveness does not simply mean the ability to accommodate choices of trimmings and frills on a basic product or service. To be competitive in the new market paradigm, businesses must also be able to anticipate radical changes in consumer preferences brought on by other fundamental shifts in technical, social or environmental norms. Selling ice cream in dozens of flavors and as many different toppings caters well to customer wants until health consciousness creates a demand for low-fat alternatives. Frozen yogurt is a response to this need. Ice cream makers have to be flexible in adapting to this change or see their market share erode in a more competitive market. The Swiss, who perfected mechanical watches and had a commanding share of the world market through the 1960s, invented the digital quartz watch as well. However, by failing to be flexible in adapting to this change, they let the Japanese capitalize on the paradigm shift and assume dominance of the market. In the future, responsiveness and flexibility will most likely require the ability to design from scratch, produce in high quality, and deliver on short order any new product or service that a customer may need. If you don't, someone else somewhere else can, and will take that business from you.

Figure 4.3   Business Key Words: Past and Future

AGE→	Industrial	Financial	Information
KEY ↓	1950	1990	
Focus	Mass Production	Bottom Line	Customer Wants
Success Factors	Economy of Scale	Return on Investment	Responsiveness Flexibility
Impact	Higher Standard of Living	Conspicuous Consumption	Global Prosperity

The issues discussed above capsulize, in perhaps a grossly simplistic way, the essence of American business up to the 1990s. We summarize the keywords in Figure 4.3. This scenario has tremendous implication on the structure and organization of business enterprises, the design and control of work processes, and the work and careers of every individual in the work force. In the remaining chapters of Part II, we examine the consequences and identify a new driving force toward prosperity in the age of information. Then in Part III, we see that to go with this force, we need to develop an awareness of how things get done and how information technology can help. This is the culture of B.I.O. (Business Information and Operations) Rhythm. In the meantime, we discuss another major paradigm shift that is well underway, but that may be too subtle to have drawn widespread attention.

NEW KNOWLEDGE PARADIGM

The human mind processes information, learns from it, and stores it as facts and knowledge. Through the ages, information has been archived in progressively more versatile

Figure 4.4   Old Knowledge Paradigm

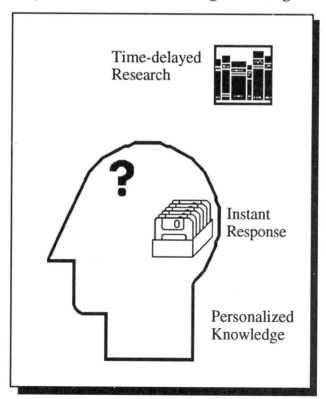

Time-delayed Research

Instant Response

Personalized Knowledge

media: from stone carvings, to hand-scripted scrolls, to printed books, to photographic and sound recordings, to full motion video. Libraries and museums are typical depositories of the collective wealth of human knowledge. While it is always possible to "look it up," the process of such information retrieval has in the past been indirect and time consuming. It is time-delayed research. For most applications of knowledge—teaching our children, analyzing a business situation, making a medical diagnosis—it is indispensable to have a human professional trained to have the requisite knowledge stored in memory for instant recall. The alternative of looking everything up as required

Figure 4.5   New Knowledge Paradigm

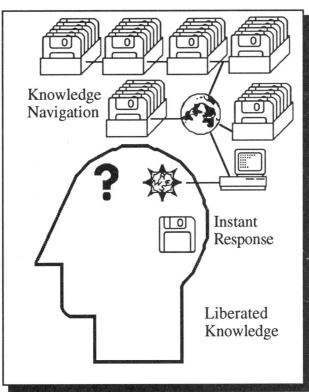

is simply not effective. This paradigm of "personalized" knowledge is schematized in Figure 4.4. With information technology, this picture is rapidly changing. It is already feasible to tap knowledge-bases around the world over computer and communication networks. With ever-improving speed and connectivity, it will be just a matter of time before the process of bringing up any information anywhere becomes virtually instantaneous. We may consider this movement as the liberation of knowledge. It has the fundamental implication of a changing role for the human being in every profession. From gatekeepers of information and knowledge, people have to become information and knowledge navigators. This new scenario is depicted in Figure 4.5. Note that we are not talking about computers directly "displacing" humans by taking over their jobs. Rather, because of technology, the role of humans has changed—a paradigm shift. Those who are unable to adapt will indeed find themselves out of the game, not so much because they cannot compete with machines, but because they insist on playing by old rules that do not apply anymore. As evidence of this shift, we are already witnessing the fate of middle managers in large corporations. Traditionally, they have been the gatekeepers of business information. They channel and filter production reports, sales figures, costs projections, and accounting records up and down the managerial hierarchy of an organization. With control over such information distributed among a cadre of middle managers, each of them can stake claim to some unique knowledge about the business. This way, they can justify their respective position as essential to the operation of the business. With technology liberating business knowledge, it does not take long for organizations to realize that many gate-keeping tasks do not add any real value to the work process. They can be eliminated as excess or waste. As we alluded to, these middle managers have not really been replaced by computers. The actual shift is toward knowledge navigation: the identification, acquisition, and processing of appropriate information as input to decision making. In business, this may appear in the form of spreadsheets and databases within a comprehensive management information system. What is happening is that workers involved with value-adding operations can now navigate easily through this information. So can top executives. As a result, the entire work process is simplified and the need for many layers of intervening gatekeepers vanished.

Similar effects of the paradigm shift in knowledge are beginning to show up in the medical, legal, and educational professions. Doctors accumulate their expertise through intelligence, diligence, and experience. The medical knowledge and acumen in judgment that they stock up are valuable assets, which allow them to command very handsome remuneration. There is as yet little fear that computerized "expert systems" can replace competent physicians. However, with the liberation of medical information and knowledge by technology, doctors who fail to avail themselves to such knowledge-base or refuse to learn how best to navigate in this sea of information will fall behind. Already, many of their judgments and procedures are being regulated by the insurance industry. The latter, armed with data spanning the entire medical profession, can perhaps rationalize its position as arbiter and auditor of quality of health care. Educators, including high-school teachers and college professors, have long assumed the role of "sage on a stage" in delivering packaged learning material to a captive audience of students. While the personal style can indeed be motivating and even inspiring, it is more akin to spoon feeding. This approach is fine in days when there was general agreement on what body of knowledge should qualify a person as educated. The situation has changed significantly when entire world and social orders are in flux, and change is the only constant in the market and workplace. Learning to learn becomes more important than what is actually taught. Again, technology offers tremendous opportunities. With multimedia presentation and interactive programs, business students can, for example, learn what it takes to operate a factory—by reacting to real life situations, and seeing simulated results of their own actions. No amount of lecturing can provide the same learning experience. Teachers must become well versed in knowledge navigation and experts in the selection of material as well as the setting up of stimulating learning programs. Having done that, they can take on the role of "guide on the side" in the typical classroom of the Information Age. Lawyers have already seen how word processing is transforming the bulk of their routine paperwork. The next step can indeed be the paperless legal profession. Although it may sound far-fetched, it can become a necessity sooner than one might surmise. Already, business transactions are executed in nanoseconds while litigations can take years to settle. Something must be missing. Just like the middle managers, physicians, educators, and lawyers will find that the new knowledge paradigm is changing the rules of their game. They must learn to navigate adroitly in the sea of liberated knowledge of their profession. With the help of information technology, the competent professionals will become even better ones. The others will find themselves unable to compete.

Throughout this discussion, we stress information

technology and the knowledge that it liberates as enabling agents for the human mind. Referring to the pictures in Figures 4.4-4.5, we can describe the old knowledge paradigm as all of human history when the mind has been used as both the intelligent information processor (symbolized by the question mark) and the medium for mass memory (symbolized by the bank of magnetic diskettes). The complexity of knowledge in most professions can easily overwhelm this mass memory. By releasing the mind of this burden, we free up considerable brain power to improve ourselves as knowledge navigators (symbolized by the compass). This can also reinforce our capacities to process information and to generate new knowledge. The whole process should be an evolutionary improvement in the intelligent use of the mind, and not a lax submission to automation.

SHAPING THE FUTURE

As seen earlier, the shift of market control from business enterprises to consumers can also be regarded as the liberation of the mass market. This, together with the liberation of professional knowledge will be shaping our future. Changes are being brought about by Information Technology, which is the convergence of computing, communications, multimedia, and solution technologies. To compete, businesses must take on a customer focus and become responsive and flexible. Top-down control with accounting numbers will no longer work well in this scenario. Instead we should see a resurgence of putting people back into the picture.

5

Emerging Organizations

CUSTOMER FOCUS

The evidence of the two major paradigm shifts—the liberation of the global consumer market, and that of professional knowledge—is mounting as the convergence in information technology takes hold. I shall proceed with the assumption that there are not too many skeptics to con-

Figure 5.1   Management Focus

Bottom Line   vs   Customers

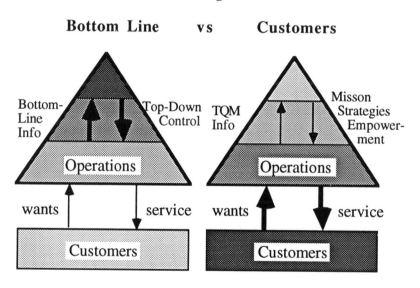

vince. With this outlook, let us start with how business organizations must cope. The focus will be customers' wants as opposed to the bottom line. The key success factors are responsiveness and flexibility. We can depict the

interactions both within the organization and with its customers as in Figure 5.1. On the left is the model of typical
business practices in the Financial Age. Top management
bases its strategies primarily on accounting numbers: costs,
profits, and volumes. These give rise to bottom-line goals
in terms of return on investment. The latter in turn leads
to performance measures, sales quotas, profit targets, etc.,
for the operations. Note that there is nowhere in managerial accounting to enter quality of product and services, and
satisfaction of customers. If we agree that this is relevant
information, then top management is quite removed from
it. Sure enough, executives may be aware of survey results
or indirect feedback from industry watchers, but certainly
do not rely on them in the top-down, remote control of the
enterprise. Meanwhile, managers of the operations and
employees who do deal with the customers directly are in a
position to listen to them, and figure out how products and
services can be improved. Unfortunately, that is not how
frontline workers get rewarded. Typically, their performance is measured by how well they serve the bottom-line
numbers, for example, by meeting sales quotas. This is
indicated by the darker arrows of internal interaction as
compared to the lighter ones for the customers. The model
on the right side of Figure 5.1 retains essentially the same
hierarchical structure. However, the focus is on the customers. Managers and employees at the operations level are
empowered to control their work processes to satisfy the
needs of customers. Their performance measures are based
on quality of work and customer satisfaction. The darker
arrows between operations and customers symbolize this
new emphasis. To keep track of how everything is going
and how improvements are being made, proper accounting
procedures and monitoring of TQM progress are the major

feedback to top management. The latter must have a clear vision of its particular business in a global perspective, and be able to articulate the mission of its organization with respect to all the constituencies of a modern enterprise. A true commitment to the customer focus, well thought out competitive strategies, and a reward structure that effectively empower and entrust employees to continuous improvement will be the trademarks of successful top management in the organizations of the future.

To illustrate the customer focus, let me recount some recent experience at two automobile repair shops. Both are well-established franchises so that the above organizational structure applies in the sense that top management is the franchise, and the individual shops are the operations. I am the customer. The first shop specializes in mufflers and brakes. I took my car in because from the noise it made, I knew some parts of the exhaust system had to be replaced. The mechanic showed me the holes in the muffler and the places in one section of the tail pipe that were rusting through. The muffler had a lifetime warranty so it was replaced for free. I paid for the new tail pipe. Within two days, I received a follow-up phone call asking about the reception and the service at the shop, and whether I was satisfied or not. I said it was fine, except that I noticed a different rattling sound that was not there before, and wondered what it could be. "No problem, bring it back and we'll take a look." It turned out to be some nonessential, original part that was coming loose. It was removed without charge. Afterward, there was another follow-up call to see if I was satisfied with the second visit. No doubt I was. Not long after, as the weather got warm, I realized the air-conditioner in the car was not cooling. I took it to the second shop that was billed as a tune-up and brake center specializing in air conditioning. The diagnosis of the air-conditioning service, which cost about $40, was that my car was flat out of freon. Three and a half pounds—over $60's worth—were put in, which provided a cool ride home. Unfortunately, it was all gone again the following day. On the return visit, I was told that the pressure valves leaked. But weren't they supposed to check for leaks before putting the freon in? (I have since learned that it is against the law to put freon in leaky air-conditioners.) "Oh, it wasn't leaking when we checked. Leaks can develop anywhere anytime, you know? There are so many places it can leak…" Ah-ha, so what options did I, the customer have? "We only guarantee our labor but not the freon," said the manager with a smirk. That meant they could try fixing it, but as long as it leaked, I had to keep paying for the freon. I decided to cut my losses and drove away.

Apart from serving as an example of the contrast in customer focus, the above anecdote can also reveal the power of the consumers through information technology. The traditional word of mouth is well known. I certainly would recommend the first shop to my friends, and tell them to avoid the second. Surveys by consumer-oriented publications have broader circulation but cannot by their systematic nature be sufficiently timely or comprehensive. Now, imagine consumers logging their experiences on electronic bulletin boards in ubiquitous computer networks. Soon enough, a customer can scan the track records of prospective providers before paying for any service. With appropriate data processing—and new forms of law enforcement to guard against fraud—the levels of detail can be mind-boggling, and yet all available instantaneously at one's finger tips. Does one shop do better in one thing but less so in another? Does it project any offensive trait:

sexist, racist, elitist...? Even if the work is fully guaranteed and ultimate satisfaction ranks high, what are the chances of getting it right the first time? Which place seems to cater better to senior citizens? What percentage of its business is from repeat customers? Do you still wonder about whether there is much substance in the new market paradigm that we talked about in the last chapter?

It should be remarked that the customer focus does not imply an obsequious servitude to public whimsies. The successful enterprise does not necessarily have to cater to the lowest common denominator in taste or aspiration. It can anticipate genuine needs and create value to help its customers succeed in their own meaningful pursuits. Products and services like the walkman, fax, and automated teller machines were not passive responses to frivolous demands by the customers. Rather, they presaged new and bona fide fixtures in the progress of living standards. By contrast, the current debate on the influence of film and television on public mores, in particular what many consider as excessive exposure of violence, is a reminder of the potential downside of this key business focus.

RESPONSIVENESS AND FLEXIBILITY

As we enter the 1990s, the status quo is still primarily the bottom line-driven, top-down approach to management that characterizes the Financial Age. There is no need to feel alienated if you find that to be the case with your workplace. It is easy for observers, whether disinterested outsiders or agenda-pitching consultants, to point to the need for change. The fact remains that changes are always difficult because they mean disruption, uncertainty, and risk: predicaments that only adventurers seem to enjoy. Well, perhaps entrepreneurs too, but often only because they see no other choice. With the customer focus, it appears that at least an entrepreneurial—if not outright adventurous spirit is necessary for managers to effect the kind of changes that can make their businesses responsive and flexible. The market is not offering much choice. It is either change or starting over, which again is an entrepreneurial proposition. There is another form of risk taking that does not involve change, only familiar rules. It is called gambling. Playing a new game by old rules is indeed a gamble, with the odds stacked heavily against the gambler.

As a simple experiment, you may wish to try the following to appreciate the kind of obstacles that stand in the way of better quality service in even rather trivial matters. I am sure you are familiar with the scheduling of service calls for the like of plumbing, electric, utility or appliance repairs. Typically, you will be told by a dispatcher to expect a service person on a certain date, perhaps specifically morning or afternoon but rarely more precisely than that. You have to arrange for someone to be at home and somehow, the average wait always seems to be at least half a day. The next time, assuming it is not an emergency, tell them it does not matter whether it will take a week, two weeks, a month even, as long as they can schedule you as the first call for the day. It sounds reasonable, doesn't it? Someone has to be first everyday and looking ahead, the schedule book must begin to have totally blank pages. Amazingly, the answer will be no in most cases, and that it just cannot be done. What happens is that the dispatcher can only book the number of calls for a service person, but not to schedule them. Then, depending on the nature of the calls and their location, the service person (or yet some other scheduler) will work out the itinerary for the day.

Although making your call the first may mean only a slight detour, it is not to be considered because it is not company policy. Unfortunately, this kind of logic can make even a tiny operation of, say, one dispatcher and several service persons behave as a large, complex, unresponsive, and inflexible bureaucracy.

Given that changes are necessary, the next question is what they should be and how to bring them about. To make sure that we are not engaged in some pie-in-the-sky discourse, let us keep the models in Figure 5.1. Therefore, the main difference between the new and the old is symbolized by the relative thickness of the arrows. We are not starting over, just considering what constitute enablers and obstacles toward responsiveness and flexibility.

SIZE

Offhand, it seems intuitive that large size is a hindrance to responsiveness and flexibility. This is true only in the following sense. From a customer's point of view, the size of a business enterprise enters into the picture only through the direct contacts made. A banking corporation may have tens of thousands of employees. However, for a customer dealing only with one particular branch, the bank can still appear as a small and effective operation. If one gets to know the tellers and officers by name, and receives friendly, personalized service rather than being treated as a case file, then it feels like a small bank. By contrast, when one calls up a typical centralized answering service for assistance, as when placing a mail order, the impersonal nature of the transaction suggests a large and inflexible operation regardless of its actual size. The same rationale applies to the internal operations of an organization. Even if only a small proportion of employees deal with external customers, everyone else has internal customers who rely on the output of one's work. What ultimately influences the perception of size is the way work is organized among employees. It also holds opportunities to be responsive and flexible in the interaction with customers. For this reason, the competitive organization of the future does not necessarily have to be small. It just has to be as nimble as a small one.

The trend in downsizing that is sweeping Corporate America has usually been heralded as a sensible effort on the part of business enterprises to adapt to the changing, competitive environment. In reality, it may only be a direct ramification of the bottom-line approach. Downsizing cuts costs, and lower costs mean higher return on investment—presumably. That may explain why in most cases when a major company announces a massive layoff, its stock price goes up. Investors in the Financial Age, just as bottom line driven as top management, welcome the news as a signal of improved return on investment a quarter or two down the road. Has the company done anything to make itself more responsive and flexible to customer needs in the long run? Not necessarily so. Indeed, some of the employees being let go, whose work may not be contributing directly enough to the bottom line, may indeed be people who can help with a truly significant shift in focus. Restructuring by accounting numbers alone may be no more than playing a new game by old rules.

COMPLEXITY

Complexity is a different issue. It is not synonymous with size, although the two often go hand in hand. It is usually indicated by the layers of management within the organizational structure. The longer the chain of command, the more complex the organization. Unlike size, complexity is a definite obstacle to responsiveness and flexibility. Time delays, chance of error, inertia to change—all contribute to missed opportunities for improvement. They go up with the amount of paperwork, explanation and persuasion, and the number of committee or signature approvals required to get anything done. Bureaucracy is a showcase of organizational complexity. In government, some see it as a necessary consequence of the expression of political power and the accommodation of subsidized employment. Government is traditionally not a competitive business, even though the politics behind it can be very much so. In principle, it serves the public, but there is rarely a customer focus. There is no need for one when the customers have no choice. This leads to waste and ineffectiveness that can seriously jeopardize the prosperity of the governed. The Clinton administration, in an effort led by Vice President Al Gore, is addressing the issue of reinventing government by reducing complexity and eliminating wasteful practices. If successful to any extent, this will represent a positive trend of introducing the customer focus into government. The irony of bureaucratic complexity, whether in government or the private sector, is that no one can really stand up to explain and justify it. It simply takes on a life of its own. Few people who fill in a form, even as a daily routine on the job, know exactly what happens to every piece of information on the form as it moves on down the line. Who uses it? What for? Is that really necessary? We do our part and pass it along. Once it leaves our desk, it is someone else's job. So the major consequence of complexity is that people can work hard without ever knowing how things really get done. Euphemistically, we call it the division of labor. Competitively, we are stripping everyone involved of the ability to contribute to the improvement of the process. Without a good understanding of the process, it is impossible to come up with meaningful ideas for higher quality, more responsiveness, and better flexibility. With this in mind, we can tell that the successful organization does not take the reduction of complexity on blind faith or in gross oversimplification. Instead, it emphasizes thorough knowledge of how things get done so that an optimal structure for the work process can either be designed or evolve through continuous improvement.

MANAGEMENT

We have already talked about the top-down, remote-control approach to management that prevailed in the Financial Age, and its almost exclusive reliance on accounting numbers and bottom-line information. Let us go back further to trace its origin and foothold. It may be easy to overlook the fact that customer focus, responsiveness, and flexibility —all the tenets of competitiveness for businesses in the future—were as old as the history of civilization. A visit to any museum or historical monument will jolt our memories that quality was not invented in Japan. In every art and craft of any period before the Industrial Age, we can witness an exuberance of quality that always seemed to surpass what we conceive to be humanly or technically feasible for the time. There was little business management as we know it. It was either governance through social domination, including the extreme case of slavery, or free artisans dealing directly with their privileged patrons. In either case, one catered to the consumer of one's skills to prosper. Work was results oriented. The methods of getting work done were in the possession of the workers, who were naturally motivated to improvement by the need to satisfy their patrons. With the introduction of mass production in the Industrial Age, the methods of getting things done became more rigidly cast in capital investments—in the form of factories, machineries, and assembly lines. Changes could be expensive, as it might involve the moving or redesigning of equipment. Nevertheless, it was quite possible for managers in charge of the work process to gain sufficient insight and knowledge to be able to think of ways to improve. The Japanese eventually used this approach to great advantage. However, in the U.S., the prospect of successful process management was nipped in the bud with the advent of management by the numbers.

It began with a group, led by Colonel Charles Thornton, that figured out how to manage various operations in the Army Air Force systematically, with data and analysis. After World War II, they approached Henry Ford II to offer their services to help the Ford Motor Company recover from the war time depression. Ford bought the idea and provided the setting for the new trend in "scientific management" that prevailed in American business throughout the Financial Age. The group, which included Robert McNamara and Arjay Miller, became known as the Whiz Kids. For their top-down, bottom-line orientation to work in manufacturing, it was necessary to have rigid control over the entire work process. Everything must be done in such a way to fit some computable model for costs, production rate, inventory, capacity utilization, and ultimately profit. The mandate from top management was to minimize cost and maximize profit. This led to the following well-known phenomenon. Overhead costs, which included amortization of capital, energy, etc., were attributed over the products in proportion to their labor content. For example, if model A was twice as labor-intensive as model B, its overhead cost was assumed to be twice that of the latter. Since these costs were fixed, the best way for a manager to reduce this overhead cost per item was to produce more of that item, regardless of the market demand. The numbers always looked better by keeping all the machines running. That this approach did not start from customer demands had of course its consequences. For the time being, we reiterate only the implication of its need for total accountability: Production processes must be rigidly controlled.

Unfortunately, this concept was soon extended to cover practically all business operations, including all kinds of white-collar and office work. American business management adopted the factory model. Work was viewed as a flow of job steps to produce some end results, with employees acting as the machinery of production. As such, their roles were quite mechanical and can indeed be programmed into manageable and accountable job descriptions. To manage people was to see that they got certain things done by following exact methods or procedures. Managers wanted not only to see results, but also to make sure that each proper step toward the results had been taken. They set the goals and controlled the methods. Just as machinery designed and placed in the production line to perform specific tasks, people are expected to produce predictable results. Whether well intentioned or not, upsetting the prescribed flow would be a blow to the apparent efficiency of the system. The adage of "paid to work, not to think" is more than a cynical reflection of the model of mass production that has permeated the workplace.

EMPOWERMENT

Perhaps enough is said about the incompatibility of top-down control by accounting numbers and a responsive and flexible customer focus. It is time to see the kind of changes that must be wrought. Once again, rest assured that we do not need a revolution. Referring to Figure 5.1, we now consider the significance of the thickened arrows between operations and customers, and the lightened ones between top management and operations. The key principle here is the empowerment of every employee to control the work process so that customers—both external and internal—can be better served. Offhand, it sounds as if top management is giving up much of its clout, at least enough to make any incumbent nervous about such change. That is really not the case. Managing by the numbers, top management does have control of the work process, details of which it does not know much of or care about. This control is simply by default since employees have no incentives to fuss with the process. To serve the bottom line, they would much rather follow instructions to produce accountable and predictable results. If the work process is perfect, then may be it is worth having a control over, just to make sure that it stays perfect. Since it is not, one might as well turn it over to those who stand a better chance of improving it, —the employees in this case. Top management retains the ultimate clout by having control over the reward structure. If customer is to be the focus, then whatever and whoever contribute to that end should get rewarded accordingly. The power structure does not have to change. It is just that different strings need to be pulled. Empowering employees is in reality putting more responsibility on their shoulders, trusting that they are able to deliver. In the factory model of business operations, this was not a logical option. After all, we did not expect machines to be able to self-organize into better assembly lines. This mental habit may be the only reason why employee empowerment seems less than natural. As soon as we can wean away from the factory model of work, it would not be unreasonable to count on intelligent people to perform according to how they are rewarded. Sure enough, there is risk involved. But can we afford not to take that risk? The market forces that are shaping our business environment seem to say no.

From the employee's point of view, empowerment is much less a political gain than a significant change in job description. From now on, it is more likely to be "paid to get results, not to follow procedures." Many in our work force will be ill-at-ease in this new game. They are hardly to blame. Our educational system, predicated on the same principles as mass production, naturally produces more solution users than problem solvers. Moreover, the traditional emphasis on individual accomplishment rather than teamwork helps shape professional workers into gate-keepers of knowledge rather than facilitator of the work process. Instead of helping with the flow, they often become bottlenecks. Fortunately, things are bound to change for the better. With the liberation of professional knowledge by information technology, which is the second of the major paradigm shifts shaping our future, well-motivated and suitably empowered workers will have much greater opportunities to become process innovators. While this may sound good, it is obviously easier said than done. How can one get managers who thrive in giving orders, and workers who are used to following them to adapt to the new game? In leading-edge companies, the urgency in responding to global challenges is perhaps sufficiently obvious. With corporate resolve, employee empowerment can indeed become showcase examples of a new style in management. For smaller organizations, the transition may not go as smoothly. There is always a risk of losing the old system before the new one can be put in place. The results can be chaotic and counterproductive. What is needed is a generic cultural movement to get everyone involved into the proper mind-set. People must be stimulated to become more interested in how things get done. We take up this topic in detail in Part III of this book.

EMERGING STRUCTURES

Suppose that by shifting away from the bottom-line orientation and management by accounting numbers, it is possible for business enterprises to adapt to the new market and knowledge paradigms. Then it is worthwhile to explore truly advantageous forms of organization that may thrive in the new environment. It turns out that there is no need to hypothesize in this regard. Market forces, global competition, and information technology have already singled out several favored candidates. Let us examine them and see what they imply in both existing and startup enterprises in the future.

The first is the flattening of the traditional pyramid structure as illustrated in Figure 5.2. This is brought on by two factors that we have already discussed. Both the liberation of professional knowledge by information technology, and the empowerment of managers and employees of front-line operations are eliminating the need for many gate-keepers in the form of middle managers. By one estimate, more than 2 million middle managers had been laid off by Corporate America between 1990 and 1993. With reduced

Figure 5.2   The Flattened Organization

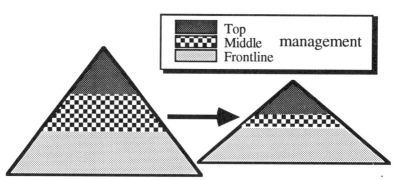

complexity, the flat organization is naturally more conducive to responsiveness and flexibility. However, as we
have already alluded to, it is important that there is a true
commitment to the customer focus, rather than simply cutting costs and increasing productivity just to stay afloat.

As organizations pare down to concentrate on what
they can do best—their so-called *core competencies*—they
cannot and should not attempt to be everything to every-
body. Instead, they will benefit from strategic alliances
with many of their external constituencies, including suppliers, retailers, distributors, investors, government, local
communities, and even competitors. This second emerging
structure is what authors Kenneth Primozic, Edward Primozic, and Joe Leben call the extended enterprise in their
book *"Strategic Choices: supremacy, survival, or sayonara."* It is schematized in Figure 5.3. Obviously, a good
working relationship between a business enterprise and all
its constituencies is nothing new. However, in the Information Age, such alliances take on new meanings. Information
technology, particularly in the form of electronic data
interchange (EDI), allows the partners to link their operations and perform their transactions instantaneously. In

short, their computers can talk directly to one another. A supplier, for example, can monitor the stock levels of its products used by the enterprise and replenish them in the most timely fashion possible. This can be done without any of the traditional paperwork. Purchase orders, production and delivery schedules, invoices and payments are all processed electronically by the respective information systems of the partners. Retail giants like Wal-Mart and Toys 'R' Us pioneered this approach and are setting the competitive

Figure 5.3   The Extended Enterprise

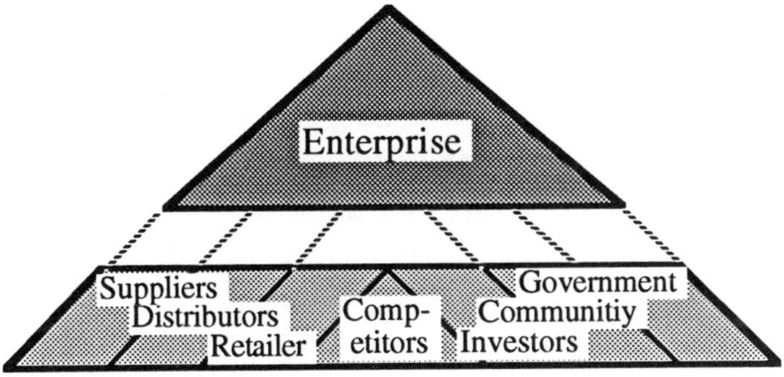

standards for the entire industry. The drive to be responsive and flexible to the needs of customers brings forth even more exciting opportunities for alliances. Mail-order houses, for example, are teaming up with overnight couriers by essentially running their warehousing operations right at the courier's distribution centers. That is how, for little more than regular postage, one can have a software purchase delivered overnight. By comparison, the venerable standard to "allow 6 to 8 weeks for delivery" now seems almost absurdly callous. Alliances among competitors are surprisingly more conventional than one might imagine. By pooling resources, primarily in research and development, competing organizations in most industries have long recognized that they can all benefit from the results of better products and new markets. With the accelerated pace of change, this becomes all the more important as major player after major player provided evidence of the precariousness of an overreliance on the status quo.

By extending the logic of getting a business enterprise to concentrate on what it does best and leave all other tasks to suitable partners, many leading business thinkers are now proffering visions of the *virtual corporation.* This is a timely and ad hoc alliance of organizations to take advantage of dynamic business opportunities. The key physical linkages are provided by information technology, which is removing most previous limitations imposed by time and distance. While the lack of distinct physical boundaries may indeed conjure up images of such a structure as a computer-generated entity, its name is not derived from "virtual reality." Rather, it referred to an older technique —Gosh! Twenty years: it must be ancient—to make computers act as if they have more internal memory than they do by the use of external "virtual memory." Likewise, by drawing on the strength of all its partners, a virtual corporation can in principle out-perform what is suggested by its physical characteristics. In a sense, it is an attempt to blend the best of all ages: industrial, financial, and information. Recall that key success factors through those eras are economy of scale, return on investment, and responsiveness and flexibility. By pooling its partners' strengths and expertise, a virtual corporation can gain scale without the size. Overhead costs are minimized with each partner focusing on its core competency. This means better return on investment. Moreover, the loose and ad hoc structure is a natural requisite for being responsive and flexible to market needs.

The ideal analog is perhaps the "Dream Team" of American basketball players put together for the Olympic games. The goal of winning the gold medal is clearly defined. The window of opportunity is extremely narrow but well known enough to accommodate precise planning. This vision of business enterprises is not really futuristic. Predecessor models have long existed in Hollywood as well as the construction industry. Teams of producers, screenplay writers, directors, actors and actresses, and film crews are brought together to make a movie. A close alliance among the partners is essential for the project. However, when it is over, whether any of the collaboration will be repeated depends largely on the needs of future projects. Developers, contractors, builders, and construction workers have similar arrangements. While these existing models serve to illustrate the basic structure of the virtual corporation, they are not quite its prototypes because of the nature of the stakes involved. The conventional approach is essentially a system of contractors and subcontractors. There are the principals, typically the producers or developers who may be backed financially by banks or venture capitalists. The other partners in the alliance work mostly under contract—even if they get to share the profits as part of the arrangement. As providers of service, they can at least in principle expect to get paid regardless of the ultimate success of the project. This is not the case with a virtual corporation. In Figure 5.4, we depict the organization of VerySoft, a hypothetical producer of software products. The ideas are generated by the creative people at Primal Concepts, Inc., who know what the market needs, what technology can provide, and how to design a product. The implementation of these ideas into computer programs is the domain of expertise at C-Shining-C Programmers. For all practical purposes, it can be located anywhere on earth with either a satellite or computer network linkage. Similarly, Hitek Writers International specializes in preparing documentation and training material comprehensible to the end-user. It is

Figure 5.4   Example of a Virtual Corporation

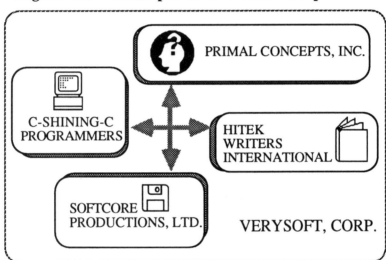

already working on a manual and tutorial while keeping close touch with both the designers and programmers via electronic mail. The design of the packaging and the production of the final product—including program discs, and the printed material in a shrink-wrapped carton—are handled by Softcore Productions, Ltd. Every partner has a stake in VerySoft, Corp., and is not simply a contractor. The product is everyone's product. All partners gain or lose together depending on how well the product sells. The exact arrangement of risk bearing and profit sharing is worked out rapidly without protracted negotiation or cumbersome legal paperwork. For such a network of companies to work, knowledge of one another's competency and a great deal of trust are essential. Most of all, everyone involved must be committed to the customer focus so that the corporation can benefit from the greatest leverage from all the individual contributions to responsiveness and flexibility. To the avant-garde, this may be the prevalent structure of business organizations in the future.

Just for completeness, we should mention that many variations of the above basic structures have been proposed and discussed in the business literature. For example, instead of reversing the thickness of the arrows in the triangles we have in Figure 5.1, one can turn them up-side-down to express the change in management focus. The result is called the Inverted Organization. Other ideas, such as Star-burst, Shamrock, Federated, and Networked organizations, are similar to the Extended Enterprise and the Virtual Corporation.

WHAT'S WRONG WITH THIS PICTURE?

Let us return to the present for a moment and reflect on the two current trends that have been drawing most attention in the business press. One is downsizing for cost effectiveness and productivity. The other is empowering employees for improvement in the work processes. When we discuss them separately, they both seem logical. Reducing complexity by removing layers of management, and shedding wasteful or ineffective practices all sound reasonable. So does letting employees take charge of the actual operations they are involved with so that they have more incentives to solve problems, remove constraints, and obtain better results. The question is then: How can employees feel motivated and truly empowered when they have to fear for the uncertainty of their very own jobs?

Imagine a conference room full of employees attending a TQM workshop. The atmosphere was charged with enthusiasm when someone walked in and spread the word that

Figure 5.5   Mixed Signals

their company had just announced another massive layoff. Even if those in the room were not affected, it would not be difficult to visualize their reaction. Can one take all these new-paradigm, people-oriented management precepts seriously while organizations treat workers simply as dispensable tools? How do we reconcile the seemingly mixed signals that some cynical observers are already calling a sham?

Once again, we end up with the top-down, bottom-line approach to management by the numbers as the root cause of the dilemma. The best analogy I can think of is the difference between being health conscious and being weight conscious. The customer focus, responsiveness, and flexibility are signs of good health while high costs, low profits, and waning competitiveness are symptoms of obesity for enterprises in the Information Age. Downsizing to cut cost by accounting numbers alone is not the way to good health. It is simply *corporate liposuction!* The surgical removal of fat tissues will indeed reduce weight, and perhaps even enhance appearance, but it is not likely to improve the functioning of the body. By contrast, a proper diet and fitness program is the key to revitalizing the organization. This is the true responsibility of top management. It should be what its vision and action plans are about. Without a careful articulation of the right size, downsizing—or restructuring, or reengineering—to improve the bottom line (no pun intended) is likely to result in return trips to the cosmetic surgeon. We have evidence in the fact that over 20% of the employers who announced layoffs in the month of September 1993 had already downsized once or more times earlier in the year. It is hard not to view such steps as passive and seemingly helpless reactions to a changing environment. Corporate America is starving for leadership that can convey well thought out plans for the future. Unless the remaining employees can be convinced that they are the muscles and not the fat, any prep talk about empowerment will be empty and wasted.

6

The Future of Jobs and Careers

We have seen in Chapter 3 that the productivity paradox is giving way to the prosperity dilemma. The tremendous investment in information technology in the 1970s and 1980s is finally paying off. Output and productivity are on the rise. Yet, the living standard of the work force taken as a whole is not improving. Nationwide, companies of all sizes are learning to improve their competitiveness by doing more with fewer people. The technology-induced paradigm shifts described in Chapter 4 are fueling this trend. As better-informed consumers take over control of the global market, businesses have to be responsive and flexible to their needs by acting as small and nimble organizations rather than complex bureaucracies. The ever-increasing accessibility of information and the liberation of professional knowledge enable the empowerment of front-line workers, and eliminate the need for layers of middle management. Massive layoffs seem the rule of the day as companies downsize and restructure. Needless to say, jobs and careers in the new forms of organizations discussed in Chapter 5 are going to be substantially different from the traditional. What are the new jobs? Where will they be? What kind of skills will be in demand? How secure will any job be? These are "high-anxiety" questions raised by many in the work force who understandably are unsettled with trepidation by all the changes occurring in the workplace.

It is easy to say that the world is changing, and so to prosper, one must learn the necessary new skills. We all know that in reality, life is a lot tougher than that.

Retraining and retooling, especially with uncertainty of what lies beyond, demand an open mind and much will power. It also takes adjustment to a sense of failure—a recognition that what one has been doing all along is not useful anymore. No one feels good about becoming obsolete, or replaceable by technology. And no one learns well when feeling defeated. For this reason, the whole concept of retraining may be counterproductive. It is rooted in the mind-set that any training has lasting value. Occasionally, a shift in demand will happen and that is the only time when people need retraining. This applied when changes occur gradually so that typically, an entire generation of workers could retire with one set of skills. Those unfortunate enough to be caught in the middle of a shift had to learn two. This is no longer the case. From now on, changes will be fast and constant. Only continuously adaptable skills will do. This may sound like hard work, but in fact should not be more difficult than anything that we have done before. Indeed, with the help of technology, it should become easier. It is the attitude that counts. Unless we are open to new ways of getting things done, there will always be mental blocks against lifelong learning and adaptation of job skills. We should probably underplay formalized retraining and start with fostering a cultural change in our attitude toward work.

THE NATURE OF WORK

Enjoying one's work has always been a true blessing but not a requisite for holding a job to make a living. Most of us are content to seek pleasure from leisure activities rather than from work. Nevertheless, a job must be satisfying in some way to keep us going. It can be a sense of belonging to some productive endeavor, of being useful, of assisting others, or simply of financial and economic security. All of these motivations are compatible with work that is well defined and well delineated. Job descriptions are carefully spelled out. As the factory model has been applied to both manufacturing and office work, clean-cut division of labor is the preferred approach to any complex task. As a result, people can work hard and be suitably rewarded without understanding much of what they are doing, or how things

Figure 6.1   Handy's Inverted Doughnut

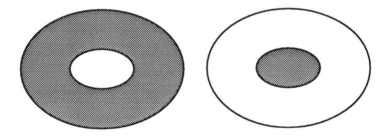

really get done. They follow orders in much the same way as in a military hierarchy. Intelligence (information) goes to the generals (bosses) who make strategic decisions and issue orders through a chain of command (middle management) to the rank and file (frontline workers). This concept of work is best illustrated by Charles Handy's doughnut model in his book *The Age of Unreason*. The doughnut on the left in Figure 6.1 is what we are familiar with: solid all around and with a hole in the middle. The solid part is the shape of traditional work, well mapped out with known boundaries but no flexibility or room to grow. With the new business paradigms, the nature of work has changed. We must now think of its shape as an inverted doughnut as depicted on the right in Figure 6.1: solid in the middle and empty all around. (Never mind that such a doughnut cannot be made. We need only the imagery for the allegory.) The solid center contains both the purpose of the work, and how it fits in the scheme of things—the big picture. It also includes guidelines and recommended methods and procedures. The worker is then expected to grow this job into the empty part of the inverted doughnut as there is plenty of room for judgment, improvement, and even innovation. The need for this "inversion" of the very nature of work is a direct result of all the new parameters in the business environment. First, there is the switch from the bottom-line focus in the Financial Age to the customer focus in the Information Age. With it comes the move from top-down management by the numbers to empowerment of frontline workers with control over the work processes. This approach will not work with the traditional doughnut of work as "carrying out orders." It needs the ability of workers to grow jobs in the inverted doughnut. But how? We shall see later that the crucial ingredients are an awareness of how things get done, and appropriate savvy in how technology can help. That's it. If this becomes the prevalent culture in our work force, there will be ample motivation for everyone to pick up new skills as needed without any depressing and disparaging transition of formal retraining.

DOES TECHNOLOGY DEGRADE JOBS?

Before we get too excited about a new era of more challenging and stimulating work, let us take a look at the hard reality of another view of what many jobs have become. In 1988, Barbara Garson wrote *The Electronic Sweatshop: How computers are transforming the office of the future into the factory of the past.* It was based on her interviews with various white-collar workers, including short-order cooks in a fast food restaurant, agents for an airline reservation system, social workers, and financial advisers in an investment firm. Operating a computer-controlled fast food production system—the fry vat that makes french fries from potatoes—the cook had only to react to beeps and buzzers just as a robot. Airline reservation agents were trained to assemble their phone conversation from precise modules to keep calls to under two minutes. Their productivity was monitored to the second. Instead of aiming to help solve problems, social workers were rated by a computerized point system that tracked their activities. The financial advisers were essentially mouthing choices made by an electronic expert system. All felt that their jobs lacked a regard for human intelligence, and that being enslaved by technology was stressful and demeaning. Both from the title and a casual reading, one could easily get the impression that Garson's accounts were the typical humanist gripes about technological progress. This would be unfortunate, for she had her finger on the root cause of the problem, as she wrote in the introduction:

> "Right now, a combination of twentieth-century technology
> and nineteenth-century scientific management is turning the
> Office of the Future into the factory of the past."

She was right, except perhaps for misplacing some labels. The nineteenth-century style of command and control was from a military tradition. Scientific management: the top-down, bottom-line orientation to managing by the numbers, was very much a phenomenon of the Financial Age of the twentieth-century. In any case, she put the blame not on computers but a "mean-spirited management that distrusted humans and their idiosyncrasies." In the conclusion of the book, under the heading of "It could be different (but it probably won't be)," she compared the computer to the sewing machine in the Industrial Age. She lamented that labor was never quite in a position to say, "We want the sewing machine but not the sweatshop." Here is her closing paragraph:

> "Computer programs can be changed. There are many ways to combine the efficiency of computers with the skills and talents of human beings. Frankly, though, I doubt that our workplaces will change simply because we start dropping pro-people ideas into the suggestion box. The pull in the other direction is extremely powerful. Still, if we insist forcefully enough, perhaps it's not too late to say, "We want the computer but not the electronic sweatshop."

Well, take heart Ms. Garson, it turns out that market forces are proving to be even more powerful than the pull that you dreaded. Henceforth, every time we hear customer focus and employee empowerment mentioned, we will witness at least a chance, if not a promise, that our workplace can become more humane.

TECHNOLOGY AT YOUR SERVICE

The electronic sweatshop conjures up the horror of people serving technology and being treated like mindless robots in the process. The question of who is serving whom is indeed significant and intriguing. The answer is not always obvious either. Consider the pilot of a Boeing 747 jumbo jetliner. The plane is a flying castle of high technology controlled by sophisticated computer systems. It can literally fly itself. The pilot responds to beeps and buzzers and pushes buttons. How is he or she different from the teenage cook at the controls of the fry vat at the hamburger place? The pay is probably a hundred times better, hour for hour. Such differential valuations of jobs can lead to opposing perceptions of the role of technology. On the one hand, the pilot is the captain in command of the plane. All the technology is at his or her disposal, including the beeps and buzzers that provide information to get the job done. We definitely see technology at the service of the human being. Obviously, to qualify for such a job, it takes years of training and experience. On the other hand, any teenager off the street can be trained in fifteen minutes to run the fry vat by listening to the beeps and buzzers. The technology is specifically designed to accommodate an extremely high turnover rate of employees. Do people leave because the job is lousy? Or does the job need to be semi-automated because people do not stay long? In any case, one gets the impression here of a dispensable human being serving the technology. For an extraterrestrial observing just the cockpit and the kitchen in isolation, there may not be much of a distinction.

Where does this leave us in terms of the meaning and demeaning of jobs? First, technology by itself neither fulfills nor demeans. The nature of the job and the way it is managed do. The pilot's job is to transport a planeload of passengers and cargoes safely and punctually to the destination, not just to act as the human interface to the technology of the plane. It is an important job that pays very well. No one will say that it demeans. How should one view the job at the fast food restaurant? Ideally, we would like to say that it is to serve the customers. This way, having technology like the fry vat on hand is a great help to get the job done. In principle, the job is no less important than the president of the United States serving the people, probably just as stressful. Alternatively, we can say that the job is to watch the fry vat and make sure that each batch of potatoes yield enough servings. In this sense, the cook serves neither the customers nor the fry fat. He serves the numbers. Unfortunately, that is how the job is managed.

It is just a matter of time that a debate such as the above will become moot. Jobs that make humans feel like robots will eventually be fully automated. For example, McDonald's introduced its ARCH (Automated Restaurant Crew Helper) program in 1992. Initially, it uses robots to run the frymaker and the drink machine. The frymaker weighs, loads, cooks, and dispenses french fries without the intervention of a human attendant. The drink machine picks the right-size cup, and fills it with ice and the soft-drink that has been selected at the cash register. Other components will be added to the program, which is aimed to automate the entire food preparation process. The company claims that ARCH is not designed to displace people, just to increase sales by providing faster service and hotter food to the customers. That sounds fine, but it remains to be seen whether workers will fare better in the future than being managed strictly by the numbers.

In all fairness, we need to point out that the fast food market is somewhat of an anomaly in the evolution of consumerism. Somehow, customers want the same old things, so long as it is fast and cheap. It is like every car buyer clamoring for the 1973 Chevette—in the same apple green no less. As long as customer demands stay within the confines of the Industrial (mass production) and Financial (cost efficiency) Ages, it is to the benefit of the industry to keep managing by the numbers.

WHAT ARE THE NEW JOBS?

Before the two major paradigm shifts in the consumer market and in professional knowledge began to reshape our future, business cycles were rather credible and predictable economic phenomena. As we emerged from the recession that ended in 1991, employment was supposed to pick up with significant growth in the GDP. Only this time it did not happen. American enterprises continued to shed jobs to increase productivity with the help of technology. Surely, statistics did show modest net increases through 1993, but they covered mainly temporary help or low-paying service jobs. Experts—confounded by this so-called "jobless recovery"—are all looking for signs of the creation of new jobs to boost the next wave of significant employment. The question is not just jobs, but quality jobs with decent wages. There is no dispute that the outlook is very bright for highly skilled, so-called knowledge workers. They are typically college-educated and represent only a small portion of the work force. How about the rest? At this point, it is anybody's guess. However, if we do believe in the shift to a more customer-focused and people-oriented business environment supported by ever-improving technology, then there is reason to expect plenty of new jobs stemming from the following examples of pent-up demands.

- People do not feel that they are getting value for basic services such as household or auto maintenance and repair.

- People do not feel that the government is spending their tax money effectively.

- People do not feel safe as society turns more violent and law-and-order enforcement fails to deter crime.

- People miss the personal touch in child care, health care, and aging with dignity.

- People are not being properly educated.

- People do not have much alternative to passive infotainment.

- People are confused by the gee-whiz hype for the convergence of information technologies.

- People care about the environment but are not sure what can really make a difference.

- People miss the pioneer spirit and the American dream.

The list can go on. The items are subjects of frequent polls. They are vignettes of public opinion that will define where the action is. Without speculating on the specific kinds of new jobs and business opportunities, it is still reasonable to predict that entrepreneurial ideas to address these needs will provide the most significant growth in employment. This view is consistent with the new paradigms for the Information Age. Instead of identifying trendy skills and products, and project job demands by their marketing success, we start with people and where value can be added or created for them. From further advancement of high technology to a renaissance of craftsmanship, from product development and manufacturing to the delivery of services and care—we are not just talking about niche markets. It is the whole market. Conventional watchers of the economy are waiting for the right signs and indicators to signal when companies will start hiring again. We are not doing that. We are waiting for responses to people's very specific needs for value added, a partial list of which is given above. That is when employment will rise meaningfully. Both you and I can be very much a part of it. To paraphrase John F. Kennedy, "Ask not what the economy can do for you—ask what you can do for the economy." Up to this point, this may simply be high-sounding rhetoric. Going over the above checklist, it should begin to make better sense.

THE WORKPLACE

Information technology is already bringing substantial changes to our factories, offices, and classrooms. So far, the benefits have primarily been in improving efficiency and productivity. Higher speed, lower cost, and less waste are the visible results. We will begin to see more profound changes in the way things get done. To be concise, let us focus on the office environment and so-called white-collar work. The offices of the future are going to look quite different from what we have now for three reasons. First, as most of the routine data and information processing becomes automated, there will be much less of the traditional desk-top activities. Secondly, with critical tasks assigned to cross-functional teams, communication and coordination among such groups become key success factors. Thirdly, due to the customer focus, contacts—either direct or electronic—with customers, both internal and external, will be increased. Simply put, there will be a lot more of different kinds of "meetings" to exchange ideas and much less filling in forms, much less sitting at one's own desk, and more moving around. This calls for new layouts and architecture for the workplace. Figure 6.2 illustrates a hypothetical layout for Primal Concepts, Inc. that, as you recall, is part of the virtual corporation introduced in Chapter 5.

FIGURE 6.2   PRIMAL CONCEPTS, INC.

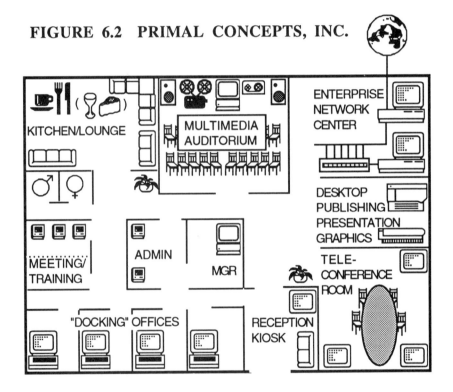

As you enter the main entrance (bottom center of picture), there is the reception area. Only there is no receptionist. Instead, a touch-screen, interactive kiosk lets you introduce yourself and indicate whom you wish to see, and whether you are expected. You have an appointment with the manager. "Please be seated. She will be right with you." Shortly, Judy, the manager, greets you and takes you on a tour of the facilities. There is the teleconference room that the company uses regularly to conduct live-video meetings with its clients in Europe, and its programming partners at C-Shining-C in Asia. Next to it is the graphics workshop. Judy explains that it is for conceptual paste-ups and rough drafts only. Production work is again handled by a strategic alliance. The computer systems room is at the corner. It houses the server computers, the network hubs and controllers as well as back-up optical storage devices, and the CD library. The computer network is based on the popular client/server architecture. However, the network manager software has the most advanced enterprise orientation. As Judy proudly shows on a monitor, a tree-structured directory represents the entire company (Primal Concepts, Inc.) as well as all its linkages to other partners in VerySoft, Corp. She points out that before the arrival of this feature, information systems were structured according to the hardware connections that typically had little to do with how the company was organized. This made it very difficult for partners in a virtual corporation to integrate their systems. With the enterprise orientation, one simply adds or deletes components to the network directory tree as changes occur in the corporation. On the way out of the room, Judy adds that obviously, the system is connected to the rest of the world via electronic superhighways. Turning right, you enter the multimedia auditorium. A meeting is in progress with a group of clients watching a demonstration of a computer-based training program developed by PCI. What is showing on the monitor of the workstation used by the facilitator is also projected onto a wall-size screen with digital stereo sound and full-motion video in vivid colors.

Judy whispers that there is always something going on in this room. Apart from formal presentations and training workshops, it is heavily scheduled by PCI employees and associates to try out new ideas or products, and even for brainstorming sessions. Next stop is the inviting and comfortable "club house." It is a combination kitchen, lounge, and dining room. Anything from continental breakfasts, buffet lunches, BYOB (bring your own bottle) wine and cheese hour (after 6 p.m. only), potluck or fully catered, sit-down dinners can be arranged here. Of course, coffee and tea are available 24 hours a day. As you put down your cup, you notice something moving over from across the room. "Would you like more coffee?" No, thanks, you say. "May I remove the cup?" It is Doro—the domestic robot. Its manufacturer has chosen PCI as a beta test site. Judy adds that Doro is being trained to handle most of the housekeeping chores. In spite of all the high-tech contraptions, she feels that the workplace is actually getting to be more people oriented, even social club-like. "As technology becomes transparent and ubiquitous, there is no longer the question of who is serving whom: people serving machines or vice versa. We all come in to interact with people, to share ideas, and to solve problems. It is important that we provide the most conducive environment," she says as you pass by the administrative offices. "My job as General Manager is to facilitate and coordinate the myriad activities, rather than to command and control them," Judy emphasizes. After peeking into a computer-based training room that also doubles as a small conference room, your final stop is the row of "docking offices." These are plush yet minimally furbished rooms that provide generic office space for associates of PCI. Everyone has a notebook computer with ample processing power and memory for one's work-in-progress. As needed, one sits down at the docking workstation, inserts the notebook computer and turns the entire office into one's own. As Judy explains, "It is a virtual office. When you are done, you take everything with you and switch it off. In typical knowledge work, you need the office setting probably only for an hour or two a day. With proper scheduling, we can minimize idle space and equipment, which used to be the major cost factors in the workplace."

Although our tour of PCI is fictitious, the workplace envisioned is only partly fictional. Most of the technology is already available in 1994 and is being put in use to various extents. We choose to look at an example of a rather small company. How about much larger organizations than PCI? What are their workplaces going to be like? Probably quite similar, as there will just be many more units—each one not much larger in size than what we have described—working together as a network.

FLEXIBLE WORKSTYLES

So far, we have seen that changes in business focus and structure of organizations, together with new opportunities enabled by information technology, are leading to new purposes and new environments for work. The latter two effects will in turn introduce substantial variations in the way people work. To start with, it is no longer absolutely necessary to do business where most other businesses are, typically "downtown" in big cities. Remember that time and distance factors are being all but removed by technology so that proximity can be replaced by connectivity. With this option, it is natural to bring work to people instead of bringing people to work. For this reason, there will be significant growth in suburban business campuses close to where people like to live. Taking a short pleasant drive, or even a bike ride to work can help reclaim tens of millions of productive hours a year currently spent by commuters in traffic. The 9-to-5 office hours are also losing their allure as symbols of business discipline. With the customer focus, the best hours are whenever customers have legitimate preferences for service. As globalization continues, it is useful to bear in mind that it is always "business hours" somewhere else. For this reason, we can expect work schedules to become more flexible. It should be emphasized that such "flexi-hours" do not necessary mean "any hours." The concept is often misconstrued by both workers and employers alike to be a laissez-faire system to work any time so long as the job gets done. This picture leaves out the customer—whether internal or external—and does not fit in the new paradigm. The proper guiding principle for flexible work schedules is to maximize coverage of customer needs. Subject to that, as much flexibility as possible can be allowed to accommodate the preferences or convenience of the workers. In other words, while flexible, a schedule must still be a well thought out plan with very definite priorities. This element is essential to maintaining the effectiveness and productivity of empowered workers.

After settling on when to work, let us consider where the work is done. The term "telecommuting" has increasingly been used to describe doing one's job at home while keeping electronic links to the office. The press has generally encouraging coverage of how such an option enables mothers with young children to keep a productive job. This is fine except that we need to expand the definition quite a bit to be consistent with our main theme. There will be less

Figure 6.3 The Transformation of Work

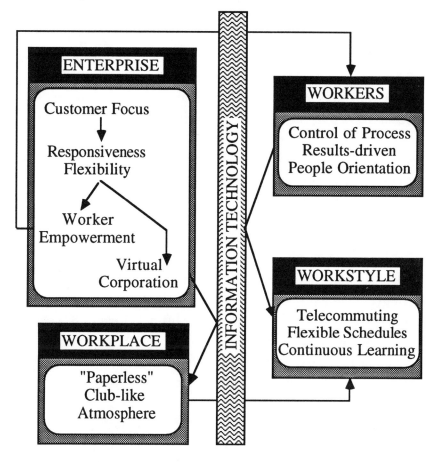

routine work around the office, and more contacts with customers, partners, and other alliances at their respective sites. Telecommuting covers all such activities away from the office as well as working at home. Many of these used to come under business travel, which brings up an interesting puzzle. As information technology in the form of video conferencing reduces the need for much business travel, the people orientation seems to call for more. Which way is it going to be? The answer is both because the nature of the business trip is changing. There will be less need for routine sharing of information, even negotiation, which can be accomplished through video conferencing. However, to better understand customers in order to anticipate their needs, to appreciate value systems different from one's own, and to gain insight into how things work and where value can be added or created—one has to be there. That is the kind of business travel, or telecommuting that we can expect to see more of.

Finally, as routine work is reduced—if not eliminated—by improved work processes and by automation, a fixed set of learned skills for a lifelong career is becoming a thing of the past. An open-minded attitude toward continuous learning will be the prime asset of any valuable worker. One can look at it in two different ways. Either all job descriptions are adaptable, or all job skills must be constantly renewable. This prospect may be unsettling for many who feel that a person's ability to learn necessarily declines with age. Moreover, people should be entitled to feel that they have earned their keeps. While neither argument is valid anymore, it should be reassuring to realize that new skills are not arbitrary switches in style or rules, but logical progressions in getting a job done better, or more easily, or both. It always pays to keep up. We now have a complete sketch of how the new business paradigms are transforming work in the Information Age. It is illustrated in Figure 6.3.

CAREER PATHS

When a job is more than just a job, offering opportunities for development and advancement, it leads to a career path. Traditionally, business organizations are structured vertically by distinct functions such as production, marketing, sales and service, etc. Within each of the business function —usually identified as a department—there is a hierarchy of job grades, ranks, and titles like rungs on a ladder. To underscore the fact that these functions are managed quite separately, the term stovepipe organization is also often used. By choice, training, or circumstance, one starts with

Figure 6.4   Climbing the Corporate Ladder

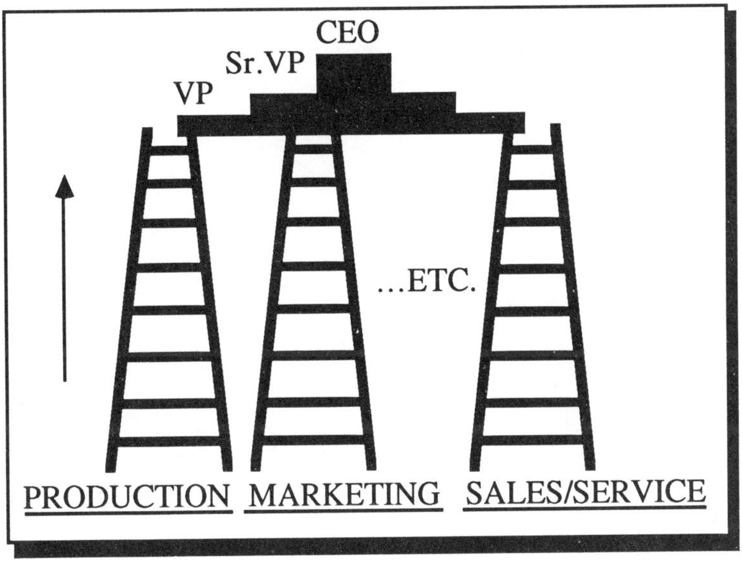

PRODUCTION MARKETING SALES/SERVICE

a position in one of these functions, typically at the bottom of the ladder. By doing a good job and getting promoted upward through the ranks, one climbs the proverbial corporate ladder. This is illustrated in Figure 6.4. With the new emphasis on responsiveness and flexibility, enterprises find it necessary to deploy cross-functional teams to accomplish specific mission-critical tasks, such as bringing out a new product. The old way had each department do its part of the job in turn: Research and Development for the design, Production for the manufacturing, Marketing for the promotion, and finally Sales and Services for the distribution. This approach was not only slow but also susceptible to letting problems in one stage slip through undiscovered till a much later stage. Backtracking to fix such problems would be both costly and time consuming. By contrast, cross-functional teams with people from each relevant department can do a better job. They can make sure that the product is what customers want, that its design can be manufactured with high enough quality and at low enough cost—all before the final decision to forge ahead. What does one get for doing a great job in such a cross-functional team? It may not necessarily be the same move up a rung of the ladder as before. For one thing, the flattening of organizations discussed in Chapter 5 has eliminated many of the rungs. More likely, the reward comes in the form of a place in a more important team, or rather a team with a more important task. I like to use sailboats to

Figure 6.5   Setting the Corporate Sails

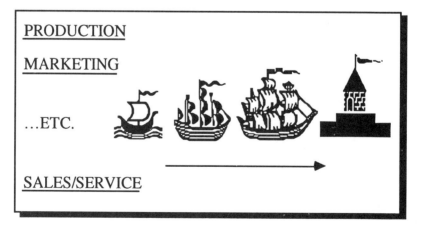

depict the team approach. As illustrated in Figure 6.5, advances in a career path in this new setting are tantamount to setting sails on larger and better boats, with more crucial missions and, of course, better pay and benefits. It is no longer climbing the same ladders, but heading to the top nonetheless. It should be pointed out that if the career path is to be one of advancement, then some form of hierarchy is necessary. As we have discussed previously, the current waves of corporate downsizing are reducing the layers of management between the CEO and the shop floor, from as high as a dozen or so previously, to between four to six. More and more, it will be which boat you are on—rather than which rung of the ladder—that counts.

LOYALTY AND SECURITY

Traditionally, these are highly held, complementary virtues in a worker-employer relationship. Loyal workers doing their best to keep a company productive and profitable are rewarded by employers who watch out for the workers' welfare and job security. This sounds great when things are going well, as in periods of uncontested growth. The old IBM with its high demand on worker conformity and no-layoff policy was a good example. With the debacles of the Financial Age, there is every reason to be cynical about the realism of such a simplistic ideal in the fast-moving and competitive Information Age. Further attempts to pro-pound these virtues are bound to turn dogmatic and are doomed to fail, much like TQM in a culture of manage-ment by the numbers. Instead, we can be totally pragmatic and redefine the same terms so that they can work in the new paradigms. With this in mind, I propose the following new-age definitions:

LOYALTY = a commitment that customers
get their value

SECURITY = a commitment that anyone who
can reduce the work in a job
will not be out of a job

In face of uncertainties brought on by constant and rapid changes, we probably cannot and need not ask for more. Indeed, if we can put these to work, they can go a long way toward rejuvenating our spirit of hard work for a good living. An employer needs look no further than workers who strive to give customers their money's worth. No dogma here, just dogged fairness. No need to preach and convert. Some have it; some don't. Pick the ones who do. An enlightened worker in the new age understands that no company can afford to keep anything that does not add value around for long. Being able to do the same old job well is no guarantee of one's usefulness. Ironically, the conscientious worker trying to improve on the work process may indeed jeopardize his or her own job. The new-age job security allays such fear. Again, it is only sensible. Yet not all companies, particularly those that continue to be ruled by the bottom line, have such awareness. The ones that do are good companies to work for.

7

The Rise of Workgroups

CROSS-FUNCTIONAL TEAMS

With the focus on mass production from the Industrial Age, work processes in both factories and offices were designed according to the principle of division of labor. To be more precise, it should be referred to as the sequential division of labor. This is because the value added by each component of the process was accumulated step by step, as in an assembly line. In this environment, while many people might be working at the same time, they did not necessarily have to work together as a team. Everyone concentrated only on a specific task. If the end product turned out to be defective upon inspection, a considerable amount of backtracking was necessary to figure out where the problems were. This was obviously a major hindrance to maintaining high quality standards. As quality became an increasingly important factor, so did teamwork. This was due to the need for better coordination among the components of the work process. Whenever a problem was discovered at any stage, one should alert those in charge of the upstream tasks to have it fixed. If necessary, the whole process could be stopped for everyone to huddle and figure out what went wrong. It was also recognized that such interaction and teamwork facilitated efforts to improve on the work process, and consequently the quality of the end product itself. Although people were brought together this way, much of the sequential flow of component tasks remained intact because of the structure of the organization. Consider the traditional way of developing and introducing a new product. First, Research and Development worked on and came up with the design. Next, Production took the design and determined how it should be manufactured. Then, Marketing concocted the promotional campaign. Finally, Sales and Services picked up the distribution of the new product. This approach was time consuming, especially if it took more than one pass for everything to work out satisfactorily.

The rigidity of the functional division of conventional organizations is likely to get into the way of their efforts to become responsive and flexible with the customer focus. For this reason, business enterprises have begun to exploit the merits of cross-functional teams. With representation from each relevant department, they can do a better job ensuring that a high quality product will be designed and produced for a profit and to satisfy customer needs. Production can help Research and Development come up with a design that is easier to manufacture. Sales and Service can suggest ways to simplify repair and maintenance. The results will be much more effective if all such ideas can be generated before plans for the product are finalized. This approach is known as *concurrent engineering* because many of the sequential tasks that used to go from department to department are now tackled in parallel by a cross-functional team. As more mission-critical tasks are handled this way, it is reasonable to adopt the view that such teams will become the basic units of future organizations.

Much research has been done and published on team building and team dynamics. As we are referring to teams of people, most such findings point to ways of motivating workers to contribute fully to cooperative work. For example, it has been observed by Jon R. Katzenbach and

Douglas K. Smith of McKinsey & Co. in their book *The Wisdom of Teams* that suitable challenges can induce more productive teamwork than rigorous team-building exercises. They found that a major obstacle to team success is the difficulty in shifting from individual accountability to a team-based reward structure. Also, cross-functional teams can do well within a hierarchical structure without supplanting the latter. It is beyond our present scope to go into further details. Let us simply bear in mind that the team concept is primarily people oriented. Indeed, it is useful to note the definition developed by Katzenbach and Smith:

> A team is a small number of people with complementary skills who are committed to a common purpose, performance goals, and approach for which they hold themselves mutually accountable.

STRATEGIC ALLIANCES

At the organizational level, we have seen that market forces are favoring a flat structure, with relatively few layers of management between the top executive and the frontline workers. It is also important to concentrate on one's "core competencies": what one does best, while leaving other tasks to someone else who can do them better. This leads to a network of strategic alliances that, depending on the exact nature of the partnership, can vary from conventional contractual relationships to so-called virtual corporations. In any case, it brings on another form of teamwork—that among cooperating organizations. While it is likely that teams of people from the organizations involved do interact, the nature of this teamwork must be quite different from that within individual groups. For one thing, we know for sure that technology will play a significant role in such alliances. For example, consider the linkage between a manufacturer and one of its suppliers provided by EDI (electronic data interchange). In this case, their computers and information systems are "teaming up," more so than their people. Many conventional concepts that apply to teams, known as team basics, are no longer relevant here. The most obvious one is proximity: that a team needs to work closely together. Another one is small size to preserve cohesiveness of the team. In other words, as the people aspects diminish in going from intraorganizational teams to interorganizational ones, contractual accountability plays an increasingly important role. What we need is a more general and comprehensive view of such new forms of teamwork.

A FRAMEWORK FOR COOPERATIVE WORK

We have seen that the essential ingredients for a team are the people. For a team to be successful, it is necessary at the very least for the people involved to be able to get along with one another. On top of that, they must also share common goals, and possess complementary skills to propel the team toward those goals. Tacit in any cooperative work process is a division of responsibility to which individuals are held accountable. When everyone does his or her part well, so does the team. We can refer to this aspect of teamwork as an understanding and agreement, or a social contract, whether it is binding in any legal sense or not. This contractual ingredient is then the basis of interorganizational alliances. The commitment to cooperate is likely to be reflected in the design of the work processes used by the partners in the alliance. An example is the use of EDI for all transactions between a supplier and a manufacturer. The vital link here is information. We are now ready to extend our process of generalization one more step. Let us take away even the contractual aspect of the cooperation. What remains is the information linkage, which in a sense gives us the most generic form of cooperative work. I use the term "workgroup" to capture its meaning as derived from teams and alliances. We now have the framework as depicted in Figure 7.1. To fix ideas, we should also venture a definition.

> A workgroup is any number of people, information systems, organizations, or combinations thereof, whose work processes, dedicated to a specific mission, are interrelated by the need to exchange information.

Figure 7.1   A Framework for Cooperative Work

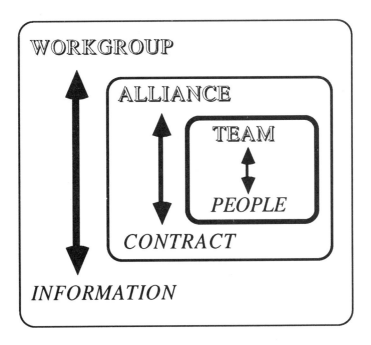

As indicated in the figure, an alliance is a workgroup linked by information *and* abiding by contractual account-ability. A team is a workgroup linked by information, abiding by contractual accountability, *and* consisting of people working closely together. So, a team is both a work-group and an alliance. An alliance is also a workgroup. However, a workgroup does not have to be either an alliance or a team. One way to illustrate the subtle differ-ences among these relationships is by the following musical analogy. A symphony by Mozart is a workgroup of sound waves interacting as music. The musical instruments used to generate the sound waves are an alliance abiding by the score for the symphony. The orchestra playing the instru-

Figure 7.2   A Musical Analogy

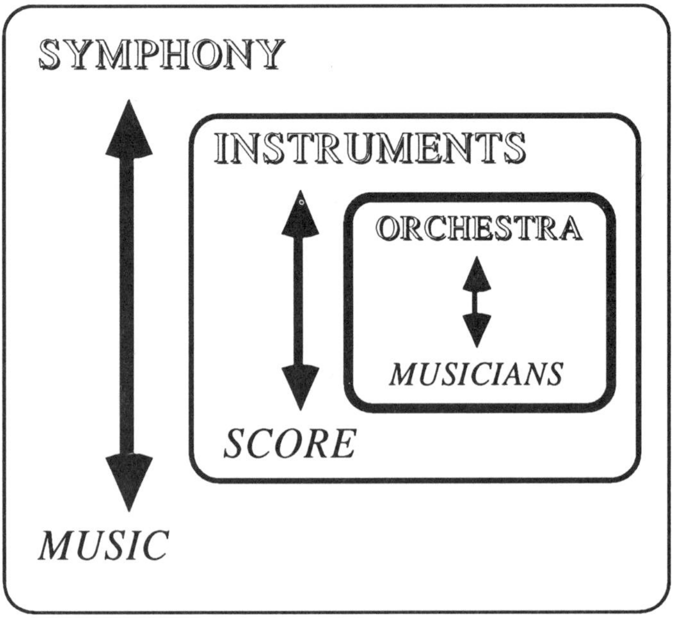

ments is a team of musicians working closely together. What happens when you play a digital recording of the orchestra's performance on a compact disc? You do not get an orchestra, not even the instruments, still you get the music in Mozart's symphony. Using this line of reasoning, we can begin to appreciate the essence of information-driven collaborative work, as removed from specific organizational or personal context. However, our purpose here is not to split hairs and analyze which group is which. Nor are we downplaying the importance of the people orientation of teams. We are well aware that with the customer focus and employee empowerment, the interpersonal aspects of work have to play a central role. Nevertheless, it is just as important to point out that, enabled by information technology, newer forms of cooperative work will be sharing the stage. The new work processes are likely to depend more on information interchange than on personal contacts. Much can be accomplished by groups of people that have never met or even talked to each other on the phone, let alone rubbing elbows as a team in the traditional sense. We can capture all these different forms of collaborative work with our definition of the workgroup.

A NEW DRIVING FORCE

We are now ready to address the prosperity dilemma: that rising productivity from the technology payoff does not lead to higher standards of living for our work force. As productivity gains imply doing more with fewer people, many of the conventional jobs, especially in middle management, are being eliminated. With better-informed consumers calling the shots in the marketplace, businesses have to be more responsive and flexible to their wants and needs to remain competitive. This calls for the uprooting of the bottom-line approach to management in favor of empowering workers to take charge of work processes for continuous improvement. To be truly nimble, collaborative efforts must integrate across boundaries of traditional business functions. Within an organization, cross-functional workgroups will become the basic units responsible for mission-critical tasks. As organizations stay within their core competencies, they find it possible, again with help from information technology, to act and compete as much more complex entities by networking into ad hoc workgroups that are becoming known as virtual corporations.

Workgroups in the Information Age are mission oriented. They are put together to meet a challenge or to take advantage of a window of opportunity shaped by fast-changing market forces. As the mission is accomplished, or when the opportunity elapses, a workgroup is disbanded. New ones are formed as the need arises. Therefore, the success of workgroups will be the driving force toward prosperity in the future. It is the source of new jobs and the best chance for higher employment rates. The success of workgroups will depend on how well they can meet society's pent-up demands for value added. This is not necessarily in the form of the next gee-whiz gizmo, but rather in dealing with the concerns that people have with the way they live, and the way society is heading. Optimistic technologists may criticize my underestimation of the potential of their next breakthroughs to create wonderful job opportunities. The truth is if an invention is any good at all, it is more likely to eliminate more old jobs than the new ones it generates. Let's say someone has perfected a computer-aided, mold-injection process for custom-designed fiberglass houses that beats conventional building methods hands down in costs, comfort, and durability. Surely, a new industry is born, but I bet it will employ far fewer people than the old one that it replaces. By contrast, fix-it-yourself supply centers, such as Home Depot, that respond to people's demand for value in home repair and improvement, do create net increases in the employment of sales clerks who are knowledgeable in the handicrafts.

For the individual, career paths will look quite different from before. From climbing the corporate ladder, we now have setting the corporate sails. This translates to *a continual reemployability in successful workgroups.* It is at once more challenging and less secure by traditional standards. No longer will one set of skills and job description make stable employment. Instead, an aptitude for lifelong learning and adaptation to new demands for workgroups is essential to a rewarding and fulfilling career. On the surface, this sounds unsettling and seems to imply that future jobs require ever-increasing technical knowledge and specialized skills. With technology displacing much routine work, there is substantial bemoaning at the massive loss of low-skill, high-pay jobs. This is accompanied by the dread for the emergence of an unemployable underclass. Indeed, we saw many back-office, paper-shuffling jobs disappear with the recession that ended in 1991. While these did not require special skills, they were decent paying, full-time, white-collar jobs. In the ensuing recovery, many of these jobs did not come back. Instead, the modest upswing in employment reflected mainly low-paying service jobs as in fast food, or temporary help with little security or benefits. What are the implications of such a trend if it continues?

THE ROAD TO PROSPERITY

At this point, there is a fork in the road to any further pondering over future prosperity. One goes uphill and follows the assumption that it is important to keep as much of our work force gainfully employed as possible. The other disappears behind a blind curve and poses the disturbing question of what if continuing increase in productivity means that eventually we can afford to keep the majority of our work force idle. These are depicted in Figure 7.3.

Figure 7.3   The Curve and the Hill

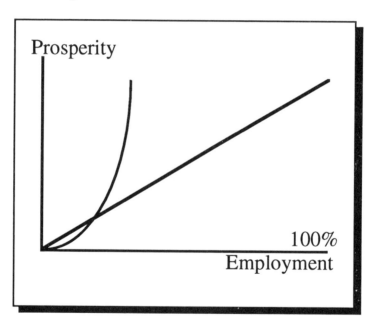

Believers in the uphill struggle are looking for ways for the economy to spawn more jobs and for the educational system to prepare our work force to take on such jobs. Those who take the curve are contemplating a scenario where there is enough wealth but not enough jobs to go around. They wonder if our society can cope with such a dilemma. Let us assume for a moment that collectively we can be productive enough to sustain a reasonably high level of prosperity, say, at the top of the vertical scale in the picture. If this is achieved with full employment, then we have just about the capitalistic ideal. The problem is that no one knows where all these jobs will come from. By contrast, if only a portion of the work force is necessary and qualified to do the jobs producing the economic output, we will end up with a two-tier society: the haves and the have-nots. Even with the most judicious system to distribute welfare, we will still be looking at significant discrepancies between the elite and the underclass. How is this different from what we have all along? Just imagine the disappearance of the entire working middle-class as we know it. Not an inviting specter, even if we manage to keep everyone well above poverty level of subsistence. The real puzzle is then what is likely to happen to this employment gap. We can always get the state to employ everyone and declare full employment. This has been tried under communism and it is well known that it does not lead to prosperity. With no incentive to be productive and competitive, the outcome—as recent history has shown—is something like the low, flat plateau labeled as the communist debacle in Figure 7.4. Everyone has a job, but the system fails to motivate the level of collective efforts necessary to take the economy beyond the Industrial Age. Contrary to popular belief, it was not so much the lack of productivity that brought down communist economies. Centrally planned systems were quite well suited to benefit from economy of scale. Output had obviously been high enough to sustain massive and progressive military build-ups to maintain the regimes as superpowers. However, without free-market mechanisms

Figure 7.4   The Gap and the Plateau

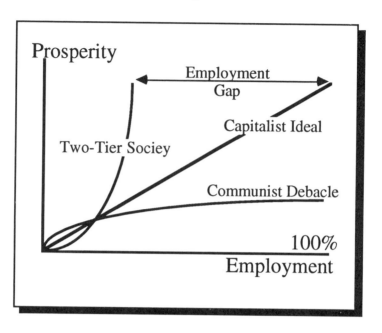

and profit incentives to nurture the crucial customer orientation, all service components of the economy fell behind and never evolved. So, it was evidence such as bumper crops rotting in one region while people were starving in another—because of a grossly ineffective infrastructure for communication and distribution—that hinted at the eventual demise of this approach.

Given the unlikelihood, or at least the uncertainty of 100% fulfilling and prosperous employment, and the two rather extreme alternatives, it is natural to see if there can still be some attractive middle ground. Fortunately, such a scenario is indeed conceivable. As a road to prosperity, it can be regarded as a multi-lane highway. This scenario is plausible, even palpable, but by no means inevitable. I am going to present it with neither prophecy nor advocacy. We have argued that in the transition from the Financial Age to the Information Age, a customer focus and people orientation will emerge and eventually prevail. The economy will be driven by a value-conscious marketplace. However, the

Figure 7.5   The Multi-Lane Highway

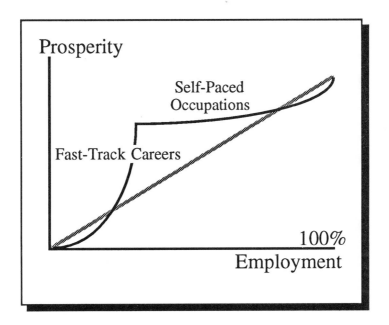

underlying values do not have to be purely materialistic. We are not expecting consumers just to become ever more fastidious. It may be that people are reverting to older-fashioned values in their pursuit of happiness. Perhaps money, prestige, and power must be better balanced by less materialistic rewards. As the abundance of single-track, 40-hours-a-week, 40-year careers subsides, other options are becoming not only viable, but even attractive. Many may choose to have multiple careers in diverse fields of interest, taking time off in between for education, family, or other personal priorities. Others may share jobs, on top of flex-time, flex-place arrangements. Yet others may wish to blend career, retirement, and volunteerism at various stages of their lives. As business enterprises adopt workgroups as their basic units of operation, such multi-track careers become fully respectable and amenable to careful planning and preparation. Since job descriptions themselves are losing permanence, the ability or desire to hold one life-long is neither as appealing nor admirable as before. Many of today's informal workstyles, such as freelancing and consulting, still carry an easy-go-lucky, hand-to-mouth aura about them. As special cases of tomorrow's "work-grouping," their roles and functions will be very much in the mainstream. Nevertheless, with technological advances and the acceleration of global competition, there will be no shortage of high-skill, high-stress career opportunities for those who prefer to stick with the fast track. Suppose fewer people than in the Financial Age opt for this approach to jobs and careers with the conventional mind-set. Some may choose to do it for a shorter time span before retiring early into other challenging and meaningful endeavors. Others may decide to go with a totally self-paced agenda. The overall effect on the economy will be something like the combined curves for fast-track careers and self-paced occupations shown in Figure 7.5. It is a way to bridge the employment gap. It can happen, but it is by no means inevitable. It hinges largely on the ability of our society to adapt to the technology payoff. The options are plain: be dexterous or be displaced. While the choice seems obvious, the actual outlook is not. The question of how to adapt will hold the key to prosperity in the Information Age. With this we come to the crux of the book. However, before moving on, a few clarifications are in order.

REALITY CHECK

Let us take stock of what we have so far and make sure that we are on the right track. The changes around us are very real. The issues we have taken up—including the outlook on business practices, labor-management relationships, and the future of jobs and careers—are the preoccupation of society as we enter the third millennium. One can hardly pick up a newspaper, watch a telecast, or listen to any politician without being reminded of some of the dilemmas we are facing. It is an uneasy feeling to sense that as a species, human society seems smart enough to take charge of its own evolution, and yet as a system it may be running the risk of falling apart. The puzzle is no less perplexing than whether the universe is ever-expanding or destined to collapse on itself. In any case, we have traced many of our economic predicaments to the top-down, remote-control, bottom-line approach to management by financial and accounting numbers that characterizes the Financial Age of the last four decades or so. Summarizing the changes we are experiencing on a global scale as major paradigm shifts, we hope to find new ways to cope. The liberation of the consumer market and the liberation of professional knowledge together point to the necessity of a customer focus as well as the empowerment of workgroups to make businesses more responsive and flexible.

Is this argument too naïve? Is the bottom-up, people orientation practicable? Worst of all, is all this talk just another round of academic exercises to make work for business scholars and management consultants? I hope not. To be convincing, I need to emphasize that there is absolutely nothing wrong with watching the bottom line. After all, one cannot stay in business by giving away the store.

Financial reward is still the best incentive for hard work although it does not have to be the only one. So let us affirm that for any business enterprise to prosper, it has to turn a bottom-line profit and deliver a healthy return on investment to its stockholders. As its basic operational unit, any workgroup should benefit from that profit in proportion to the value it adds to the process. Yes, we are all in it for the bottom line. What needs to change is not where to go, but *how* to get there. Adopting the customer focus and people orientation does not change the enterprise into a philanthropy or charity. It means a different way of doing business, just like different mechanisms to transfer the power of the engine to the wheels of a car. Top-down management is rear-wheel drive, using financial goals to push the car forward. Workgroup empowerment is front-wheel drive, letting customer wants pull the car forward. Just as front-wheel drive has proven to give better traction in rain and snow, it now appears that empowered workgroups are the way to go in the business paradigms of the Information Age. They are the new driving forces to prosperity in the future. What we shall attempt to do next is to identify critical factors to make this whole approach effective. Remembering how movements such as TQM were doomed to fail when preached like a religion on top of a bottom-line culture, we know better than simply looking for the next fashionable banner. Instead, I present a very natural concept of balancing the awareness of how things get done and how information technology can help. I call this B.I.O. (Business Information and Operations) Rhythm and argue that it is the key to prosperity for workgroups of tomorrow.

Part III

B.I.O. Rhythm

A Key to Prosperity for Workgroups of Tomorrow

- Do fax machines and desktop publishing really change the way people work?

- Why is home banking so slow to catch on while Automatic Teller Machines flourish?

- Why do retailers get suppliers to manage their inventory; and overnight couriers let customers track their own packages?

- Is there a way to explain all these and other recent developments in business?

- What is the key to prosperity at all levels of a business enterprise?

- What are the ways to get hold of this key?

8

B.I.O. Rhythm

Competitive market forces are moving businesses toward a customer focus. Consequently, there is an increasing need to entrust control of the work process to frontline workers who deal with the customers. The rapid development of information technology is providing the opportunities for workgroups at all levels to find better ways to get things done—not just doing things faster. While these two formidable currents are bound to set our bearings into the Information Age, smooth sailing is by no means automatic or guaranteed. In fact, the two have perhaps diametrically opposite characters. Information technology is dynamic and volatile. Like waves in a rough sea, today's state-of-the-art is quickly pushed over by new standards of tomorrow. Operation of work processes, by contrast, is habit forming and routine oriented. Like ripples in a calm pond, it propagates its influence in a steadfast pattern. It should then come as little surprise that IT and business operations are unlikely to work in perfect harmony without significant efforts to ensure that the two are in sync. Moreover, as long as either party of this yin-yang relationship is evolving—as IT certainly will be—the whole must keep on changing. This precludes any static perspective for the design of business operations that rely substantially on IT. To make best use of available technology, one must rethink how work gets done. The reengineering of work, and the innovation of business processes have become popular pursuits in Corporate America in recent years. It is important to note that these should not be treated as one-time, fix-up projects. Once a higher level of effectiveness is achieved, new demands and opportunities will in turn be open to take advantage of further advances in technology. For this reason, I call the mind-set for continual improvement—in business operations with the timely support of information technology—*B.I.O. Rhythm.* A visual aid to this concept is given in Figure 8.1. The initials stand for Business Information and Operations. That they spell out the physiological phenomenon of biorhythm is unintentional, but perhaps not altogether inappropriate. Current management thinking does accommodate the view of business enterprises as

Figure 8.1   A Graphical Display of B.I.O. Rhythm

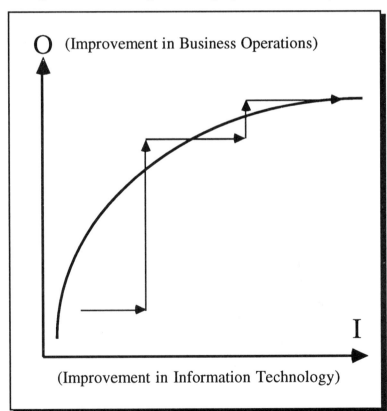

dynamic organisms capable of growth, learning, and evolution. To minimize confusion, we will stick with the capitalized initials and pronounce this coinage as "bee-aye-oh" rhythm. In Figure 8.1, the upward sloping curve is used to represent an ideal path of balanced and effective improvement. Things are getting better and better as we move from the lower left toward the upper right of the picture. The zigzagging lines about this B.I.O. Rhythmic path indicate that typically, long-term improvement can be considered as the combined results of steps taken in both the directions of information and operations. While any sequence of steps is conceivable, those with alternating directions enveloping the ideal path reflect conscious and successful attempts to attain B.I.O. Rhythm. Through a series of examples, we are going to see how this chart can be used to describe and interpret many developments in our business environment.

WHAT'S YOUR FAX NUMBER?

In just a matter of years, the fax machine has gained widespread use and has become a standard feature in most business offices. More people are asking directly for your fax number instead of first inquiring whether you have one or not. This must certainly be significant progress, right? Well, probably not as much as it may appear at first sight. While it helps transmit documents much faster than, say, the mail, it does not really change what we do with such documents. In most cases, business is done the same way as before. Depending on the situation, the time savings from expediting certain paper transfer may or may not be critical to the underlying work process.

I have relatives who own and operate a small manufacturing outfit for certain specialty consumer products.

For decades, they do all their accounting manually. Every time there is a change in the cost of raw materials, wages for labor, or freight rates, it will take days to prepare new price quotes. Back in the mid-1970s, when personal computers were just becoming popular, I demonstrated to the owners how easy it would be to update their price quotes with an electronic spreadsheet. Somewhat nonplused, they simply told me that given such a small and traditional operation, any fancy high-tech would be an overkill. Another ten years passed by. Prices of low-end PC clones had dropped from the thousands to a few hundred dollars. Just to prove a point, I offered one as a gift to the factory. It was very politely turned down; and so I gave up. Within a month, a note came over the fax: "…Fax machines just became available on the local market. We bought one last week and have been using it everyday. It's great!" The same people who would not have anything to do with a computer snapped up the fax. What is the difference? With the fax, they did not have to cope with any real changes in the way they worked. In our chart, this is a horizontal step without an accompanying move upward. For this reason, we should not expect much by way of advancing along the B.I.O. Rhythmic path. While our example may be a little bit extreme, the same kind of resistance to change—conscious or otherwise—can be found to various extents in most existing work processes.

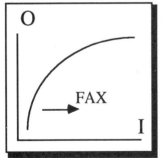

Figure 8.2   Fax

In all fairness to the fax technology, it should be pointed out that there are situations in which a step in the vertical direction can indeed be made. For instance, many business people used to phone the corner coffee shop to order a take-out lunch. Now they can fax the same order. For the coffee shop, a fax order does not require someone to answer the phone. This is a real change in the operation and hence can be considered a move up in the O-direction. Next time you fax something, think of whether it really changes the way things get done. If not, ask yourself what it would take (even if it is pie-in-the-sky) to do a better job.

THAT'S WHERE THE MONEY IS

By the time personal computers developed a substantial user base, the banking industry was eager, willing, and able to provide home banking services. With the use of a

Figure 8.3   ATM   vs   Home   Banking

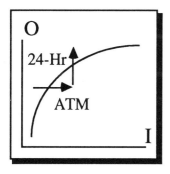
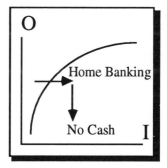

modem, one can take care of all kinds of financial transactions in the comfort and convenience of one's own home. Some banks, at one time or another, were ready to provide customers with the necessary hardware to get started. Yet, even to this day, home banking has never quite caught on. Meanwhile, automatic teller machines (ATM) have sprung up everywhere and become part of many people's regular routine. Why would people rather get out of the house, even in foul weather, and drive up to a hole in the wall to use essentially the same technology? The only reason is that they cannot get cash over the phone line. In what is still primarily a cash-based economy, this drawback is enough to negate other operational advantages, such as round-the-clock availability, and the convenience of one's own home.

ALL THAT GLITTERS

Information technology is basically electronic. It holds the promise of eventually eliminating the use of paper at work. Apart from saving trees, this prospect will also go far in streamlining the cluttered workplace. Then came desktop publishing. It has been considered as one of the triumphs of IT. By enabling personal computer users to produce documents, presentations, newsletters, and reports, which only years ago required graphic designers and typesetters, it opened up the floodgate for creativity and expression. Does it really make us work better? That is not obvious. We do know for sure that it has raised the expectation and superficial quality of paper output. With the increasing ease of production, there is no doubt that the quantity of such output has also increased. As a professor, I am no stranger to absolutely professional-looking reports, which on closer examination, turn out to be devoid of meaningful content or signs of coherent thought. What happened is that desktop publishing has set higher quality standards for the presentation of paper output. In business correspondence, no less than laser printing, sprinkled with **bold face** and *italics* for emphasis, is expected nowadays. The B.I.O. Rhythmic curve has been raised from the dotted line to the solid one in Figure 8.4. By taking control of creativity and expres-

Figure 8.4   Desktop Publishing

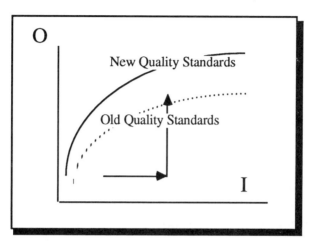

sion, we might indeed have made a move up in the O-direction. However, unless there are further changes to help us produce better *content*, we have not really gotten anywhere in terms of the new expectations. In any case, if the paperless office is to be the ultimate goal, desktop publishing could prove to be quite an engrossing detour.

TEACHING ELEPHANTS TO DANCE

We have seen how a B.I.O. Rhythm curve can shift in one direction. It can also happen in the other dimension, as shown in Figure 8.5. This is typical of projects to "modernize" venerable bureaucracies such as the Internal Revenue Service. It is not unusual to see ten-year schedules and multi-billion-dollar budgets for these tremendously complex undertakings. Apart from the IRS, agencies like the Federal Aviation Administration, the U.S. Patent and Trademark Office, and the National Weather Service have all experienced explosive cost overruns and lengthy delays

Figure 8.5   IT for Mega-Bureaucracies

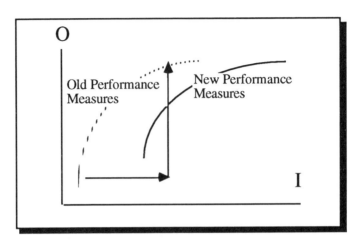

in their IT projects. Technical and managerial difficulties aside, these systems are likely to become obsolete by the time they are completed. This is due to the simple fact that ten years can easily translate into three or four generations of technology. With luck, they may still work well enough to serve their intended purposes. However, the curve for matching up the needs of the times with state-of-the-technology has changed. Another cycle of modernization will be in order. Unfortunately, the very scope of the project will again preclude the system from ever becoming truly B.I.O. Rhythmic. In the present context, we can substitute "Bureaucracy" for "Business" as the "B" in "B.I.O."

MORE BANK FOR THE BUCK

Lest you think that all efforts to improve on business processes are initiated by technology, we will look at examples where steps are taken first in the O-direction. Traditionally, banks are in the business of transactions: checking accounts, savings deposits, loans, etc. As records are kept separately in information systems specific to different transactions, a bank does not necessarily know much about its customers—not even those who deal extensively with it. The emergence of the customer focus and the need to be responsive and

Figure 8.6   Relationship Banking

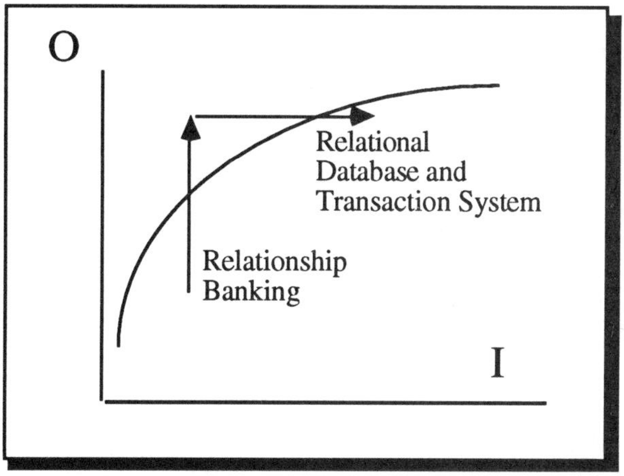

flexible to compete in the new market paradigm give rise to the concept of "relationship banking." The bank wants to keep complete profiles of its customers so that it can market individually tailored services and products. With this move up the O-direction, pioneers like Banc One Corp., the Columbus, OH-based banking conglomerate, decided that they are in the information business rather than the transaction business. The step in the I-direction involves replacing the disparate information systems with an integrated customer database and transactions processing system. The bankers may decide that customers with high balances in their checking accounts can be better served by higher-yielding savings accounts. They can now readily generate a list of customers who qualify and who might be interested in such services.

YOUR MARTINI, MR. BOND, STIRRED, NOT SHAKEN

Similar steps to attain B.I.O. Rhythm are taken by the travel and hospitality industries. As a weary business traveler, you might consider it a treat to be greeted without waiting in line at the front desk; pick up a key knowing it will be for a smoke-free room facing the courtyard; have your favorite newspaper waiting at the breakfast table; and not to have the coffee refreshed until you have finished the cup. To improve on customer service, hotel chains take a step in the O-direction so that you do not have to repeat the ritual of expressing your likes and dislikes at every stop. Instead, the frontline workers, including desk clerks, bellhops, housekeepers, operators, and waiters will know about a repeat customer's preferences and cater to them accordingly. For pioneers like Ritz-Carlton, the Atlanta, GA-based luxury hotel company, the I-step is in the form of a guest-recognition system. The employees feed back what they have learned about a customer into the system. They also have on-line access to the system for information on customers they are serving. While such level of sophistication can only be found initially at luxury hotels, lesser versions of preference tracking—more categorical than anecdotal—are already commonplace among airline frequent flyer programs and car rental agencies. They know, for example, if you prefer a window or an aisle seat, a full-size or a compact car.

YOUR SIZE IN STOCK, GUARANTEED

If not, you get one free! This paradoxical offer has actually appeared in advertisements. Whatever it means, we can sense the retailer's effort to be responsive to customer needs. Running out of an item in demand will turn away customers—with loss of sales as well as good will. Over-stocking items that are not moving is also costly—by tying up capital and taking up space. Increasingly, retailers are taking the O-step to shoot for just-in-time replenishment of merchandise. The practice has become known as Quick Response. It involves a strategic alliance with a supplier to provide frequent and timely shipments. For the I-step, sales

Figure 8.7   Quick Response

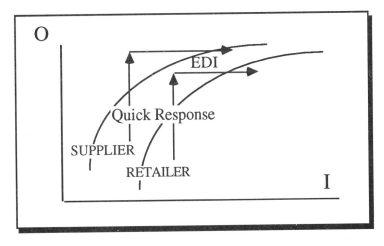

trends and inventories are continuously monitored by point-of-sale (POS) information systems. The information is shared by the supplier through electronic data inter-change (EDI). This helps the supplier with its O-step of just-in-time production planning and delivery scheduling.

In many cases, no conventional purchase orders or invoices are processed. Billings and payments are done by electronic fund transfer. VF Corp., maker of Lee and Wrangler jeans, actually manages the inventories of its products sold at JC Penney stores. Dupont, the chemical giant, works similarly with many of its suppliers. These are examples of B.I.O. Rhythm in a strategic alliance.

ARE WE THERE YET?

So far, we have seen only examples of single sequences of I- and O-steps. For something that truly begins to resemble

Figure 8.8   Overnight Couriers

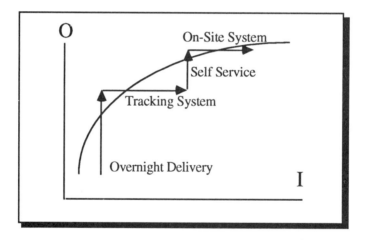

a rhythmic pattern of improvement, we can look to the most progressive overnight couriers: Federal Express, followed closely by United Parcel Service (UPS). Initially, the O-step is summed up clearly by a guarantee of delivery by 10:30 in the morning. The massive operations of package pickup and sorting, fleet scheduling and dispatching, billing, and accounting are made possible by some of the most successful information systems in use. These tracking systems—the I-step in our chart—are a showcase of IT: incorporating bar-coding, hand-held and truck-mounted computers as well as satellite communication. Still, there is no room for complacency as alternative forms of communication, notably the fax and voice-mail of today, and the digitized video of tomorrow, can easily alter the landscape of the express mail market. This calls for continuing improvement in the standards and level of service from the standpoint of the customers. It comes in the form of another O-step that will make it easier for customers to use the delivery services. Both Federal Express and UPS can now provide customers with complete PC-based systems to store address databases, to print bar-codes and labels, to tap into the courier company's tracking systems for the status and verification of delivery, and to keep account of shipping volumes and expenses. By empowering the customers, the industry enhances its flexibility and responsiveness to their needs. With the new technology, the customer can tell instantaneously when a package was delivered, and who signed for it—should a dispute arise with the recipient. This saves an extra layer of communication by eliminating the need for the customer to make inquiries with the help of service personnel of the courier company. Apart from promoting the customer focus, this approach apparently is cost-effective enough to allow the companies to equip their customers with the hardware free of charge. It may not be easy to predict their next moves up the curve in Figure 8.8. Nevertheless, I believe we can count on these competitive enterprises to seize the moment when a new combination of opportunities arrives.

BACK TRACKING

Through the 1970s and the 1980s, the New York Life Insurance Company has been a leader in investing in information technology. For development on mainframe computers, it moved early into computer-aided software engineering (CASE). It caught one of the first PC waves. For decision support, it got a jump start on expert systems. As an even bolder initiative, it had planned to convert practically its entire business into paperless transactions through imaging technology. Every check, form, and report would be scanned and digitized to become electronically manipulatable. It is an environment that most technologists believe to be the way of the future—although estimates of when it will happen may vary significantly. In any case, as an undertaking to rebuild the business platform, it represented a wide stretch on our B.I.O. chart as depicted by the dotted arrows in Figure 8.9. By early 1992, the company decided

Figure 8.9   Overreaching vs B.I.O Rhythm

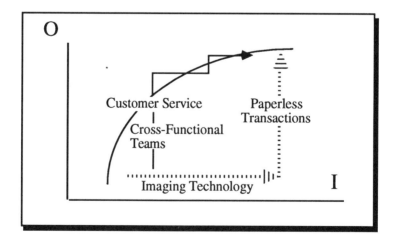

that it was overreaching in this I-step for cutting-edge technology. In the process, it may have lost sight of other critical success factors for its core business. It has since been refocusing on customer service: restructuring by empowering cross-functional teams to deliver and enhance the value of its products and services. The ambitious goal has not been abandoned though. The company is still aiming for it by taking one manageable step at a time. This change of tack can be succinctly captured as a realignment with the B.I.O. Rhythmic curve.

AHEAD OF THE GAME

In the chronicles of IT, there have been many projects that suffered from technical setbacks and managerial snafus. Not surprisingly, they eventually got smothered by runaway budgets and missed deadlines. However, there have also been some nicely done ones that nevertheless missed their mark. What could have gone wrong? In our framework, the cause of the problem is very often a dubious O-step. The nature of such missing links can vary from case to case and we should look at a few examples. The simplest one is the dust-collecting home computer. I am often approached with the question: "Which computer should we buy?" My stock response is that it depends on what you need to or wish to do. The underlying assumption is that unless you have an O-step, it may not be necessary to take an I-step. Chances are there is a need, if for nothing

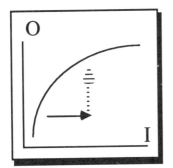

Figure 8.10   Missing Link

else, at least to become computer literate. The real question is then: What is best suited to your needs? In the early days of PC's, a decent system cost around $5,000. As new models were introduced, they still cost that much, except that one got progressively more performance for the money. By the late 1980s, both the technology and the industry have matured to a point that there began to have real choices. Today, one can set a budget of anywhere from $1,000 and up, and then find a system to fit. If you decide to splurge on a $5,000 system just to balance your check book, much of your investment will be sitting idle. Unlike a Ferrari in the garage, computer hardware depreciates rapidly. We illustrate this lack of B.I.O. Rhythm by a substantial I-step and a shadowy O-step in Figure 8.10.

Then, there is the short-lived debut of the Postal Buddy. This is an interactive, multimedia information processing kiosk that double-duties as a vending machine. It's

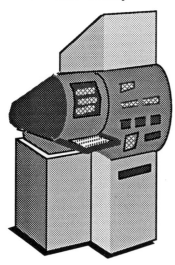

Figure 8.11
The Postal Buddy

primary purpose is to process address changes, a function of the U.S. Postal Service that costs $1.3 billion a year. It talks the customer through options on a touch-screen and gives instructions to key in the necessary information. It verifies the transaction using an internal database on a CD-ROM. The collected information is retrieved nightly by a system in San Diego, CA, that performs further verification before forwarding to USPS's National Address Information

Center in Memphis, TN. According to the Postal Service, if the 10,000 planned installations were to handle half of the over 40 million address changes made each year, the estimated annual savings on labor for data entry alone would be around $50 million. As a vending machine, Postal Buddy also sells stamps, customized cards and stationery as well as other mailing accessories. Financially, it is a joint venture with private business, for which the Postal Service is to share revenues above $42 per kiosk per day. It is a good idea, and the choice of technology is perfectly sound and timely. The first kiosks were introduced in December 1992 and the debut went without a hitch. Indeed, the project has such a smack of showcase potential that Vice President Al Gore used it as an example of how IT can help reinvent government. This makes it all the more surprising that in the Fall of 1993, less than a year after the launch, the Postal Service terminated the venture. The reason cited—that actual revenue of $15 to $30 per kiosk per day missed the projected levels of $35 to $55—showed a muddled intent for the O-step. Was it to streamline address-change notifications, or was it a new product line? For the former, the I-step taken is indeed a laudable advance to make a nontrivial government service more user-friendly, reliable, and in our terminology, B.I.O. Rhythmic. For the latter, all that technology may indeed be an overkill for a vending machine that perhaps does not have real market demand. For the time being, we can only chalk up a shadowy arrow in the O-direction to account for the setback of the Postal Buddy.

An even more complex case is Globex—the world's only computerized, 24-hour trading system for options and futures as of 1994. It is an intercontinental network of computers and workstations developed and operated by

Reuters Holdings, the British information processing conglomerate, under contract with the Chicago Board of Trade (CBOT) and the Chicago Mercantile Exchange (Merc). The $100 million system has a network of some 400 trading screens over the globe and provides round-the-clock transactions. It is aimed at attracting financial markets worldwide to list their products on the network for a fee to the CBOT-Merc venture. Major customers include the Marché à Terme International de France (Matif) in Paris and the London International Financial Futures Exchange (LIFFE) in London. Launched on June 25, 1992, Globex has failed to generate enough business, in terms of contracts traded per day, to be profitable after 18 months of operation. In the view of CBOT chairman Patrick H. Arbor, "Computerized after-hour trading has a sexy ring to it. But before screen trading can take hold, it has to reach a critical mass." In other words, while the I-step may be a resounding success, the technology may be ahead of the game. However, Merc and Reuters believe that it is the O-step that is holding Globex back. In particular, the system is not exactly "seamless." After the day time open-cry bonds trading session is over, CBOT has its own night session and does not list contracts on Globex until 10:30 p.m. John F. Sandner, chairman of Merc as well as the Globex joint venture, also realizes the need to strengthen the alliances by making participants like Matif full-fledged members—to share the costs and profits. Meanwhile, CBOT has plans to expand its open-cry operations with a new trading facility. It also has it own electronic trading network under development. All these factors add to the murkiness of the O-step for Globex. They jeopardize its potential for B.I.O. Rhythm and cast doubts on its continuing viability.

CATCHING THE WAVE

We have seen how the concept of B.I.O. Rhythm can be used to describe many contemporary developments in business enterprises and bureaucracies. Successes and setbacks alike can be cast within our framework of interaction between business operations and information technology. These forces are so intertwined that neither alone can determine the outcome of an activity to create economic value. Since both are subject to constant changes caused by progress, politics, or plight—the timing of events becomes a crucial factor. That is why we use, at least metaphorically, the dynamics inherent in rhythms to capture the essence of their synergy. The B.I.O. Rhythmic curve that we have drawn is largely symbolic. For our present purpose, there is no need to quantify its exact form or shape. It is reasonable though to assume a curve with a diminishing upward slope. This reflects naturally the narrowing of opportunities for new benefits on successive steps down a trodden path. As Kent 'Oz' Nelson, chairman of United Parcel Service, put it in an interview with Computerworld, "We've knocked out a lot of the easier ones. The [IT projects] now are much tougher." How about steps that open up new doors? With those, we will be shifting to a new curve and start climbing there. Now, we can clarify the difference between catching the wave and missing one. In the example of unwieldy projects that become obsolete by the time they are finished, we pointed out the need to start over just to keep up. The first wave is gone and so is the opportunity to make the best of it. The most one can do is to try harder for the next one. In the success stories of the overnight couriers who are taking a second step up the curve, it is trying harder too. However, it is riding on the same wave after catching it the first time around. This is the rhythm that will hold the key to prosperity in the Information Age.

SPELLING IT OUT

Even if we are not going to theorize about this central concept of the book, a concise definition may be helpful to fix ideas.

> B.I.O. Rhythm is seizing the moment
> to realize improvement in business operations
> with appropriate information technology;
> and the ability to do so continually
> as new opportunities for such match-ups arise.

9

A Key to Prosperity

If the world economy during this first half of the 1990s is any indication, the path to prosperity in the Information Age will not be straight or smooth. The liberation of the mass market and of profession knowledge, along with global competition, have essentially locked the gates on the way of doing business in the industrial and financial eras. So far, we have spotted several guiding lights to help us make the way through. They include putting the emphasis back on people by focusing on customers and empowering employees, taking risks in the entrepreneurial spirit to create value, and striving to be flexible and responsive to constant changes. These new approaches are requiring an ever-increasing level of connectivity and communication. It is perhaps of academic interest to debate whether information technology is the horse that is driving us to change our ways, or the cart that is being pulled by our collective aspirations. Pragmatically, IT and business operations are becoming inseparable yet distinct dimensions of any economic activity. For this reason, there can be no breakthrough to prosperity without the key of B.I.O. Rhythm.

Since we have considered workgroups to be the fundamental units of business enterprises of the future, the latter cannot be B.I.O. Rhythmic without their workgroups being so. As workgroups themselves can be teams of people or similar alliances, we must also have individuals who are B.I.O. Rhythmic. We shall see what that means in this chapter, and show that our concept can indeed provide a rather general framework for many popular tenets of current business thinking.

B.I.O. RHYTHM AT THE FRONTLINE

Let us start with the individual. To be B.I.O. Rhythmic, one has to be aware of how things get done, and how IT can help to do a job better. Obviously, expansion on this theme has to be done in context. For instance, someone who has the job of preparing letters to notify customers with overdue accounts may or may not be aware of the fact that what is involved is a form letter. Each letter differs in the specific contents, such as the customer name and address, account number, and the amount overdue. Other than that, they are essentially the same letter, and as such, should be amenable to systematic processing. Independently

Figure 9.1   Rudiments of B.I.O. Rhythm in Mail Merging

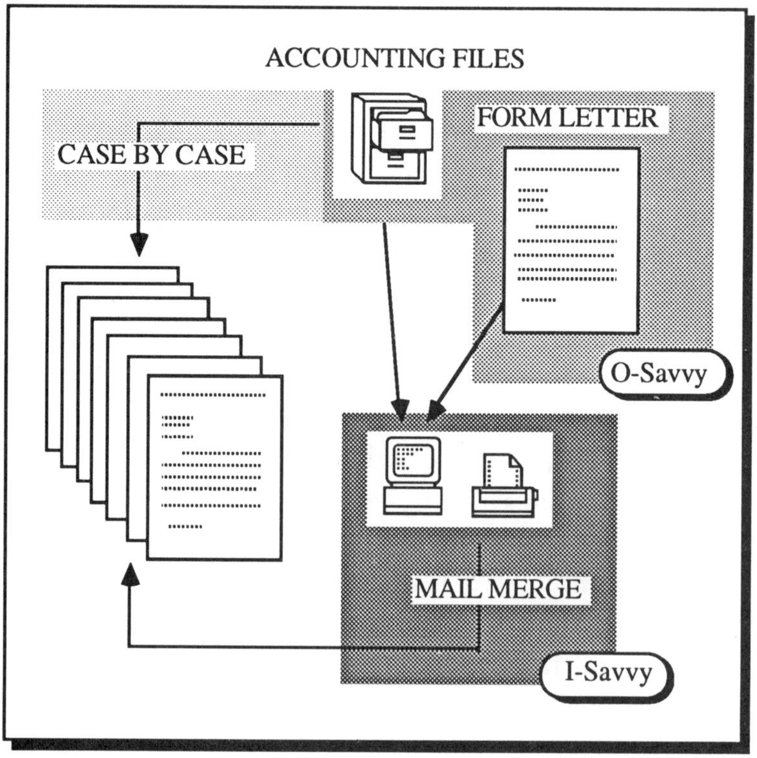

of the awareness of this particular work process, the individual in question may or may not know about the existence of mail-merging software. For anyone already familiar with this process, this example must appear trite and trivial. After all, mail merging is by now a standard feature in most word processing software. However, for the uninitiated, each piece of the picture in Figure 9.1 can indeed come as a separate revelation. I have seen many eyes light up when this topic is introduced in computer literacy workshops. More than learning a new trick, the experience is genuine savvy. In our framework, we distinguish between savvy in operations (O-savvy) and savvy in IT (I-savvy). In mail merging, the appreciation of the idea of a form letter is O-savvy. The awareness of the capability of software to get it done is I-savvy. Together, we have B.I.O. savvy that can then lead to B.I.O. Rhythm.

B.I.O. RHYTHM AT THE MIDDLE

Next, consider the case of a manager of customer service. Traditionally, when a customer calls to make an inquiry, the call is directed to the department that has the appropriate information. If there is a question on the delivery schedule for an order, it goes to the shipping department. A question on billing is handled by accounting, and so forth. If one asks about the account after checking on a shipping date, the likely response will be: "I'm sorry I cannot help you with that. Let me transfer you to..." This may not sound like much, but the following scenario is not at all uncommon. Suppose you place an order for various quantities of several different items. Some items are in stock and shipped immediately. Some others are out of stock and backordered. The remaining ones may come as partial shipments. Even if there are detailed and accurate records of all these bits and pieces of your order kept with the different departments, you may be surprised how long it will take the company to come up with an exact status of your account. O-savvy for the manager here can be the awareness that it would be much more convenient for the customer to be able to get all the answers at one stop. After all, it is one account dealing with the same company. The suitable I-savvy can be the appreciation of the power of relational databases. With this technology, records can be

Figure 9.2   One-Stop Customer Service

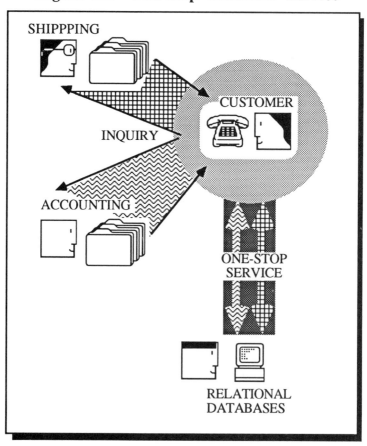

kept in logically and functionally separate files: inventory in stock, backorders, shipping dates, orders, customer accounts, etc. However, the files can be linked by appropriate keys, such as account numbers, enabling speedy queries involving multiple files. The B.I.O. savvy manager is now ready to implement such systems to allow customer service representatives to deal with any inquiry over the phone as depicted in the bottom part of Figure 9.2.

These incidental examples of individual and managerial B.I.O. Rhythm are used to illustrate the significance of evaluating the balance between operations and information in any given context. There is no absolute measure of accomplishment here. Everything should be viewed with respect to what needs to be done, such as various aspects of dealing with customers. Like the notion of "keeping up," it means different things to different people. For a retiree, reading the daily paper is a fairly relaxing way to keep up. For a practicing physician, it calls for the studying of medical journals. Even with our example of mail merging, the application is so commonplace in larger business organizations that it probably no longer counts toward any individual's B.I.O. savvy in such an environment. Whereas, for many small business startups, this match-up of technology with operational needs may still require a conscious effort on the part of the enterprising individuals to become B.I.O. Rhythmic.

B.I.O. RHYTHM AT THE TOP

By addressing the questions of how things get done and how IT may help, we can speculate on what it means to be productively savvy in any particular individual job situation. Let us see how things look for top executives with titles such as Chief Executive Officer (CEO), Chief Operating Officer (COO), Chief Financial Officer (CFO), and Chief Information Officer (CIO). With information technology becoming a seemingly inevitable trend toward progress, Corporate America has been spending heavily on computer and telecommunication systems as well as the necessary maintenance and technical support. To oversee the planning, implementation, and operation of such systems, most companies now have their designated CIO, or at least a Director of Information Systems. Typically, these are people with a technical background. Many are veterans in the computer industry—steeped in management of large projects in hardware and software development. There is a natural tendency for them to measure progress in terms of technological advances. As IT neither comes cheap nor off-the-shelf, the size and budget of an information systems department have become yardsticks for the influence of the CIO. Meanwhile, CEOs, COOs, and CFOs are usually much less technologically oriented. Many still equate IT with the personal computer, and regard the latter simply as a souped-up typewriter or calculator for the clerical staff. That the keyboard has been the standard human-machine interface certainly does not help getting over a mind-set of "secretaries type; executives don't." While it may indeed not be crucial that top executives get their hands on the technology, this detached attitude does stand in the way of critical evaluations of IT as a whole. Unlike decisions on office buildings, warehouses, manufacturing plants, or production lines, spending on IT has to date not been amenable to comparable cost-benefit deliberations. Much of the top-level approval to plow ahead is based on promises of improved efficiency or better still, competitive advantages. The latter can be most convincing whenever there is evidence that one's competitors are heading the same way. As competitors tend to watch each other very closely nowadays, it is not difficult to imagine how easily self-reinforcing trends take hold. Exactly how much better can one do? That is one question CIO's, IT consultants, and vendors alike do not yet seem to have to respond to, at least not with any great precision or guarantee, before getting the nod for their latest projects. Why would top executives, who are unlikely to sign off on the acquisition of a major product line without careful analysis, do so with IT spending? For one thing, it is never quite clear exactly what role IT plays in most business enterprises. Is it an operational expense? If so, it may be regarded as a cost of doing business—a necessary evil to be put up with and kept in check as much as possible. Just like electricity that keeps the lights on, and water that keeps the toilets flushed, there is not much to think too hard about. Or is it a capital investment? In this case, IT can be viewed as an assembly line that cranks out the products of the business. Advocates have pitched the use of IT as a strategic investment to build the very platform that supports the business. Frederick W. Smith, Founder and CEO of Federal Express, thinks the computer has become as important, if not more so, than the airplane in the business of overnight freight. Apart from such glamorous examples, IT is most often a combination of both operating cost and capital investment; and it takes a B.I.O. Rhythmic CEO to see the whole picture. Such talent at the top is still a rare breed. Observers of the industry can point out that success stories, which tend to be rehashed over and over, account for only a small fraction of the total experience with IT in Corporate America. Why are business enterprises having such difficulties making IT work to their advantage? To start with, the benefits of IT are notoriously illusive and difficult, if not impossible, to measure. This is perhaps particularly true if one sticks to the traditional economic and accounting practices of the Financial Age. Many IT projects are justified as efforts to cut costs, as in computerization to reduce paperwork and personnel. However, this is done at the cost of purchasing and maintaining the computers. To cut these costs, the sharing of resources and information by computer networking seems promising enough. But how about its costs? At what point does it become trying to put out fires with fuel? According to a survey of top executives conducted by Computerworld and Anderson Consulting in 1993, the majority (52%) do not feel that their company is getting the most from its IT investment, although most (91%) expect IT to have a significant impact on profitability. With the shift toward the customer focus, an approach of examining how any spending on IT adds value for the customer should be a particularly appropriate way to guide such development. Strategic needs for the creation of value, rather than generic cost cutting, must be articulated and well understood by both the operational and IT people. To achieve this, senior management has to become sufficiently B.I.O. savvy. In this case, it means an awareness of how value is created and delivered to customers, and how IT can help. In a comment on how businesses are using accurate information on shipment to streamline distribution and eliminate costly inventory, Fred Smith said, "If you go and talk to people that are running these new types of logistic solutions to add value to their product or service, they understand. And the people who don't understand, they're going to die." That is perhaps as emphatic a remark as we can adapt to stress the importance of B.I.O. Rhythm for top executives.

PROSPERITY OF WORKGROUPS

After illustrating the concept of B.I.O. Rhythm in the familiar setting of frontline workers, middle managers, and top executives, we can venture to expand it to what we believe to be the fundamental building blocks of future business enterprises. These are the workgroups introduced in Chapter 7. Recall that a workgroup is any number of people, information systems, organizations, or combinations thereof, whose work processes, dedicated to a specific mission, are inter-related by the need to exchange information. Because of the need to be responsive and flexible to customer needs in a dynamic and competitive environment, the mission of a workgroup is ad hoc in nature. That means there is probably not much by way of standard procedures or even common practices to model after. The window of opportunity for a workgroup to accomplish its mission is typically small. Seizing the moment precludes drawn out planning or experimentation. Unlike conventional teams of people, a workgroup can involve human-machine as well as machine-machine and interorganizational linkages. All these add up to the need for a keen awareness of work processes and the capability of IT—what we call B.I.O. savvy. To prosper in the Information Age, an individual has to attain continual reemployability in viable workgroups. To grow and turn a profit, business enterprises have to deploy effective workgroups, perhaps in the form of virtual corporations, to adapt to the customer focus. On the basis of our arguments and observations, workgroups have to be B.I.O. Rhythmic to succeed. Collectively, they create the economic values that sustain a prosperous society. For this reason, we believe B.I.O. Rhythm to be a key to prosperity in the Information Age.

FROM WORDS TO ACTION

So far, our approach has been descriptive. By identifying the distinct dimensions of business operations and information technology, we pointed out the importance of striking a balance between the two, and seizing the moment to match up opportunities for continual improvement. From extensive observation of developments in the business envi-

Figure 9.3 It takes B.I.O. Savvy People to build a B.I.O. Rhythmic Workgroup

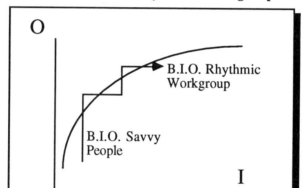

ronment, we found that our viewpoint can be a powerful framework for explaining successes as well as setbacks. B.I.O. savvy, as ascribed to an individual, is a state of mind. It says that within a particular context, such as a given job situation, one is sufficiently aware of how things get done, and knows enough about the potential of relevant information technology. Similarly, B.I.O. Rhythm is a state of affairs for a workgroup, or the organizations with which it interacts. It is the attainment of a timely balance between IT and business operations. By extension, we also regard the people who are instrumental in bringing about such a status as being B.I.O. Rhythmic themselves. There is no esoteric theory being postulated here. Hence, there is nothing to prove. The only question is whether it seems to make good sense. Assuming that it does, the next step is to see if we can turn some of the words into action. Having seen the goal line, how can we get the ball across it? The answer is step by step, although detailed strategies may vary. Since it takes B.I.O. savvy people to build B.I.O. Rhythmic workgroups, we start with people. The first step is simply to get the point across. One way to raise this consciousness is to have people read this book. If that seems too comprehensive or cut and dry, perhaps a repackaging

---

The People Agenda:

   I. **Raise awareness of B.I.O. Rhythm**

  II. **Help nurture B.I.O. Savvy**

III. **Empower in Workgroups**

---

of the pertinent messages into some customized presentation will be more appropriate and effective. In any case, we want them to first see the light. The next step involves a commitment to motivate, facilitate, and even entice them to a mind-set of continual learning. Depending on the situation, this process can be as informal as casual sharing of information, all the way to well-organized training workshops or educational programs. For this to work, it is important that a management style that leans toward

employee empowerment be in place. To whatever degree
ownership of the work process is conferred to those
directly involved, the traditional barriers of "need-to-
know" or "minding one's own business by job description"
must be brought down. Moreover, if the customer focus is
truly adopted and reflected in the reward structure, then it
is just a matter of instinct for people to become O-savvy. It
does not take any unnatural mandate to encourage employees to pursue their curiosity and get in the know, to
take control of how things get done, and to be rewarded if
they come up with better ideas. It simply goes with the
flow of human nature. Similarly, by stripping some of the
intimidating façades that cloak even the most sensible technology in forbidding "technospeak", the road to I-savvy is
no rougher than browsing through a mail-order catalog
that offers squirrel-proof bird feeders. As IT vendors and
professionals themselves catch on with the customer orientation, one can expect better communication and more
inviting settings to update one's awareness of what is available. In any case, an internal champion of B.I.O. Rhythm
can take on the role of a navigator to help sort out the
plethora of enabling technologies—preferably in plain
English. In time, we have on hand B.I.O. savvy workers,
all ready to set the corporate sail. In the third step, they are
assigned to mission-critical workgroups. Before we look at
workgroups, it should be remarked that the People Agenda
can also be individualized. This is necessary for people who
are either not yet employed in an organization, or who are
interested in our approach without much support from
within an organization. Steps I and II will have to be do-it-
yourself exercises that—with hope—may eventually lead to
a suitable Step III somewhere.

Workgroups have the following agenda. First, based

```
The Workgroup Agenda:

   I.  Identify Mission and Strategies

  II.  Match up Work Process and IT

 III.  Seize the Moment for Improvement
```

on the mission and strategies, which are typically initiated by senior management, goals and performance measures are set. Next, the work process most suitable to attaining the goals will be put together. This step will likely draw on the cross-functional constituencies of the workgroup. Here is also where B.I.O. savvy kicks in for the match-up of the workflow with enabling information technology. This will put the workgroup in a favorable starting position on the B.I.O. Rhythm chart. In keeping with the dynamic nature of the curve, the third step essentially sets off an iterative process of continual improvement. When opportunity presents itself, Step II can be repeated, and so on.

   Finally, by allowing the pieces to fall in place, we have an agenda for a B.I.O. Rhythmic enterprise.

```
The Enterprise Agenda:

    I.  Enable the People Agenda

   II.  Enable the Workgroup Agenda

  III.  Chart the Path of Improvement
```

WE ARE NOT ALONE

While the above agendas can be stand-alone campaigns for improvement, they also fit very well into all the better-known managerial precepts that are in more or less currency. As the latter tend to come and go, it is reassuring to see that B.I.O. Rhythm can provide a consistent backdrop, thereby staking claim to somewhat more enduring significance. That would be a useful feature if it is indeed to be a key to prosperity as we contended.

- *Total Quality Management (TQM)*

This is a process of continuing improvement geared toward the delivery of value to the customer. The quality aspect evolved from the application of *statistical process control* (SPC), which monitors the variations in the output and prompts for adjustments to maintain a target level of consistency. SPC was pioneered by Walter A. Shewhart at Bell Laboratories in the 1920s, and popularized by W. Edwards Deming in Japan—leading to the quality movement that changed the world of business. TQM is the extension of quality control for the end products to the entire process of delivering value to the customer. In Chapter 4, we explained why most TQM efforts in Corporate America were doomed to failure. As long as the bottom-line approach to management by financial numbers prevails, workers will have to serve the numbers to be rewarded. Most of the banner waving and drum beating for TQM can be little more than lip service. For TQM to work, it takes a business environment where workers feel that they are in control of the work process. They must be empowered to pursue the tenets of quality, customer satisfaction, and continuing improvement. This is what we have assumed for empowered workgroups. So, at least we are off to the right start. What to do next? It turns out that this is the toughest part of TQM. After all the motivational hypes and hopes, it

Figure 9.4   B.I.O Rhythm & Management Precepts I

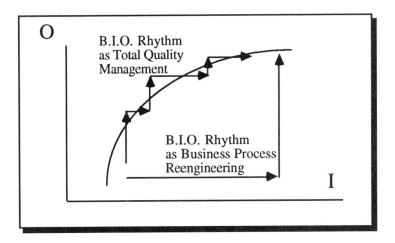

is often difficult to come up with a tangible agenda of action. Typically, brainstorming sessions are held for employees to suggest projects that can improve on customer satisfaction. Often, initial attempts are at the level of "returning all phone calls by the end of the day," or "starting all meetings on time." Surely, every bit helps but it is no surprise when enthusiasm quickly wanes. Now, B.I.O. Rhythm can be a formidable yet viable agenda for TQM. We just need to align the curve in Figure 9.4 with the satisfaction of customer needs.

• *Business Process Reengineering (BPR)*

While TQM is content with a continuous process of incremental improvement, there are situations in which a more radical and dramatic breakthrough is sought. These can arise from desperation, as when the process in place is so hopelessly antiquated; or from ambition, as when the goal is a distinctive edge over the competitors. As pioneered by Michael Hammer, coauthor of *Reengineering the Corporation: A manifesto for business revolution*, Business Process Reengineering (BPR) is not streamlining or cost trimming that shoots for percentage improvement. Rather, it advocates starting with a clean slate, dismantling the existing system that is likely the culmination of irredeemably bureaucratic practices. The process is completely rethought and redesigned, incorporating all the appropriate IT that can possibly lead to order-of-magnitude improvements. That sounds good, and the plot for revolution is often well laid out. Work should be organized around process results, such as the fulfilling of a customer order, instead of conventional business tasks like invoicing, or business functions like accounting and shipping. However, the main ingredient for a successful revolution is often missing. This is a cultural foundation, as found in, for example, democracy. The old way is likely based on top-down management. Operations are run by a hierarchical system of command and control. While this is being thrown out, what do rank-and-file workers have to hang on to? What can nudge them along to contribute to the overall effort in their own way? B.I.O. Rhythm is a plausible candidate. As a culture of awareness in operational and technological opportunities, it lends natural support to the challenge that things can be done differently. Note that in our chart in Figure 9.4, BPR is represented by a bold stride. As we have already seen in the example of overreaching in Chapter 8, such a move is not without risk, and may not be suitable for every situation in which improvement is sought.

• *The Learning Organization*

MIT's Peter Senge maintains that business enterprises, like people, have different capabilities to learn from their experiences. Learning disabilities can be a significant handicap to the prosperity of a corporation. Simulation games and exercises in a so-called practice field can be devised to help people think more creatively about problems that arise in

Figure 9.5   B.I.O Rhythm & Management Precepts II

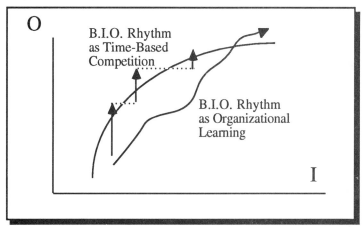

the performance field, namely, the real environment of business. While ideas for generic training abound, it is often more difficult to arrive at a systematic program for learning. B.I.O. Rhythm is a continuing process of self-study. It motivates frontline workers and executives alike to constantly extend one's knowledge in the intricate interaction among the constituents of a workgroup and the linkages within a work process. While by no means comprehensive, it can at the very least be a significant component of a productive learning process. In Figure 9.5, we illustrate this interpretation with the wavy line to indicate all the thoughtful practices associated with organizational learning that do not necessarily translate into discrete I-steps and O-steps.

• *Time-Based Competition*

All the O-steps along a B.I.O. Rhythmic curve represent improvement in how things get done. Much of this gain can come from the reduction of the time required to complete the sequence of tasks defining a work process—the so-called *cycle time*. For product development, this is the time it takes to get a new product to the market. Cycle time reduction has become the basis of an approach to stream-lining business operations that management consultant George Stalk, Jr. calls Time-Based Competition. Many automobile manufacturers, for example, can produce an all-new model in just three years, compared to the five- to ten-year cycle time that was common a decade ago. Black & Decker, the household appliance manufacturer, used to take three years to develop products such as irons and handheld vacuum cleaners. Using cross-functional work-groups, it has reduced the cycle time to two years by 1994, and is aiming to cut it down to one year. In our frame-work, such improvements can be captured as part of all the vertical O-step arrows as depicted in Figure 9.5. This allows for a broader perspective for this particular focus.

The list is far from being exhaustive. However, we hope to have demonstrated the robustness of B.I.O. Rhythm as a descriptive as well as practicable framework to im-prove business operations using information technology. In particular, it can become a tangible agenda in Total Quality Management, provide a cultural foundation for Business Process Reengineering, serve as a systematic program for the Learning Organization, and enhance the perspective for Time-Based Competition.

10

B.I.O. Savvy: The Close-Up

Having observed a variety of successes and setbacks in recent business history as manifestations of B.I.O. Rhythm, we argued that the latter is a key to prosperity in the Information Age. To attain such a state of affairs, we set the appropriate agenda for individuals, workgroups, and enterprises. The foundation throughout is the B.I.O. savvy individual who is aware of how things get done and how IT can help. How can we nurture this mind-set? By a true commitment to the customer focus that is reflected in the reward structure, we can encourage employees to pursue their curiosity and get in the know, to take control of work processes, and to be rewarded by coming up with better ideas. We need to provide an environment in which it is just a matter of instinct for people to become O-savvy. Similarly, we claimed that by stripping some of the intimidating façades of "technospeak," we can help sort out the plethora of enabling technologies, and raise awareness of what is available in more inviting manners. In this chapter, an example of this approach is given in the form of a glossary. It is a brief yet close-up look at selected topics of current interest and relevance to B.I.O. Rhythm. For ease of subsequent reference, the material is presented in alphabetical order. Therefore, when read in order, *some forward-referencing may be necessary.* However, since many items —typically the briefer ones—are included primarily to make the collection self-contained, it is strongly recommended that the reader first browse through the list for topics that strike one's fancy. Cross-referencing will then lead to the rest.

ATM (Asynchronous Transfer Mode)

A method to transmit data efficiently over information networks. Together with high-bandwidth lines such as fiber-optic cables and sophisticated data compression techniques, this will allow high enough throughput of data to realize many of the promises of the information super-highway. This ATM is not to be confused with Automatic Teller Machines, which is much better known as an information technology.

Bandwidth

The capacity for transmission of data, analogous to the number of lanes on a freeway. Technically, it is the difference between the lowest and the highest frequency that can be carried on a network. The higher the bandwidth, the more traffic can be handled.

Baud Rate

Old telegraph terminology for the speed of signal transmission, as measured by the number of times a signal changes per second. Nowadays, such rates are more commonly expressed in bits per second (bps). Telephone lines made of copper wire have baud rates ranging from 300 bps to 64 Kbps (Kilobits; Kilo = thousand). Hence, the early designs for modems were rated at 300 baud; they then progressed to 1,200, 2,400, 9,600, 14.4K-baud, and so on. Fiber-optic cables can potentially transmit at speeds of several Gigabits per second (Gbps; Giga = billion).

CBT (Computer-Based Training)

Self-paced training with programmed material on a

computer screen has been in use since the early 1980s. Initially, it was mostly text-based—with perhaps rudimentary graphics—and focused primarily on training for computer and software skills. With the arrival of multimedia and eventually virtual reality, this approach offers previously untapped potential. The audio and video components enhance the effect of simulation. Airlines are using CBT to familiarize flight attendants to new aircraft configurations. Steel mills can train operators with interactive visual results of how they set the controls. As U.S. companies spend around $30 billion a year on training, any success in increasing the cost-effectiveness of such programs will be of tremendous value.

In terms of how things get done, CBT has raised interesting organizational issues. Traditionally, employee training and development are in the domain of the Human Resources (HR) department. However, computer-based training programs naturally require the technical expertise of the Information Systems (IS) department. Which department should be responsible? With our emphasis on cross-functional teamwork, the logical answer is neither. The workgroup that needs the training should own the process, get the support to fund the investment, and coordinate its design—with representation from both IS and HR.

CD-ROM (Compact Disc—Read Only Memory)

The same 4.75" plastic diskettes popularized as audio compact discs can be used to store some 540 megabytes of data (or about 300,000 pages of text). The data is recorded by burning holes in a coating material that become nonreflective spots on the disc. A laser in the reading head of the CD-ROM drive picks up the reflective pattern as the stored information. The registration in the coating material is per-

manent and not susceptible to accidental corruption or era-
sure as with magnetic discs. The drawback is that it makes
read-write devices much more difficult to design. For the
foreseeable future, CD-ROM is expected to be the preferred hardware medium for the delivery of computer-
based, digital data in multimedia.

Client/Server (computing; networking; architecture)

A trend in business computing and information processing that emerged in the 1980s and expected to continue
through the 1990s. It is an integral part of downsizing
from centralized mainframe computing to distributed processing over a network of smaller and more cost-effective
computers. A few minicomputers or high-end workstations
are usually designated as the servers to maintain databases,
process queries, and perform resource-intensive computa-

Figure 10.1   Host/Terminal vs Client/Server

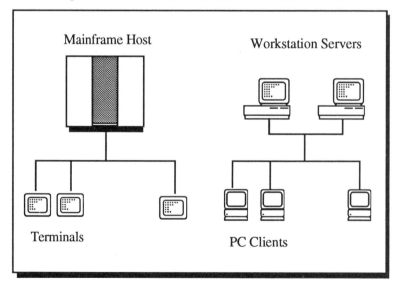

tions. A larger number of lower-powered PCs on the network are the clients. They are used to display information, process work in progress, and access the resources on the servers. In Figure 10.1, we sketch the simplest example of both the host/terminal and the client/server environment.

The decentralized approach in general, and the client/server architecture in particular, are very compatible with our notion of workgroups as ad hoc teams of people, organizations, and information systems working on a common mission through the exchange of information. In principle, the client/server environment can contribute significantly to the responsiveness and flexibility of empowered workgroups. In practice, the experience from the late 1980s through the early 1990s still constitutes only the rising portion of a learning curve. While many success stories are being written, still more on growing pains can be found. See *System Integration* for some of the issues involved.

Cyberspace

The realm of IT as the convergence of computer, telecommunication, multimedia, and solution technologies. It stems from *cybernetics*, the methodology of control and communication mechanisms common to brains and computers. The high-speed, fiber-optic communications network envisioned to be the infrastructure for the Information Age can be perceived as a system of superhighways in cyberspace.

DES (Data Encryption Standard)

With huge volumes of data transmitted over wired or wireless telecommunication networks, measures must be taken to ensure that only intended recipients get the message. Recipients on the other hand need to be able to verify the authenticity of the message. This is usually done by data encryption—more commonly known as scrambling. Many methods have been devised, using mathematical algorithms to encode and decode messages. The keys are secret codes in the form of a long string of numbers. To crack the code by trying out the astronomical number of possible combinations would take billions of years, even with the help of the fastest supercomputers. This allows experts to claim that certain encryption methods are virtually unbreakable. The algorithm adopted by the U.S. federal government is known as the Data Encryption Standard (DES).

Digital Data

Information that has been converted to a stream of bits (binary digits of 0s and 1s) for processing by computers or transmission over communication networks. For text data, binary codes are used for the letters in the alphabet, the

Figure 10.2   Digitizing Image and Sound

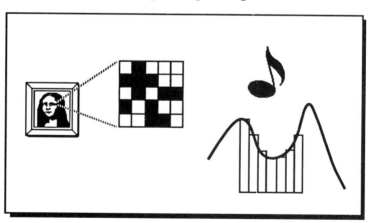

numbers, and other symbols and special characters. The most common convention is the ASCII (American Standard Code for Information Interchange, and pronounced "As-kee"). The letter "A" is "1010 0001," and the number "7" is "0101 0111," for example. For images, the picture is represented by a grid of pixels (picture elements). In black-and-white, each pixel is assigned one bit. Grayscale and color images require more bits per pixel to indicate the associated shade of gray or color. Sound waves are digitized by sampling the wave form. With both sound and images, the accuracy of reproduction increases with the resolution, as measured by the frequency of sampling and the density of pixels, respectively. To transmit high definition, full-color, full-motion video in digital form, the volume of data becomes astronomical. It would strain the capacity of even high-speed, high-bandwidth, fiber-optic networks. Compression techniques are therefore crucial to the feasibility of providing multimedia services over the information superhighway.

Downsizing

Used in both the operational and IT contexts. Many companies, especially the large ones, are downsizing to streamline operations. As part of the same effort, they are also likely to downsize technologically, migrating from a host/terminal environment to a client/server network of workstations. As we pointed out in Chapter 5, downsizing to cut costs does not necessarily make an organization more responsive or flexible. We likened such moves to corporate liposuction. "Rightsizing" is a word coming into use to reflect a more thoughtful and deliberate process of restructuring.

EDI (Electronic Data Interchange)

The processing of business transactions using direct communication between the information systems of the partners. As illustrated in Figure 10.3, EDI eliminates much redundancy in data entry and paperwork, whether the latter is sent by mail or by fax. It is more than e-mail, which would also have to be interpreted once received. Rather, the order transmitted through EDI is used to trigger automated responses by the supplier's system for inventory control, production and shipment scheduling, credit checking, billing, and so forth. The EDI cycle will be complete if the customer's account is also to be settled through Electronic Fund Transfer. Many large companies are already requiring their partners to do business with them using EDI. Essentially, it is "our computers will talk

Figure 10.3   Electronic Data Interchange

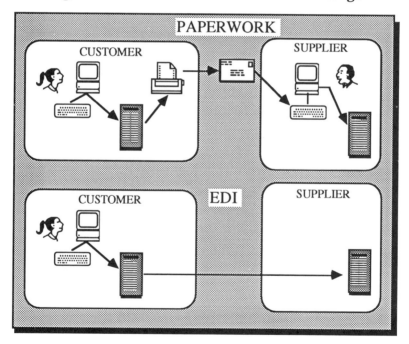

to your computers," which can facilitate Quick Response strategies to achieve just-in-time production and delivery of goods and services.

EFT (Electronic Funds Transfer)

Financial transactions through EDI.

EIS (Executive Information Systems)

Another one in the parade of seemingly endless varieties of business information systems that include TPS (Transaction Processing Systems), POS (Point of Sale Systems), MIS (Management Information Systems), DSS (Decision Support Systems), and OAS (Office Automation Systems). Traditionally, most business data represent facts and numbers. They are the professional bread and butter for accountants and financial analysts. Summary statistics and graphical presentation of such data constitute the bulk of information percolated to executives. In the era of bottom-line focus and top-down management by the numbers, this seemed appropriate enough. Initial attempts to design information systems for senior executives primarily concentrated on making it as easy and as "foolproof" as possible for them to get to these numbers. In our terminology, these are mostly I-steps, involving the adoption of available information technology, including interactive graphical user interfaces (GUIs), hypertext, and flexible queries of relational databases. With the shift toward a customer focus and responsibility to a broadened constituency for the enterprise, there is need for more than numbers. This calls for O-steps that may expand the scope and nature of data to include what has been considered "soft" information—in contrast to hard numbers. Opinions, creative thoughts, speculations and the like are processed mentally on a routine basis by executives, and yet are not taken into account by current IT. The development of future EIS may hinge on advances in new models for our mental processes, such as Fuzzy Logic and Neural Networks.

E-Mail

Electronic mail. On a LAN or WAN, this requires appropriate software to run within the network management system. It is a standard service provided by VANs, and a distinctive feature of the Internet, which connects many LANs, WANs and VANs.

Enterprise Networking

An IT design philosophy to align the configuration of the computer network for a business enterprise with its organizational structure, rather than with the physical connections of the hardware in the system. In other words: The network is the enterprise. This distinction is illustrated in Figure 10.4, where the same computer network is viewed as an enterprise network and as a client/server network. The advantage of the enterprise architecture is that management of the network can follow more closely and logically the workflow of the workgroups, making it more conducive to B.I.O. Rhythmic improvement. Suppose a new workgroup is created with representatives from the engineering and service departments to improve on the product repair process. This addition will be reflected by a new configuration of the enterprise network. The directory has to be modified to indicate the new workgroup, with the connectivity and resources that it will need. The change may lead to ideas to facilitate its workflow. By contrast,

Figure 10.4   Two Views of the Same Network

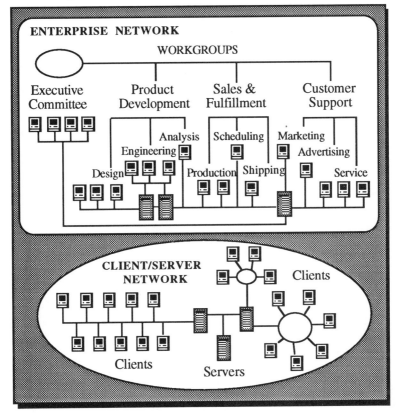

there may not be need for any physical change in the actual client/server network. So, from that perspective, nothing new appears to have happened. This is likely to obscure opportunities to move up the B.I.O. Rhythmic curve. Traditionally, network management software tends to focus on the hardware configuration. However, new products with the enterprise orientation are beginning to be introduced.

Fuzzy Logic

The extension of black-and-white logic to many shades of gray—to be discussed in more detail in the next chapter.

GIS (Geographic Information System)

Database systems that integrate spatial information, map drawing software, and traditional business data to produce geographical display of distributions and statistics. For example, a GIS can be designed to use census data to plot the map of a city, with the city blocks color-coded to indicate, say, average household income. As the market for GIS grows, the costs of mapping systems incorporating multimedia, spreadsheets, and relational databases are becoming affordable. Many GISs run on microcomputers, using databases available on CD-ROMs, including TIGER (Topographically Integrated Geographic Encoding and Referencing), a street-level mapping database from the U.S. government.

These are powerful tools to support the analysis and selection of retail site locations, transportation and distribution logistics as well as consumer market research. They can also help businesses monitor their environmental impact for compliance with government regulations.

Groupware

As applied to the early generation of software products that fall under the category of Workgroup Technology, this includes e-mailing, file-sharing, data-linking, conferencing, and scheduling programs. E-mail and file-sharing are already common features of networking. Dynamic data-linking allows timely updating of information used for work-in-progress. For example, if you are preparing a report that includes sales figures, you can link those to data maintained by the sales department. This way, your figures will be updated automatically each time a change is made by the owners. Conferencing capabilities can range from

Figure 10.5   Examples of Conferencing Groupware

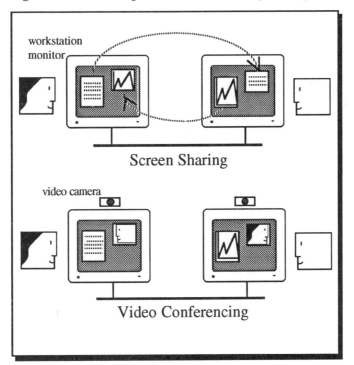

screen-sharing to facilitate collaborative work, to video interviews as a substitute for face-to-face meetings, as illustrated in Figure 10.5. Whether meetings are in the traditional, same-time-same-place; or the high-tech, same-time-different-place formats, they all need to be arranged. Scheduling groupware helps to set up meetings by accessing individual date books over the network to make appointments, and track confirmations as well as regrets.

GUI (Graphical User Interface)

The user interface is what you see and do to use a computer. Early interfaces were all text-based. You read text prompts on the screen, and typed in commands on the keyboard. Efforts to be terse led to arcane lingoes that made computers unfriendly to many people. To see the names of the files you have, it is "dir" in DOS and "ls" in UNIX systems. GUI (pronounced "gooey") uses familiar metaphors like the desktop, file folders and cabinets, menus, and windows as the working environment. Objects found in this surrounding—including files, tools, and trash cans—are represented by icons. With a pointing device such as a "mouse," simple operations are also made intuitive by imagery. To make a copy of a file, you drag it into a diskette. To delete a file, you drag it into the trash can.

How far can one take this line of reasoning? At what point does friendliness become fuss? This is again a question of B.I.O. Rhythm—a balancing of how things get done and how technology can help. Beyond GUI, watch for voice and even gesture interfaces.

Hypertext

The presentation of information with options for linkages that allow nonsequential perusal. A story with many different plots, depending on a reader's choice at various points, can be programmed as hypertext. A book is linear, with the page following this one already fixed. Hypertext is nonlinear. The next page depends on your conscious choice or prescribed preferences. Since it makes the transfer of knowledge more flexible and responsive to the needs of the learner, hypertext will be an important B.I.O. Rhythmic O-step in education and training. The I-step is multimedia.

Imaging

The transformation of documents from paper to electronic formats that can be manipulated on computers. Unlike previous technologies, such as the microfiche, that primarily archive condensed pictures of the documents, imaging aims to turn them into working files for subsequent processing. For textual documents, a key technology is Optical Character Recognition (OCR). Widely considered to be the bridge to the paperless office, imaging is still in the early stages of development.

Internet

This is to date the world's largest and fastest-growing computer network. By 1994, it connects over 2 million computers through 21,000 LANs or WANs, with an estimated 15 million users in 60 countries. Originally intended for research and educational institutions to share both information and computing resources, its popularity has grown among business organizations. To use the network, you have to lease a line or pay for dial-up access through a network-service provider, usually for a modest monthly fee. Once your computer is on-line, you can start "knocking on doors" by connecting to any other computer system with an address on the network (using the TELNET feature). Of course, to gain entry into that system, you must have a valid account or appropriate privilege there. Many such systems at libraries, universities, government agencies, and some companies provide public access to catalogs, research data, and public domain software that can be downloaded (copied to your own system using the FTP feature). Internet also provides a very efficient electronic mail service that can encapsulate fax, sound, and video data. It carries many newsgroups, mailing lists, and public servers, through which your organization can obtain or share specialized information. In Figure 10.6, we illustrate the use of e-mail over Internet. Dan teaches at BIGU, a university that is a member of the network. His e-mail address can be

Dan@BIGU.edu, with the suffix indicating the domain, which in this case is an educational institution. Similarly, Bob works at INC, a company that is also a member, giving the address of Bob@INC.com. Meanwhile, Kim operates out of her own home by subscribing to a networking service provided by NetServerX. She dials up using a modem

Figure 10.6   Electronic Mail over Internet

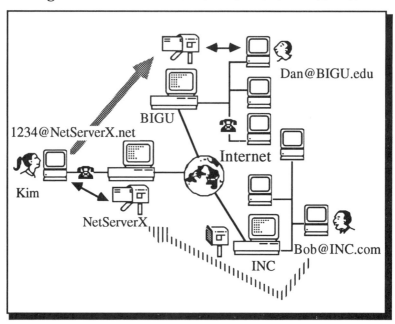

to connect to the network. Her address will be something like 1234@NetserverX.net, which acts as a rented mailbox. Other domain categories are "org" for professional organizations or special-interest groups, "mil" for the military, and "gov" for non-military agencies of the government. The Internet address for the President of the United States is president@whitehouse.gov.

Potential benefits include improved communication with customers and business partners for product announcement, updates, etc. Cooperative work can be facilitated for geographically dispersed workgroups and alliances. Although Internet is far from what the much heralded Information Superhighway is slated to be, it does give a taste of the benefits of plugging into the ever more interactive cyberspace of the IT cognoscenti. It is also a very good example of B.I.O. Rhythm in its own right, being a timely and dynamic match-up of user needs and available technology.

LAN (Local Area Network)

Network of computers that are located in relative proximity, say, sharing the same street address. Technically, it reflects a limited level of sophistication in the hardware and software required to support the network.

LANs are very useful for workgroups to share information and resources such as printers and scanners. However, bear in mind scalability issues if the operation is expected to expand, or compatibility issues if it is to link up with other business alliances.

Legacy Systems

Most large organizations that have been in operation for a while started out with the centralized approach to data and information processing using mainframe computers. Current trends to migrate to networks of smaller computers either cannot make the switch all at once for technical and practical reasons, or include plans to keep these large systems around as a special type of server. In any case, these mainframe systems become known as legacy systems. By all accounts, their glory days are over. However, with an estimated $1 trillion worth of installed-base worldwide, they give rise to a dilemma for aspiring as well as veteran IT professionals. Many entry-level jobs require legacy-system skills, typically COBOL programming, which is necessary to maintain the aging technology. Meanwhile, like having to coach tennis players to use the old wooden rackets, forward-looking programs in both technical and academic institutions would rather have their students trained on more cutting-edge skills. Similarly, the lingering legacy may be depriving many veteran professionals the motivation to keep up with developments in the field—to be B.I.O. Rhythmic in our context. Many are facing the prospect of becoming virtually unemployable the day their mainframes get unplugged.

Micro-, Mini-, Mainframe-, Super-, etc., Computers

As relative terms to classify the size and power of computers, these designations have no specific or consistent meaning. Here are some rules-of-thumb that should be valid through the 1990s. Micros fit on a desk. Minis fit in a closet. Anything that requires air conditioning is a mainframe or higher. How about the difference between a PC (personal computer) and a Workstation? If it makes you feel more important, it's a Workstation.

Multimedia

On a computer, multimedia is a user interface that combines text, graphics, sound, and video. Multimedia implementation of hypertext, drawing on vast resources accessible over the information superhighway, will become B.I.O. Rhythmic teaching tools at all levels of education and professional training.

As a component technology of converging IT, multimedia refers to the entire industry of purveyors for various forms of digital data. This includes providers of interactive television, home shopping, electronic newspapers and magazines, financial information services as well as educational and training programs. In Chapter 1, we likened multimedia to the fuel that will sustain traffic on the information superhighways of the future.

Neural Networks

Networks of logical switches whose pattern of connections can be used to represent memory or knowledge. Neural networks (or neural nets in short) are trained by reinforcement of the connective patterns that reflect what they are supposed to learn. Many experts believe this to be a more realistic model than any based on formal logic for the way our brains work. The impact on IT will be discussed in more detail in the next chapter.

OCR (Optical Character Recognition)

The scanning of a printed textual document and its reconstruction as a working file for a word processor. Note that simply scanning such a document for a digital image, as done by a fax machine, does not automatically make it recognizable by word processing software. Much work in data entry is still expended on the duplication of transferred information. While advances in pattern recognition technology have boosted the development of OCR, the challenge remains to improve on accuracy and speed.

OOP (Object Oriented Programming)

An approach to information system design and computer programming that emphasizes interaction among reusable modules, called objects, that contain both code and data. In conventional programming, code and data are separate domains. The code instructs the computer what to do. The computer then does it to the data. This is known as procedural programming. Take accounting, for instance. Traditionally, all the accounting procedures are coded in software. The actual financial numbers are kept as data. What is an invoice in this system? It is not *viewed* as a self-contained entity because the customer account, item purchased, dollar amount, date, etc., are stored in databases while the processing procedures are parts of the accounting software. The process is depicted in the top part of Figure 10.7. This separation makes it difficult to think of ways to streamline the invoicing process. Before long, one can get locked into a vicious circle. Software designers produce programs to work only with existing data structures while accountants adopt only data structures supported by available software. Where does one start to change?

With OOP, the invoice is treated as one object comprising both data and procedures, known as methods in OOP terminology, as illustrated in the lower part of Figure 10.7. The invoice object interacts with the rest of the system through messages. When a payment arrives, a message is sent to the appropriate invoice triggering its method to process the payment. Physically, this corresponds to retrieving the invoice and pushing its "Process Payment" button. Because of the need to communicate with external events and other system components, the designs of objects are specifically geared toward ease of interfacing. This way, objects are like Lego toy pieces that can be put together to build a complex information system. Such a modular architecture is more conducive to B.I.O. Rhythmic improvement through either I-steps for individual

Figure 10.7 Procedural vs Object Orientation

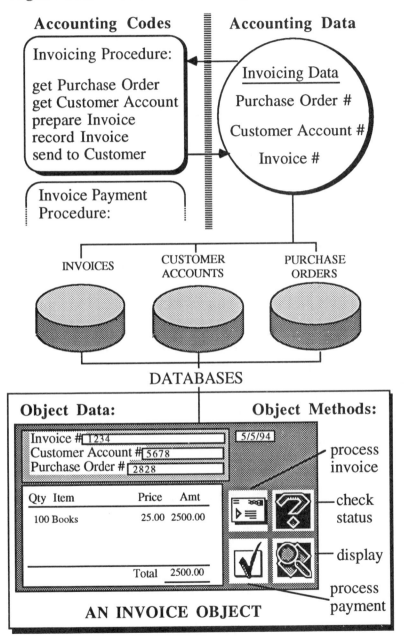

objects, or O-steps in how they are put together, or both. It also suits the needs of flexible and responsive workgroups with work processes that may be subject to rapid change.

Much more than a software design philosophy, OOP has the truly significant potential to drive businesses to think hard about the information content of their operations. What are the core objects that create value for customers? Questions like this will lead to a language that allows better communication among IT and business professionals. Rather than dwelling on codes and data, clients and servers, standards and protocols—the focus can now be on the articulation of needs and opportunities. This new mind-set is a crucial factor for B.I.O. Rhythm.

Open Systems

Information systems that are based on nonproprietary, industrywide standards. Hardware designed in compliance with those standards is interchangeable in open systems, so that there is no need to rely on a single vendor as the supplier. This makes the market more competitive, and provides better value for the users.

To the consumer, it has always been an obvious question why so much of the IT on the market cannot work together. Why does incompatibility seem more the rule than the exception? It started out with the perception among vendors that to gain market share, they must differentiate their products and keep their design and functions proprietary. This fits the old market paradigm that we discussed in Chapter 4, with a few players dividing up the whole pie. Once consumers are locked into one vendor's standards, they are expected to remain loyal customers. The race to establish different standards also fostered creativity, innovation, and eventually choices for consumers.

With the liberation of the mass market, well-informed customers are judge and jury of how well any product suits their needs. That IT vendors are beginning to pay close attention to making everything work together is yet another clear signal that businesses are indeed shifting to a customer focus in the Information Age.

OSI (Open System Interface)

This is an effort to establish guidelines for the development of standards for computer networks to communicate with one another—regardless of specific hardware or software used in the individual components.

Outsourcing

The farming out of entire business processes to external alliances. To focus on the things it does best—its core competencies—a business enterprise might find it more productive to outsource some of the other functions to specialists who may be able to carry them out more effectively. Examples range from payroll and accounting to information systems. Much debate on cost-benefit tradeoffs as well as myriad pros and cons have ensued in the last few years. In our framework for workgroups, outsourcing can certainly be viable. Whether it makes good sense as an O-step depends on its impact on the creation of value for the customers.

Parallel Processing

The use of computers with multiple processors working simultaneously on different pieces of the same task. While the power and performance of individual processors keep on improving at a tremendous pace, the leading-edge of technology has also to be the most costly. By ganging up a collection of lesser and cheaper processors, it may be possible to do as well, if not better. Machines with a large variety of configurations have been on the market for over a decade. Some have from dozens to hundreds of relatively powerful processors, each capable of handling complex tasks independently. The approach is known as coarse-grain parallelism or distributed processing. Others have tens of thousands of low-end processors that can only perform simple instructions. The approach is known as fine-grain or massive parallelism.

The potential for cost-effectiveness through parallel processing is quite real. The challenge lies in matching the technology with suitable applications, and to program the machines to work together. In principle, it is most suitable for handling the workflow of our new-age workgroups, since much improvement from process innovation is achieved by converting sequential tasks into parallel ones. Once such an O-step is identified, the I-step can be implemented using parallel-processing computers.

PDA (Personal Digital Assistant)

Palm- or pocket-size computer serving as date book, rolodex, and note pad that may incorporate voice and handwriting recognition, wireless modem, fax, and printer. Apart from providing a miniaturized and portable office for executives on the go, a PDA can also facilitate customer service by providing instant references to product specifications and repair manuals. Specialized designs are already in used by car rental agencies to expedite rental returns, and by restaurants to coordinate customer services and kitchen operations.

Privacy

With increasing connectivity through IT, the monitoring of the flow of information within an organization has become a much debated ethical issue. For instance, do employees have the right to privacy of their electronic mail? Or do employers have the right to monitor communications since the networking medium is company property? How about employees playing electronic solitaire or trading stocks on their computers at work? While many philosophical arguments along traditional lines have been put forth in support of both sides of the debate, the cultural foundation we have laid for B.I.O. Rhythm does cast some new light on such matters. From the employer's perspective, if there is a true commitment to empower employees and to entrust work processes to workgroups, then there should be no reason to intrude on their privacy. For employees, new-age loyalty translates to only one golden rule: Whatever activity that does not add value for the customers, directly or indirectly, is inappropriate. Within this framework, there may still be much room for disagreement. However, it would become easier to tell whether one is sincere or just paying lip service to the customer focus.

At the societal level, the issue of privacy of information gets even broader and more complicated. First, it involves the question of ownership. Information, unlike most other commodities, allows nonexclusive transfers. When I give you some, I do not have to give it up. For this reason, it is only worth what you are willing to pay, which in turn depends on the added value that you may expect. So, a stock tip is worth something; telling the time is usually not. As IT makes people more and more interconnected, the question of what has value and who owns it becomes murky very quickly. Many businesses you deal with—including supermarkets, credit card, phone and cable companies, magazine publishers, department and video stores—can compile a complete profile of you as a consumer and sell it to other merchants. Who owns that information? A second question concerns the privacy of individuals as well as organizations. It is outlined below in the discussion of security.

Quick Response

A strategic approach to optimizing the supply of seasonal or fashionable goods as the uncertainty in market demand unfolds. For example, orders from retailers for ski clothing for the Christmas season have to be placed by February. Traditionally, there is no provision to replenish items that turn out to be in demand because of the long lead time in the manufacturing process. With Quick Response, the supplier-retailer alliance attempts to adjust the production quantity according to initial marketing results in, say, the month of September. Typically, the partners use EDI to expedite communications.

Relational Databases

Databases represented by a collection of two-dimensional tables, each one called a relation, that can be linked by common keys when queries are performed. A simple example is given in Figure 10.8. Data for customer accounts is stored in the top table. Since each record relates an account number to a customer and a phone number, it is called a relation. Similarly, the second table is a relation for the balance-due in various accounts. Now, suppose we wish to make a list of overdue accounts and contact the delinquent customers by phone. This is accomplished by a query that results in a new relation by linking the two already in place. In commercial relational database systems, which are widely used in the client/server environment, the creation of tables as well as the formulation and displaying of queries are done through the Structured Query Language (SQL).

Figure 10.8   Example of Relational Database

Customer Relation

Account Number	Customer Name	Phone Number
1001	V. Chap	257-8974
1002	J. Suet	835-7621
1003	B. Wond	835-4096
1004	H. Kola	257-9387
1005	M. Yudi	254-5812

Balance-Due Relation

Date Due	Amount Due	Account Number
2/15/94	240.00	1004
2/28/94	375.00	1002
3/31/94	68.50	1005
3/31/94	47.00	1003

QUERY: Get customer name, phone number and balance for accounts overdue by 3/15/94

Overdue Relation

Date Due	Amount Due	Customer Name	Phone Number
2/15/94	240.00	H. Kola	257-9387
2/28/94	375.00	J. Suet	835-7621

RISC (Reduced Instruction Set Computing)

All computer processors are endowed with an instruction set. It is the bag of tricks that they can do. As computers become more powerful, the bag gets larger to accommodate more fancy features. This Complex Instruction Set Computing (CISC) tends to slow the processors down because they must spend time on picking out the right trick to perform. RISC is a design philosophy (or architecture) that prefers a reduced number of tricks, which are built directly into the circuitry. This makes each trick much faster. The missing fancy features can then be produced by programming appropriate sequences of these fast tricks. The overall trade-off is such that RISC is currently favored over CISC for cost-effectiveness.

Raw power—as measured by clock speed in megahertz and instructions per second—may not translate directly into superior performance in actual applications. Like owning a car, it is how it handles in different kinds of weather and road conditions that counts, not just horsepower.

Scalability

An issue common to both the operational and the IT aspects of the design of a work process. Typically, a design may be conceived for and demonstrated with a small workgroup. If it proves to be useful, extension to larger groups and more complex applications will be attempted. However, the results in terms of performance or even feasibility may not be scalable. For example, if two servers work well with fifteen clients over a network, it does not necessarily imply that adding two more servers can provide a total of thirty clients with the same level of service.

Security

With the Information Age come new forms of crime. These include pranks to gain unauthorized entry into computer systems; malicious planting of computer viruses, and other destructive or disruptive agents; fraudulent transfer of data, as in the stealth of electronic funds; and piracy of intellectual property. Data encryption will play a key role in safeguarding against such intrusion of privacy and propriety. The technology can already provide virtually unbreakable schemes to protect data transmission. The question arises as to whether the government should reserve the right to eavesdrop on electronic communications by keeping a trapdoor into a standard for encryption. The debate is still ongoing as of early 1994.

Solution Technology

One of the four converging components of IT. This comprises decision-support methodologies that have been highly developed over the last five decades in specialized fields such as Operations Research and Management Science. There is ample opportunity to realize the full potential of this approach to problem solving by assimilation into IT, as will be discussed in more detail in the next chapter.

SQL (Structured Query Language)

An industry standard for the interface to relational database systems. In a rare case of universal compatibility, SQL is supported by all vendors although each one may add its own extensions to provide additional features. SQL programs are used to create, view, modify, and make queries on data tables, as illustrated in Figure 10.8.

System Integration

Information systems in all but the smallest organizations can involve hardware from different vendors and software developed for specific functions (e.g., accounting, marketing, and manufacturing). Traditional data processing functions are likely to be centralized on mainframe or minicomputers. With the proliferation of PCs and LANs to handle individualized as well as team tasks, many islands of technology may result, making it difficult for seamless coordination of the flow of information. System integration is the process of making all the pieces fit. Many issues may be involved, including compatibility, scalability, privacy, and security.

An example is the migration from a centralized mainframe environment to the client/server network architecture. The client PCs may be running under the DOS operating system while the servers are RISC machines running UNIX. On top of that, the network connecting all these components has to be managed by yet another network operating system. Much as vendors are striving to support open systems, it is difficult to guarantee so-called plug-and-play (success on the first try) compatibility for the myriad possibilities of different configurations. Successful integration can make the whole more than the sum of the parts. It involves the timely match-up of many variables in IT to make things go the way a work process is envisioned. It is a workbench for B.I.O. Rhythm.

TCP/IP (Transmission Control Protocol/Internet Protocol)

Method used by the Internet to multiplex mail messages over common carrier linkages such as phone lines. It provides continuous connection at low cost by maximizing bandwidth use. It should be noted though that TCP/IP is not compatible with the OSI model.

VAN (Valued-Added Network)

Network service providers that offer dial-up connectivity, e-mail, and specialized information resources such as stock quotes, travel reservation, etc.

Virtual Reality

Life in cyberspace. Technically, it is digitally programmable—rather than less controlled, chemically induced—hallucination. As a nascent technology, it is mostly heralded as the medium for total-immersion, three-dimensional entertainment, and full-action games. The real potential is in computer-based training (CBT) and education at all levels.

WAN (Wide Area Network)

Telecommunication network of geographically dispersed information systems. A business enterprise with divisions, alliances and customers in different cities or countries may use a WAN to serve the operational needs of workgroups drawn from all of its constituents.

Wireless

With computers and telecommunication networks, white-collar work is no longer confined to a fixed office location. Telecommuting is made feasible. Notebook and laptop computers, as well as PDAs further increase the mobility and portability of work. Wireless modems will complete the picture of the worker who is totally untethered yet fully connected.

Workgroup Technology

IT in support of the work process of workgroups. We have identified workgroups as the fundamental units for the creation of economic values in the business enterprises of tomorrow. Since B.I.O. Rhythm is a key to their prosperity, workgroup technology is of obvious importance and will be discussed in more detail in the next chapter.

Zero Zero (The Year 2000)

January 1, 2000 may well be doomsday for many mainframe-based business information systems. The majority of software applications that run on them to process transactions, payroll, accounting, etc., were written in the dated COBOL language. Back in the 1950s—when computer memories were rather limited, and perhaps also to reduce efforts in data entry—IT professionals adopted the MM/DD/YY format using only the last two digits to record the year. For example, 1994 is simply 94. With almost half a century to go, they did not worry about what would happen beyond the year 2000. For anyone born in 1948, these programs can tell his or her age in 1994 to be 46, by subtracting 48 from 94. How old is that person in 2000? The answer will be -48! Now, imagine what will happen to all the calculations for interest on loans and mortgages. Can the problem be fixed? Not easily, if at all. This is because the flaw is structural rather than data specific, and there are millions upon millions of software applications and complex databases involved. Many experts are estimating industrywide costs in the tens of billions of dollars, even if technically feasible solutions can be found. As to the bleak prognosis for systems running on COBOL, it is not an exaggeration since many are using compiled software (known as object codes) inherited from older machines. Often, the original program (source code) and its documentation are no longer maintained. This makes significant modifications all but impossible. If your business relies in any way on such legacy systems, either directly or indirectly, it would be prudent to make contingency plans before the blip disappears from the B.I.O. Rhythm chart altogether in just a few years.

11

B.I.O. Savvy: The Long View

Our list of IT-related developments relevant to B.I.O. Rhythm is by no means exhaustive. The purpose of the selection is to stress the importance of our viewpoint. None of the items should be taken as inevitable, as if it is thrust upon us by irreversible forces of progress. Each should have its place in the mind-scape of how things get done and how technology can help. Obviously, some technical exactitude has to be traded off for making everything fit in the bigger picture. Nonetheless, it may be what is needed to help bridge the communication gap among executives, end-user employees, and IT professionals. I have witnessed numerous meetings of representatives from these three groups. The executives are typically nonchalant about the technical details wielded by the IT pros as well as the specific needs and concerns pleaded by the end-users. Their interest is mainly in ensuring that a project stays within given head counts and dollar figures. The end-users might thinly veil their cynicism toward IT's ability to deliver on time and as required. After all, the last two projects scheduled for completion a while back may still be pending. Meanwhile, the IT pros would try in earnest to highlight the intricacy of the technology involved, such as the need to mesh protocols for multiple platforms. That the end-users cannot fully articulate their needs on the outset and keep changing their minds in the course of a project does not seem to help matters. This may come as a shock, but it is a fact that one seldom hears IT and operations discussed in the tone of our close-up look in the previous chapter.

Assuming that our B.I.O. savvy viewpoint can be helpful, let us take a somewhat longer-term outlook. We examine four topics that are likely to have fundamental impact on the way we work, learn, share ideas, and conduct business as we progress into the Information Age.

FUZZY LOGIC

That may sound like an oxymoron because we are so used to logic that is crisp and clear. True or false, yes or no, on

Figure 11.1   A Glass of Lemonade

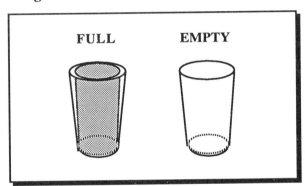

or off, zero or one, black or white—are all manifestations of binary logic: Out of two possibilities, only one is experienced at a time. Practically all of our science and mathematics are built upon this Aristotelian reasoning. As explained in Chapter 1, it is also the principle governing the operation of all digital computers. Now, imagine filling up a drinking glass with lemonade, as shown in Figure 11.1. The one on the left is full, and the one on the right is empty. Can you remember the last time you drank out of such a "full" glass? If you ask for one, you probably expect

Figure 11.2   "Full" Glasses

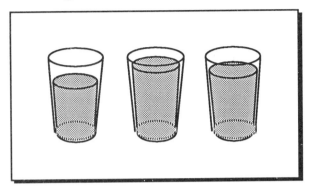

something out of Figure 11.2. While none of those is exactly full, they can be "pretty full," "almost full," "quite full," and so on. There is then a degree of fullness. In this particular physical situation, one can of course measure precisely how full a glass is in terms of, say, percentage of capacity. The first one may be 70% full, the second 95%, and the third 82%, for instance. However, we also have constant need to deal with qualitative and descriptive evaluations, such as customer satisfaction, user-friendliness, political trustworthiness, etc., for which there are no precise and quantifiable measures. While we may feel comfortable rating such things on a scale of 1 to 5, or score them out of 100 points, we must realize that basically it is all very fuzzy. Fuzzy logic is a philosophy that formally accommodates this kind of ambiguity, and it leads to new ways to deduce solutions from problems that are extremely complicated by conventional reasoning.

The distinctive feature of fuzzy logic is the recognition of overlapping contradictions. That means a glass can be both full and empty at the same time, but to different degrees. As you drink up, it becomes less and less full, and more and more empty. When it is half full, it is also half empty. A shade of gray is both black and white; the darker the shade, the more it is black than white. A customer can be both elated and disgruntled when having mixed feelings about a product or service. Someone who is 6' 2" is tall by most standards but short for basketball players. Put under this light, almost all the adjectives we use day in and day out are fuzzy. It is not the fault of murky thinking, a condition many teachers believe to be curable by a good dose of scientific education. Nor is it the result of chance, which can be aptly handled by the theory of probability. To fully appreciate fuzzy logic, it is important to tell the difference between ambiguity and uncertainty. When we say there is a 70% chance that you will get a full glass, that means if you keep asking, you get it 7 out of 10 times on the average. But what do you get each time? It is still either a totally full glass, or a completely empty one, as in Figure 11.1. There is no provision for your ever getting a glass that is 70% full. While there is uncertainty as to which one you will get, there is no ambiguity in what it is once you get it. Therefore, we cannot use probability to explain fuzziness.

Why is fuzzy logic going to be important to B.I.O. Rhythm? The short answer is because it works. As it turns out, this conclusion was neither obvious nor arrived at without twists and turns. The study of multivalence logic (more than the two values allowed in binary logic) was pioneered in the 1920s and 1930s. However, it was not until 1965, when Lofti Zadeh of the University of California at Berkeley published a paper titled "Fuzzy Sets," that the field was christened. Not surprisingly, just the name itself is enough to turn off those in mainstream science. In the words of Bart Kosko, a younger authority in fuzzy thinking, "It forced the new field to grow up with all the problems of a 'boy named Sue'." Subsequently, not unlike many good ideas invented in America, and largely ignored —if not jeered—at home, fuzzy logic found a fervent following in Japan. Whether it is due to pure pragmatism or a cultural acclimation to ambiguity (as in Tao and Zen), or a symbiosis of both, the Japanese moved quickly to tap this "dubious" science for commercial use. Washing and drying machines can now offer one-button operation by picking their own cycles. Video cameras can compensate for shaky hands. Cars have ignition systems, automatic transmissions, anti-lock brakes, and cruise controls that can function smoothly by adjusting to their environments automatically. Elevator systems can sense patterns of traffic to move people more efficiently. Subway trains can speed up and stop on a dime without jolting or tugging their passengers. Microwave ovens, rice cookers, air conditioners, copying machines, dehumidifiers, dishwashers, toasters, vacuum cleaners, refrigerators, televisions, and shower heads are on a long list of appliances that are controlled by fuzzy logic programmed on microchips. By 1991, the market for fuzzy-equipped products has already exceeded $1 billion in Japan. On the service front, fuzzy logic is gaining grounds in portfolio management systems, health management systems, language translators, and shopping guides—just to name a few. U.S. business and industry are once again playing catch-up (remember Quality?). In recognition of its significance, the U.S. Department of Commerce has labeled fuzzy logic as a key technology for future competitiveness in 1991.

How does it work? How much do we need to know with regard to B.I.O. savvy? Let us find out by way of an example. Suppose we wish to follow the fuzzy logic of a value-conscious shopper, as capsulized in Figure 11.3. This may sound perfectly reasonable and familiar. However, if

Figure 11.3   Logic of a Value-Conscious Shopper

**If poor value, buy a little;
if good value, buy more;
if great value, buy a lot.**

we have to pick it apart to analyze the meaning of each word, we are faced with ambiguity all over. Value can perhaps be captured in a price-quality relationship. Looking at a pile of oranges of certain quality at a particular price, how does a shopper evaluate? According to fuzzy logic, any price-quality combination can be a poor, good, and

Figure 11.4   How Good is the Value?

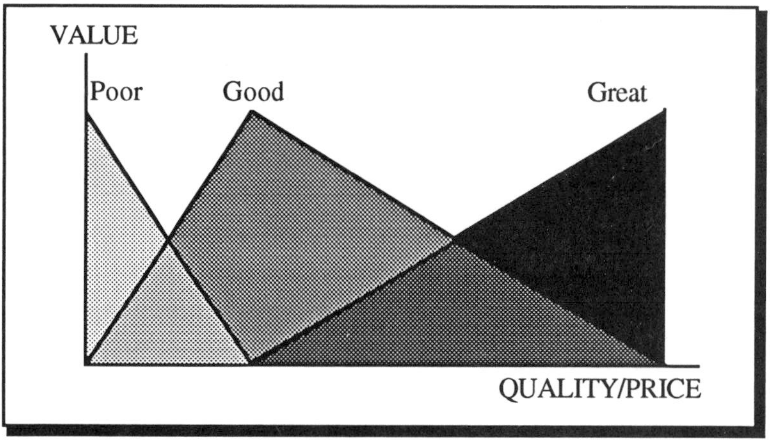

great value—at the same time, but to various degrees—as illustrated in Figure 11.4. As the ratio increases to the right, the oranges become more and more of a great value, and less so as just plain good. By our choice of terminology, there is no need for "poor" and "great" to overlap. In general, any overlap is acceptable as long as it makes sense. Next, we look at the decision on how much to buy. The physical quantity may be measured in pounds, or

Figure 11.5 How Much to Buy?

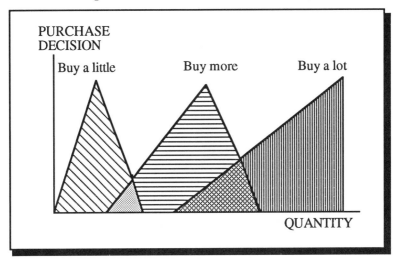

dozens. One pound can be somewhere under "a little," two pounds between "a little" and "more," five pounds between "more" and "a lot" while twenty pounds is primarily "a lot." This is depicted in Figure 11.5. Note that the evaluations are totally subjective, depending entirely on the perspective of the individual shopper. What we have shown are just generic examples. In any case, we now have a *fuzzy system* to map out the buying logic of the shopper by lining up the fuzzy values with the fuzzy quantity to buy, as in Figure 11.6. The rules listed in Figure 11.3 essentially fire a decision (little, more or lots) according to a condition (poor, good or great). Because of the overlapping of the conditions, the rules are allowed to fire simultaneously, but to varying degrees. The results must then be superimposed to arrive at an actual decision. The process is known as "defuzzification" and can be accomplished by a gamut of mathematical techniques. The appropriate choice depends on the application. The fuzzy rule here is whatever works

Figure 11.6   Fuzzy Logic of the Value-Conscious Shopper

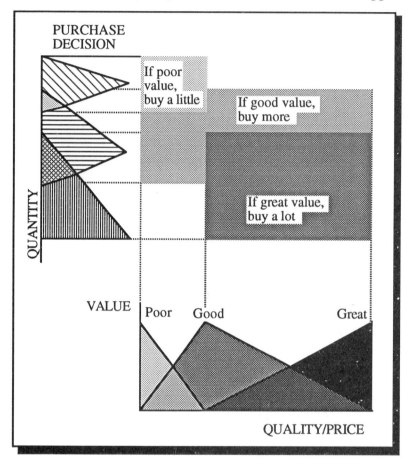

best. Once proven, it can be programmed into a microchip. To continue our example, let us consider a value condition that is, say, 0.7 "good" and 0.3 "great," as indicated by the arrow in Figure 11.7. One method to sort out the decision is to add up the "buy more" triangle with its height reduced to 70%, and the "buy a lot" triangle with its height reduced to 30%. The center of mass of this lumped-up area can then be used as the quantity to buy under the given condition. Is it magic? Not exactly. A lot of hand waving? Perhaps. Just

Figure 11.7   Defuzzification of Decision Rules

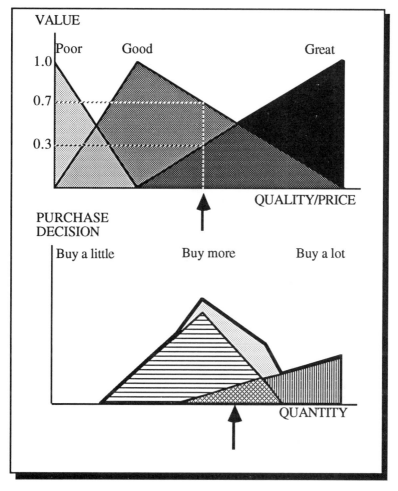

keep in mind that the car you drive and many appliances in your home may already be under the control of similar fuzzy systems. If you like the way they work, you would have to be a believer. In the context of B.I.O. Rhythm, there is tremendous potential for fuzzy logic to smooth out the kind of rough edges in business information and operations brought on by computerization. This will be in keeping with the customer focus and people orientation.

NEURAL NETS

None of the computers in use today, from micros to super-mainframes, can really think. No matter how powerful, they are hardly smart machines. Nonetheless, they can perform some functions of the human brain, such as logic and arithmetic, with lightning speed and perfect accuracy. Such processing power brings hopes that eventually, computers can be taught to reason as humans and become intelligent. This is the holy grail in the field of Artificial Intelligence (AI). For decades, computer scientists, psychologists, philosophers, and mathematicians have worked hard on understanding how human minds think and learn—in order to mimic such behavior with digital computers. As humans are capable of such sophisticated reasoning as to be able to deduce the laws of nature and other universal truths, most attention has been focused on models of intelligence based on logical foundations. This can be regarded as the theory of the mind as software. It is a belief that by stringing together enough logical operations, step by step, we can replicate everything that our minds do. Then, computers with enough power and speed can be programmed to do the same. More recent research has cast some doubt on this scenario. It becomes apparent, for example, that using sequential logic, there is not much hope for computers to recognize a face as effortlessly as most of us do, even with processors more complex and speedier than the brain. The prospect is looming that the human mind, while capable of doing formal logic, is not put together with such logic. Rather, it is the result of neurological activities in the brain, leading to what may become the theory of the mind as "wetware." In any case, significant progress with eye-opening results has been made in recent years to build brainlike machines—rather than mindlike software.

The most promising are neural nets comprising networks of switches that mimic the activities of the neurons in the brain. There is substantial evidence that the brain learns and memorizes by building up connected paths among neurons. Therefore, it seems plausible to "train" neural nets along the same lines. There are now prototypes that can learn to read. Given a text, the machine will attempt to match sounds with the words, by adjusted connections among its artificial neurons, over and over again. If it pronounces a syllable correctly, a corresponding connected pattern is reinforced. What come out at first are random drones, turning to babyish babbling, then bursts of gibberish, and after only about ten hours, comprehensible though not necessarily perfect speech. Other neural nets are trained to retrieve information, for example, by connecting names to phone numbers. Compared with conventional databases, they stand a better chance of getting the right number, even if the name is not spelled exactly the way it was entered into the directory. Another feature of neural nets is their ability to keep functioning, at least partially, even when parts of the networks are damaged or removed. This is also a known characteristic of the brain. By contrast, most digital computers are disabled when even the tiniest component fails.

One of the areas of AI with significant impact on business, health care as well as law and order, is Expert Systems. This involves the encapsulation of expert experience and judgment in computerized systems to dispense advice and opinion as automated consultants. Applications range from financial planning, credit checking, medical diagnosis, to legal counseling. Most existing systems are rule-based. A collection of if-then rules are synthesized from expert opinion, and then programmed into software. A financial expert system may have a rule saying that if you are over 40 years of age, with income of over $40,000, and an outlook for rising interest rates, then you should put so much of your investment in stocks, and so much in bonds, and so on. Typically, if you look inside an Expert System, you see all the rules spelled out. Neural nets, on the other hand, can be trained on the same expert opinions. Yet, if you look inside, there are no explicit rules—only complicated patterns of connections. This difference is already making them more like the real experts who know what to do without consciously following any precise rules. This "connectionist" approach, as it is called, to program machines to help with knowledge rather than data retrieval, can play a major role in information systems for all kinds of applications. For this reason, its development should be high on the to-watch list for the B.I.O. savvy.

Figure 11.8   A Neural Net

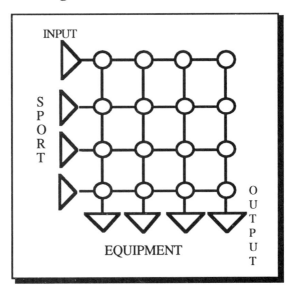

To get an idea of how neural nets work, we look at a very simple example. We take a network of 16 neurons, laid out in a 4-by-4 grid, as shown in Figure 11.8. The left side of the net is connected to input signals, indicated by the triangles pointing into the network. Output signals are sent through the four triangles at the bottom. Suppose we wish to train this network to match up a sport with its principal equipment. First, we need a code for the sport to be used as input. Since there are four input switches that can be either turned on or off, we can use a four-digit binary number to

Figure 11.9 Input and Output

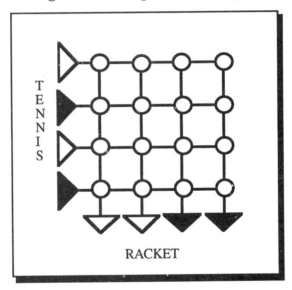

RACKET

represent the sport. "Tennis" can be arbitrarily assigned the code [0 1 0 1], for example. The output can be similarly coded, say, [0 0 1 1] for "racket." Using white for "0" and black for "1," we have the input-output pairing in Figure 11.9. With a black input switch turned on, a current flows across the net. To have this current contribute to the output, the neuron at the appropriate junction must be

Figure 11.10   Input-Output Connections

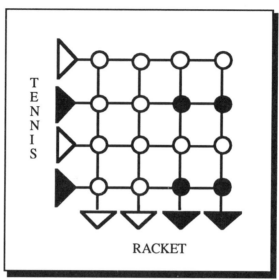

switched on for the connection. This is shown in Figure
11.10 for the "tennis-racket" association. Now, whenever
the input pattern for "tennis" is applied, the output pattern

Figure 11.11 Additional Connections

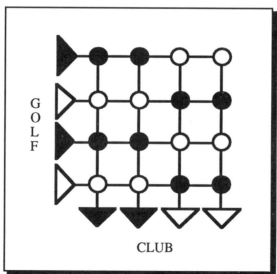

Figure 11.12   Output Threshold

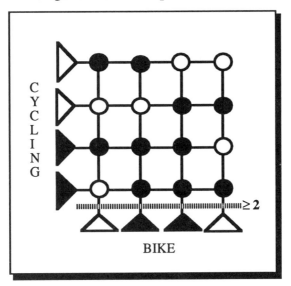

will be that for "racket." So, the neural net has learned or memorized that the equipment for tennis is the racket. Let us teach it more. Using [1 0 1 0] for "golf" and [1 1 0 0] for "club," we add more connections, as in Figure 11.11. Is there room for more? Let us try [0 0 1 1] for "cycling" as input, and [0 1 1 0] for "bike" as output. The new connections are included in Figure 11.12. Now, we have a problem. Because of previous connections, the "cycling" input will now send current to all four output switches giving [1 1 1 1] instead of [0 1 1 0] for "bike." This happens when networks get overloaded, as with our mistaking someone for another in a rush. To get around this, we can set a threshold for the output switches. In this case, requiring at least two signals before the switch is turned on will resolve our problem. As a matter of fact, there is still capacity to learn on this net, so that we can include [1 1 0 0] for "surfing" to turn on [1 0 0 1] for "board." The simple neural net that has learned the answer to four ques-

Figure 11.13   The Trained Neural Net

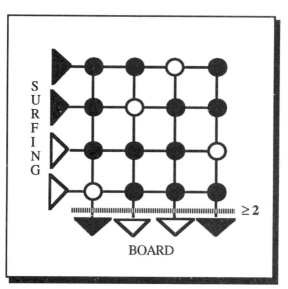

tions now appears in Figure 11.13. Remarkably, this threshold strategy is also a known phenomenon with neurons in the brain. If you are underwhelmed by this trick with 16 artificial neurons, just remember that our brains have a hundred billion or so real ones as well as much more complex mechanisms for their connection. Also, while we have "force-fed" the answers to questions in our example to illustrate the building up of connections among the neurons, neural nets are more typically designed to learn by examples, trial and error, and reinforcement. This type of learning can indeed result in knowledge in some sense. Once the connections are there, a neural net can respond to questions it has not encountered before. Even in our case, the as yet undefined input of [0 1 1 0] will produce the new output of [1 0 1 0]. Since our assignment of coding is quite arbitrary, this could be any other combination of sport and equipment. However, in more complex situations where inputs are logically related, the new answers are also likely to make good sense. The outlook for neural nets is that even networks with just a few hundred or perhaps thousands of switches can already become very useful tools of information technology.

SOLUTION TECHNOLOGY

The bulk of problem solving in the business environment involves decision making. We need to make decisions only when there are choices or options. Among all the possibilities, perhaps there is one that is best in our judgment. Therefore, central to the process of solving business problems is the evaluation of what is available according to criteria that reflect our goals and preferences. Beyond simple situations where the choices are few and obvious, the amount of information involved and the complexity of the interacting factors make it impossible to list all the options, let alone identifying the best as solution. Fortunately, most of these problems are amenable to quantitative methods that have been steadily developed and improved over this century. Contributions from economists, mathematicians, engineers, and scientists cumulated into the two relatively new fields of Operations Research (OR) and Management Science (MS). They are predicated on the belief that whatever you set out to do, there must be a best way to go about it. Airlines with thousands of crews to assign aim to cover all the scheduled flights without having to shuttle off-duty workers as passengers (a practice known as deadheading). Meanwhile, myriad work rules as well as employee preferences must also be taken into account. Managers of an advertising campaign must allocate a total budget over various media to maximize results from the coverage. Financial firms seek to balance risks with returns from their portfolios of investment. Manufacturers of multiple lines of products sharing common raw material, parts, labor, and machine capacities need to determine the proper mix according to customer demands and profit margins. The logistics of supplier-retailer alliances practicing Quick Response have to be worked out to achieve just-in-time replenishment of stock. Without sophisticated schemes to route traffic, communication and transportation networks alike can easily be bogged down by unpredictable buildups. Let us also not forget the "agent" introduced in Chapter 1 that can pick a movie best suited to your mood, or the "analyst" that can describe the most optimistic scenario by the deadline with the given budget for the project. All these situations involve *solution technology* in action. Their common thread is the idea of constrained optimization: doing the best under given conditions.

Once again, the basic principle can be illustrated with a simple example. Suppose you manage a small bakery and have on hand 10 lbs. of flour, 3 lbs. of sugar, and 3 dozen eggs. Your pound cake takes 1 lb. of flour, 3 oz. of sugar, and 4 eggs; and brings a profit of $2. Your sponge cake takes 1 lb. of flour, 6 oz. of sugar, and 1 egg; and brings a profit of $3. What should you bake to make the most profit out of the available ingredients? Since sponge cakes are more profitable, how about going all out for them? Ten is the most you can make with the flour, but that will require 60 oz. of sugar—12 oz. more than what you have. Should you settle for 8 sponge cakes at a total profit of $24 then? Or can you do better? (If your reaction is to go get more ingredients, you are way ahead of the game and should seriously consider managing a bakery as a career!) To see how this problem is viewed through solution technology, we sketch the given conditions in Figure 11.14. On the hor-

Figure 11.14   Feasible Combinations of Cakes to Bake

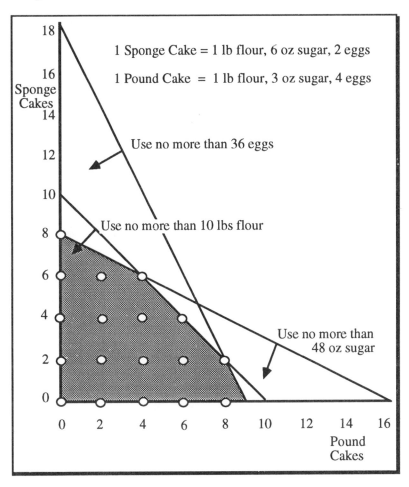

izontal axis, we count the number of pound cakes; and similarly for sponge cakes on the vertical axis. With 10 lbs. of flour, we can make 10 pound cakes and no sponge cake, or vice versa. These two extreme combinations correspond to the points (10, 0) and (0, 10), respectively, on the graph. If we draw the line joining these points, any combination below it will also be allowable by the supply of flour. The arrow pointing from the line indicates the side containing combinations that use no more than 10 lbs. of flour. The supply of sugar gives rise to the extreme combinations of (16, 0) and (0, 8) which lead to their own line delimiting allowable combinations. Finally, there is a third line corresponding to the condition for the eggs. Each such line represents a constraint. Taken all together, the feasible solutions to the problem must lie on the allowable side of *all* the constraints. This leaves combinations within the shaded

Figure 11. 15   Optimal Combination of Cakes

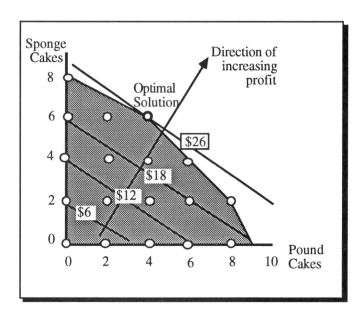

area in the figure. Next, we observe that just as all combinations that use up the same amount of an ingredient lie on a line, so do all combinations that return the same profit. We can then identify such lines and the direction in which they are improving. The feasible combination that is in the frontier gives the highest profit achievable under the given conditions. Hence, it is the optimal solution. In our case, 4 pound cakes and 6 sponge cakes should be baked to earn $26. That is $2 more than the all-sponge-cakes alternative.

Quantitative methods to address constrained optimization problems are also known as Mathematical Programming, as pioneered by George B. Dantzig of Stanford University while working for the Air Force in the 1940s. Since then, their extensive development provided the foundation for both the academic disciplines and professional practices of OR and MS. With the bottom-line focus of the Financial Age, and the arrival of digital computers, the quantitative approach attracted much attention and became an integral part of business education. Yet, after five decades, its success can only be qualified as mixed. The shortfall is not due to the lack of power in the technology, but rather the mindset that it has helped to foster in the era of management by the numbers. Specialists who are much better versed in the methodology than the understanding of real situations in business often ended up fitting solutions to superficial problems instead of resolving any inherent difficulty. Many costly projects have produced results that are quickly shelved because they simply cannot fit in the bigger picture. By now, the lesson has been learned that few problems can be "optimized" in isolation, and that true measures of best solutions are often more complex than costs, time, and profit considerations.

With the shift to the customer focus and people orientation in the Information Age, one can no longer assume away the inexact nature of human judgment, or ignore the need for soft information in the process of IT-assisted decision making. For MS/OR professionals who are B.I.O. savvy, there are great opportunities to expand the scope and realize the full potential of their fields. By embracing advances in fuzzy logic and neural nets, for example, quantitative methods may become much more relevant and robust. Even more significantly, like all other components of IT, the emphasis should be on getting people to use it, rather than to do it. We have been insisting that all business students learn to formulate constrained optimization problems as well as to solve them. My guess is less than 5% will ever put it to use. It is like trying to get people to adopt certain driving skills and habits that will help improve fuel efficiency in cars. It won't get far. The thing to do is to put the appropriate technology on a chip and under the hood. The performance of the car can now be optimized automatically. That is the reason for my view of quantitative methods as solution technology—one of the four converging components of IT, as discussed in Chapter 1. They must become robust modules that can help sort out options on demand, without the user doing more than stating the facts and asking the questions. *Ultimately, real people don't compute—they contemplate, comprehend, and communicate.* Does it seem too far-fetched? It won't be if the Japanese find a way to commercialize it first.

The B.I.O. savvy individual, for his or her part, must also outgrow the numbers-oriented mind-set of constrained optimization, even as the latter matures as solution technology. It was not totally facetious in remarking that the answer to how many of each kind of cake to bake is to get more flour. Indeed, the mark of a responsive and flexible business enterprise is its ability to remove constraints and open up new opportunities, not just doing the best under externally imposed conditions. The technology can also be of great help for this purpose. For example, you can ask how much an extra pound of flour is worth to you. The answer, incidentally, is $1 in our bakery example.

WORKGROUP TECHNOLOGY

For our purpose, we have defined a workgroup to be any number of people, information systems, organizations, or combinations thereof, whose work processes, dedicated to a specific mission, are interrelated by the need to exchange information. We argued that workgroups are the fundamental units for the creation of economic value in the Information Age, and that their effectiveness will determine the prosperity of society at large. A key to their success is B.I.O. Rhythm—seizing the moment to realize improvement in business operations with appropriate information technology; and being able to do so continually as new opportunities for such match-ups arise. Having gone this far, it is obvious that every component of IT can directly or indirectly facilitate the functioning of workgroups. However, there are tools and systems specifically designed to enable responsive and flexible work processes. We refer to these as *workgroup technology*. In the previous chapter, we discussed some initial features that are already becoming commonplace under the category of "groupware." They include electronic mail, conferencing, and scheduling systems. However, a backbone concept for workgroup technology is just now emerging in the form of workflow automation systems. In Figure 11.16, we sketch a simple work process for an employee to, say, purchase a book. Suppose the request has to be approved by the leader of the workgroup to which the employee belongs. Once approved, the employee has the choice of buying the book directly and be reimbursed, or having the book ordered by the Purchasing Department. In the first case, the Accounting Department will be alerted to initiate an expense voucher. In the second, the necessary information is for-

Figure 11.16   A Workflow Automation System

warded to the Purchasing Department to place the order. What a workflow system does is to enable the specification of such a work process, usually schematically. Once in place, the eventual generation of tasks, and the routing of data and documents can be handled automatically by the system. In an enterprise-networking environment described in the previous chapter, this allows reviews and modifications to the underlying process to be made easily. For example, if the employee is reassigned to a different work-group, a few changes will have to be made to the directory of the enterprise network to reflect the new configuration. Otherwise, the processes remain the same. Suppose all requests to purchase books will now have to go through a librarian who keeps track of the company's collection. The schema of the work process for book acquisition will have to be changed. The addition of the appropriate flows of information to and from the designated librarian is shown in Figure 11.17. Once this is in effect, the new process will

Figure 11.17   The Modified Work Process

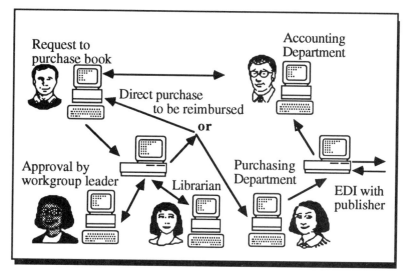

again be guided automatically by the system. For business enterprises with workgroups that need to respond to rapid changes in missions and operational procedures, workflow automation systems will play a major role in their efforts to attain B.I.O. Rhythm.

Most of the other elements of IT on our watch list are also likely to come together to contribute toward workgroup technology. The workflow systems in the not-so-distant future will be object-oriented, interactive multimedia, and enterprise-networked. They will be linked to Executive Information Systems that incorporate fuzzy logic and neural nets for soft data, as well as solution technology for decision support. If all these seem to make sense to you now—but would have sounded no more than technological mumbo jumbo before you picked up this book—then you are well on the way to becoming B.I.O. savvy. What do you think the mailrooms and boardrooms of tomorrow will be like?

Part IV

Beyond Business

A New Culture

- Why are the education, health care and government sectors not yet in the Information Age?

- What must we do so that society can truly benefit from technology?

- How can government bureaucracy become B.I.O. Rhythmic?

- What is the key to reducing the costs and improving the quality of heath care?

- How can information technology help us learn and teach better?

- How can we all become part of a solution?

12

Good News, Bad News

At this point, it is worth reflecting on what brought business and industry into the Information Age in the first place. Was it all the technology that they have been adopting? Not exactly. In retrospect, the move to automate and computerize turned out in most cases to be reactive rather than proactive. This was especially evident in the considerable languish in rethinking work processes. What drove every competitor in the same direction was the liberation of the mass market. With ever-improving access to information and distribution channels, customers are essentially upping the ante in the form of more sophisticated demands and critical judgment of value added. To prosper, businesses must first redirect their focus on the customers and be responsive and flexible to their needs. This commitment is crucial to the effective move away from a bottom-line orientation and top-down managerial control, to an emphasis on empowered workgroups. Employees involved in the latter should be fully aware of how things get done. The answer to the question of why something is done in a certain way must be in terms of how value is added, and not because it has always been done that way. In this view, work processes can be under constant evaluation and reengineered as necessary. Being aware of how information technology can facilitate such work processes, B.I.O. savvy workgroups are capable of seizing the moment to realize improvement in business operations with appropriate technology. Their ability to do so continually as new opportunities for such match-ups arise puts their enterprise on a path of B.I.O. Rhythm. This is our scenario for business to prosper in the Information Age. That is the good news. The bad news is that we cannot yet extend our principle to cover the other major issues in modern society: government, health care, and education. Here, appearance can be most deceptive. After all, we do see massive evidence of

Figure 12.1   Where We Stand

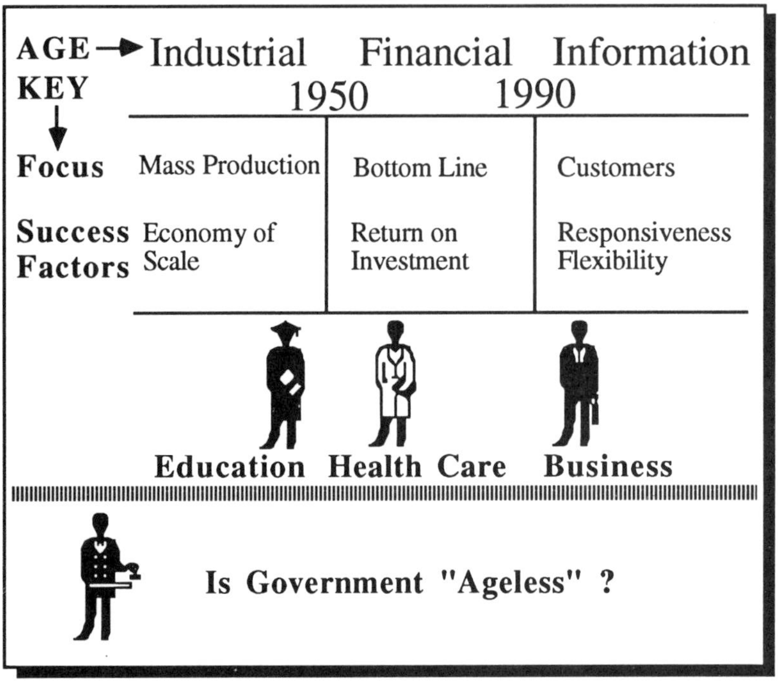

AGE →	Industrial	Financial	Information
KEY ↓	1950		1990
Focus	Mass Production	Bottom Line	Customers
Success Factors	Economy of Scale	Return on Investment	Responsiveness Flexibility

Education   Health Care   Business

Is Government "Ageless" ?

the introduction of IT into what we shall refer to as the "Big Three" sectors of the economy. So why can they not follow the same path of B.I.O. Rhythm as business does? Simply put, none of the "Big Three" sectors has really entered the Information Age. Shocking as it may sound, the reason is quite obvious. There has never been the same concept of the customer as in business. It seems unnecessary somehow. While our automakers, steel mills, and garment factories were scrambling to satisfy their customers or risk losing their business to the Asians or the Europeans, the "Big Three" sectors have rather captive audiences. Apart from not having foreign competition, these sectors do not even have real threats from domestic competitors. Sure enough, people may have the nominal freedom to switch schools, pick hospitals, and vote public administrations in and out of office. In reality, they are locked in by invisible yet impregnable confines of bureaucratic dogma. Let us see where we stand in each of these sectors.

WHY JOHNNY CAN'T

The educational system that we adapted from the Old World worked remarkably well for the Industrial Age. Unfortunately, that is where it has remained, as illustrated in Figure 12.1, in spite of relentless changes in every aspect of its environment. The public schools today were founded on a century-old assumption that government should provide a standard education for all children. This approach was well suited to the key focus of mass production and the critical success factor of economy of scale. Learning by memorizing and regurgitating information was adequate for the needs of workers of the early assembly lines. As society's need shifted to knowledge workers and problem solvers capable of managing dynamic change, the shortfall of our educational system became all the more apparent. Indictments by vocal critics might have raised public awareness just enough to garner support for meager attempts at quick-fixes. Examples are campaigns to close the gaps in test scores by our students and their international counterparts. However, as long as government is both the producer of service and arbiter of whether the consumer's interest has been served, there can be no market mechanism and no customer to speak of. Two commonly used arguments against letting parents have a free-market choice of schooling for their children are: i) they would not know how to choose; and ii) they should not be burdened with the choice, especially for disadvantaged families already preoccupied with other problems. Can this be the Information Age? Higher education is not faring that much better, with serious questions being raised regarding its relevance and accountability. In any case, there is no need to get too involved here in the ongoing political and ideological debate on this subject. The point is that without a customer focus, measurements of improvement can become dubious. Imagine the following breakthrough: "New breed of horses can double efficiency of pony express." This might have meant something for customers of the service in the late 1800s, but definitely not for users of the information superhighway. For this reason, we have to be careful evaluating any apparent pursuit of B.I.O. Rhythm in the absence of a customer focus. Is all the technology going into dressing up the same old ways of doing things? In the case of education, high-tech classrooms, for example, do not necessarily translate into improved learning and better-prepared students who can prosper in the future.

THE CARE IN HEALTH CARE

Health care presents a somewhat different enigma. It started out with a customer focus in the days when family doctors delivered newborns, watched them grow up, and continued to help them stay healthy. Doctors knew their patients, personally and medically. They understood individual needs and exercised their own judgment to best meet those needs. In return, they had the trust of the patients who were well aware of their own mortality and quite content with the guidance on the journey with an inevitable end. With advances in modern medicine, the focus has shifted dramatically from the customer to the products. Boasting a seemingly endless list of medical procedures, many no less than true miracles, the health-care industry is out peddling its wares instead of care. Of course, like any other sophisticated and valuable products, advanced medical procedures are costly to develop and to deliver. There is then little surprise that health care actually finds itself smack in the middle of the Financial Age. There, the key focus is the bottom line and the critical success factor is return on investment, as indicated in Figure 12.1. The only way to sustain expensive medicine is to do more of it. The way to do more is to convince customers that they need it. This was exactly how businesses pushed their products in the 1980s and created the wave of conspicuous consumption. When the choice involves life and death, it is not difficult to be persuasive. Another outcome of this development is the need for specialization. The general practitioner (the closest remnant of the family doctor) provides little more than a referral service to the specialists. In the process, no one really gets to know the customer. So much for the customer focus. If this is not enough to take the care out of health care, the insurance industry has most certainly finished the job. By buffering its big business self between the medical professions and consumers, it has added layers of bureaucracy and management by the numbers. Its bottom-line focus naturally chooses to provide coverage only for those consumers that can maximize its return on investment. All together, the insurance-medical complex has escalated the nation's health-care costs to 14% of GDP by

1992, while leaving some 37 million Americans without any medical insurance coverage. Since health care is not exposed to the same kind of market forces that drove other businesses into the Information Age, it can only compound the problems if left to its own device.

Figure 12.2   Health-Care Reform: the Debate

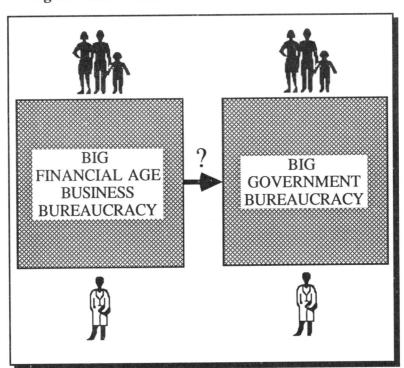

President Bill Clinton's administration, in a monumental effort spearheaded by First Lady Hillary Rodham Clinton, has proposed its plan for health-care reform in 1993. One of its slogans is "putting people first," a reprise of the theme of the 1992 presidential campaign. Critics and skeptics alike are equating the plan to the substitution of "Big Government" for "Big Business." If that is the case, it may do little to untangle the bureaucratic mess, as shown in Figure 12.2. Which way is it? What does the B.I.O. savvy think? You guessed it. It all comes back to the customer focus. The existing system is hopeless, as it has all but disregarded the basic needs and interests of the consumer. Putting people first sounds right, but if it has to be done by political decree, it may not lead to the kind of market incentives and competitive forces that naturally reward continual improvement. However, it is still a good start. Ultimately, the success of any reform will hinge on how well it puts the customer in the driver's seat. Assuming that this can be done, at least to some meaningful extent, we can begin to contemplate health care in the Information Age. There, the opportunities for improvement through B.I.O. Rhythm abound. Almost every aspect of the bureaucratic buffer between the patients and their doctors can be streamlined. Even the practice of medicine and the delivery of care can benefit significantly from information technology as we shall explore in a separate chapter.

"NEXT!"

Where can we place government on our time scale in Figure 12.1? Based on our experience of being handled like inventory parts waiting for their turns on an assembly line, the Industrial Age may be the first to come to mind. However, the perpetual budget crises that seem to plague all levels of government are more like nightmares of the Financial Age. Perhaps government is indeed ageless. As if to further distinguish it from business enterprises, we seem to have granted it a license to be ineffective in serving our needs. The label of bureaucracy has been pitched as both a curse and an excuse. Why? Because we never consider ourselves as customers. Although we foot every penny of the bill, we do not demand that government earn its money's worth. While it is put in place to serve, we perversely defer to it as the seat of unmitigated power and authority. Yet, we haplessly resign to its inadequacy in enforcing law and order and protecting us from crime. If we were customers with a free-market choice of providers, we would have shopped around to evaluate competing services. Since that has never been the case with government, we adjust by setting embarrassingly low expectations. Unfortunately, by tolerating inefficiency we are indirectly condoning waste and abuse of our resources. Cynics may say that society will always have its problems, and there are so many that it

Figure 12.3   Government Policies and Social Issues

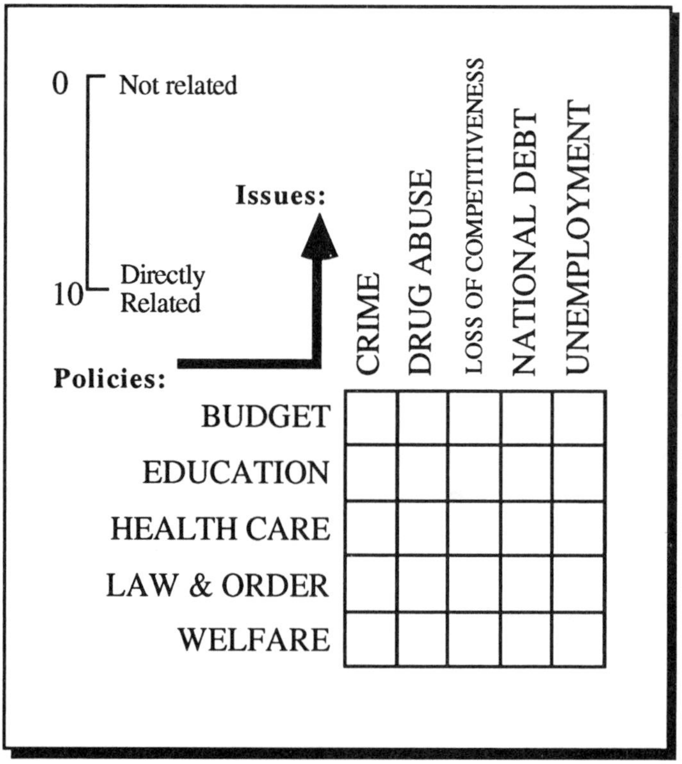

Policies:	CRIME	DRUG ABUSE	LOSS OF COMPETITIVENESS	NATIONAL DEBT	UNEMPLOYMENT
BUDGET					
EDUCATION					
HEALTH CARE					
LAW & ORDER					
WELFARE					

Issues:
0 Not related
10 Directly Related

is a lost cause to expect our government to do much about solving them. It is true that problems are plenty. What is often overlooked is how they are all interrelated. Here is an exercise that may help us see things in a different light. In Figure 12.3, some major areas of governmental policies are pitched against a selection of issues high on the list of contemporary social concerns. Obviously, certain pairs of policy and issue are directly related, such as BUDGET and NATIONAL DEBT, LAW & ORDER and CRIME. Put a 10 in the corresponding entries of the matrix. Next, fill in the rest with your rating, on a scale from 0 to 10, of the extent to which a policy area and an issue are related. Just think about it and record your gut feeling. There is no need to be very precise. Finally, add up all the numbers you have in the matrix. If your total is over 100, you have probably uncovered some relationships that were not obvious before this exercise. On the other hand, if your total is well below 100, you are probably unaware of facts like the following.

- It may be easier for public schools to get budget approval for metal detectors than for computers.

- Health-care costs add over $1,000 to the price of every car made in America.

- Most welfare recipients would be worse off working at minimum wage.

- Product liability insurance constitutes 95% of the cost of a flu vaccine.

These may have the appearance of random trivia. However, the list can be extended until they add up to the realization that all our socioeconomic problems are closely intertwined. Moreover, the greatest difficulty in dealing with them stems largely from our forfeiture of the role of customers for governmental services. This leads to the rude awakening that the days of minding your own business as an innocent bystander are over. *In the Information Age, if you are not part of a solution, then you are part of a problem.* The pervasive connectivity that transcends any

Figure 12.4   Citizens as Consumers of Dogmas

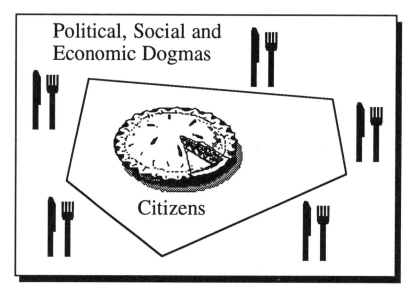

barrier in time and space is setting the stage. Although it may sound ominous, this revelation is actually good news. It has been pointed out that putting people first can work only if people know what they want. How are they to tell? Traditionally, it has only been through their allegiance to political, social, and economic dogmas pitched one against another by competing leadership, as depicted in Figure

12.4. Not surprisingly, it is the same picture we used to illustrate the old market paradigm in Chapter 4. As we discussed there, the bottom-line approach led businesses to push for conspicuous consumption that resulted in the overdrawing of our economic means. Bureaucrats, even those with the best of intentions, have been following the same path all along. To have an effective and customer-driven government, citizens must assume the role of well-informed and value-conscious consumers. We recall the picture of the new market paradigm to draw the analogy as

Figure 12.5   Citizens as Customers of Government

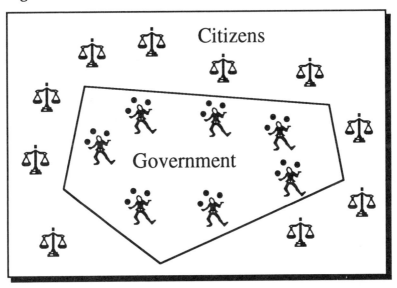

in Figure 12.5. Henceforth, the so-called silent majority must be relabeled as gullible customers. They are part of the problem of letting government get by without creating value to the potential of society's resources. The customer mind-set is not revolutionary. As customers, we know better than to expect something for nothing. The same reasoning can keep political and ideological excesses in check.

B.I.O. RHYTHM FOR SOCIETY

Can we really do better if we try? Definitely. The reason behind this optimism is the tremendous help we can count on from information technology. However, from hard-learned lessons in the business sector, we can also predict that using IT to automate existing bureaucracies alone will not get us too far. The way things get done must be closely scrutinized, starting from their purposes and following through the procedures to see how values are added. Only no-nonsense processes should be enabled and enhanced with suitable match-up with technology. It can be done, as evidenced by promising results that are transforming business enterprises adapting to dynamic changes brought on by global competition. To realize similar B.I.O. Rhythmic improvement in education, health care, and government—corresponding driving forces must be called into play. (Incidentally, it is convenient to substitute "Bureaucratic Information and Operations" for "Business Information and Operations" in "B.I.O." in the present context.) Where are these forces going to come from? Probably not from political or ideological mandates. We learn from history that forces of that nature can only push us to trade one set of bureaucratic dogma for another. Regardless of which dogma has currency, the ineffectiveness, waste, and abuse of bureaucracy can still proliferate. Market forces, as determined by consumers' collective value judgment, are more reliable drivers.

While there is much hope, the process will not be easy. Even the reengineering of basic business operations can prove to be nontrivial as old habits die hard. The revitalization of the fundamental processes of society is perhaps the greatest challenge we must face if we aspire to prosperity in the Information Age. As in business process reengineering, it is crucial to have a cultural foundation to build on. This can again be found in B.I.O. Rhythm. A citizenry that is aware of how things get done and how technology can help will provide the positive market forces if given the opportunity to behave as well-informed and value-conscious customers. It is the same savvy that people will need to prosper in the workplace of the future. Its extension to public interests is quite natural. For this reason, it can indeed be the new culture of tomorrow.

To bring education, health care, and government into the Information Age, the majority in a democratic society will have to agree that these sectors should take on a customer focus. How and when this can happen is beyond the scope of this book. My vision is that as the work force becomes B.I.O Rhythmic to prosper economically, the new culture will eventually take hold. As more of us realize that not being part of a solution is to be part of a problem, the right kind of change is inevitable. It is up to us to bring good news, as the status quo can only be counted on for more bad ones. In the rest of the book, we survey some early examples of how IT *can* in principle contribute to the improvement of these sectors. Remember that fundamental reforms are necessary to remove many structural barriers to responsiveness and flexibility to customer needs. Otherwise, the benefits of technology, no matter how sophisticated, will be no more than cosmetic.

13

Reinventing Government

On March 3, 1993, President Bill Clinton announced a National Performance Review (NPR), remarking that:

> "Our goal is to make the entire federal government both less expensive and more efficient, and to change the culture of our national bureaucracy away from complacency and entitlement toward initiative and empowerment. We intend to redesign, to reinvent, to reinvigorate the entire national government."

The six-month project, which was led by Vice President Al Gore, resulted in a report titled *"From red tape to results: creating a government that works better and costs less."* The four chapters in the report bore the headings: Cutting Red Tape; Putting Customers First; Empowering Employees To Get Results; Cutting Back To Basics, respectively. The impact of IT on efforts to improve government was also specifically recognized. This is very much in line with what we have discussed in the previous chapter. Whether, or how well the talk can be turned into action remains to be seen. It serves at least as one blueprint for a B.I.O. Rhythmic government. For this reason, it will be of interest to us to examine the list of recommendations that fall under "Reengineering through the use of information technology" in the Gore Report. In the following, the action items identified in the NPR are quoted in *italics*. Interpretation, comments, and promising examples from the perspective of the B.I.O. savvy are inserted. Note that these independent opinions do not necessarily reflect those of the NPR.

IT01   Provide clear, strong leadership to integrate IT into the business of government.

A high-level workgroup that fully appreciates the significance of B.I.O. Rhythm should be established to articulate the vision of balancing effective work processes in public service with enabling technology. Its most important mission is to promote the cultural foundation that is essential for citizens to become knowledgeable customers, and for service providers to become responsive and innovative. It must also make sure that the tail does not wag the dog, as happened often in the past. In what we called "over-reaching" in Chapter 8, many previous IT projects with unwieldily long lead times and runaway budgets eventually fell on their own bureaucratic weight. This leading workgroup can benchmark best practices and coordinate the integration of efforts at the federal, state, and local levels into a coherent infrastructure. It should guide us toward government as a seamless, and perhaps even transparent service provider.

IT02   Implement nationwide, integrated electronic benefit transfer.

This is the analogy of home banking and automated teller machines (ATM) in the financial services sector. The caveat here, as we learned from earlier attempts, is whether we are ready to be a cashless society. Before the latter becomes a reality, the ATM model is definitely more practical for programs such as welfare and food stamps. The model could be the state of Maryland's system to dispense such benefits from 1,800 ATMs and the checkout terminals at 3,000 grocery stores statewide.

IT03   Develop integrated electronic access to government information and service.

This can become an important use, as well as justification for the information superhighway. It will put government services as major resources accessible over the digital networks. The NPR pointed out one-stop "help desk" and integrated "kiosk" services as examples. As we have seen in previous chapters, the technologies of relational databases and distributed processing are already widely applicable. However, as the story of the Postal Buddy serves as a reminder, the purpose and value of such services must be clearly identified. This way, their performance can be meaningfully measured in subsequent reviews of their cost-effectiveness. Nonetheless, promising projects at the state level have emerged. For example, integrated databases that support one-stop service are already in place for welfare services in Hawaii, children's services in Illinois, and employment services in New York. In the spirit of B.I.O. Rhythm, further success along these lines will depend on how well diverse services, from local to federal, can be integrated to minimize confusion from having to deal with too many different systems.

IT04   Establish a national law enforcement/public safety network.

The scope of such an information network extends from traditional searches of criminal records—outstanding warrants and fingerprints—to multimedia display of patterns, trends, and even clues to help with law enforcement. Geographical Information Systems (GIS) linked to relational databases can be designed to correlate crime sprees with the activities of known criminals. The potential of using fuzzy logic and neural nets to sort out evidences is also promising. At a more mundane level, using IT to reduce paperwork and simplify record keeping alone can free officers several hours a day from desk work. This can give them more time to prevent crime or enforce the law.

In a related action item for the Department of Justice (DOJ09), the NPR recommended to "make the Department of Justice operate more effectively as the U.S. Government law firm." It further remarked that "justice should undertake several improvements in the way it manages its litigation functions to improve service to its customers and better manage its case load." This is of considerable interest to the B.I.O. savvy. Even without getting into serious debate over our judicial system, the following irony cannot be ignored. While transactions can take place in a nanosecond in the Information Age, it may still require years of scribbling and babbling by dozens of lawyers, costing tens of millions of dollars to settle a litigation. Something must be out of sync here. In business, IT liberated professional knowledge from middle managers who used to play the role of gatekeepers. A similar development is possible in the legal profession, leading to significant improvement in productivity.

IT05   Provide intergovernment tax filing, reporting, and payments processing.

This is a good example of our workgroup framework. Recall our definition of a workgroup to be any number of people, information systems, organizations, or combinations thereof, whose work processes, dedicated to a specific mission, are interrelated by the need to exchange information. See also the remarks on enterprise networking and workflow systems regarding *IT09* below.

IT06   Establish an international trade data system.
IT07   Create a national environmental data index.

Along with several other recommendations for the Department of Commerce (DOC08-10 in the NPR report: to establish a manufacturing technology data bank; to expand the electronic availability of census data; and to improve the quality of the national trade data bank), these will provide useful resources for business enterprises and academic institutions alike. They supply further evidence of the liberation of professional knowledge, which was presented in Chapter 4 as one of the two major paradigm shifts that are reshaping our future.

IT08   Plan, demonstrate, and provide governmentwide electronic mail.

The trend to date has been for individual agencies to build their own e-mail systems, which are then connected to larger networks such as the Internet. As a result, even agencies that have very close working relationships may end up communicating through messages that are routed halfway around the country. Also, the different systems cannot support a single, easy-to-use directory. Until these difficulties can be removed, efforts to significantly reduce the amount of interagency paperwork will be hampered.

IT09   Establish an information infrastructure.

As in other large and complex organizations, disparate computer and communication networks have sprouted up all over the landscape within the public sector. As we have seen, the hardware view of such systems usually does not mirror the organizational structures, making it difficult to locate and share resources. The perspective of enterprise networking, in which the network *is* the enterprise, provides better flexibility and adaptability to changes in work processes. Workgroup technology, especially in the form of workflow automation systems, will be particularly useful for government operations.

IT10   Develop systems and mechanisms to ensure privacy and security.

As pointed out in Chapter 10, before systems and mechanisms can be devised, the issues of privacy and security have to be carefully resolved. On the one hand, there are questions regarding ownership of information such as customer profiles collected as a byproduct of business transactions. On the other, the right of employers to monitor employees' communications, or the prerogative of government to eavesdrop on suspected criminal activities will have important bearings on how business is conducted in cyberspace.

IT11   Improve methods of information technology acquisition.

Relative to bureaucracy, IT advances at phenomenal speed. This year's leading edge is next year's antiquity. With its notoriously inefficient procurement procedures, government is prime candidate to be stuck with overpriced and outdated technology.

IT12   Provide incentives for innovation.

In a sense, this sums up much of what we have been talking about: to follow a path of B.I.O. Rhythm. To do it, we have to start with a customer focus to set missions and goals, a reward structure to motivate positive change, and empowered workgroups who have control over their work processes and who are aware of the potential of technology. Then, the opportunity to seize the moment to improve on operations with the help of IT leads to continual innovation.

IT13   Provide training and technical assistance in IT to federal employees.

Initiating them to the true meaning of the Information Age and the culture of B.I.O. Rhythm will be a good start. Debunk the myths. IT is neither a godsend nor a necessary evil. By itself, it does not liberate or enslave. It is a tool that can help serve customers better—and yes, federal employees do have customers. Lifelong learning is an integral part of work not because of individual inadequacies, but because of changes in customer needs as well as new opportunities to improve with better technology and more effective ways to get things done.

14

Rationalizing Health Care

DIMINISHING MARGINAL RETURN

The fundamental difficulty with thinking rationally about health care is the following dilemma:

Figure 14.1   The Dilemma of Life

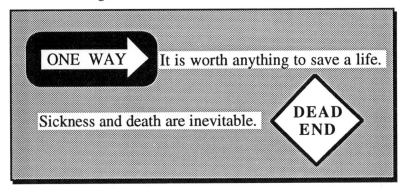

Advances in medical science and technology have been pushing the envelope in our ability to preserve and prolong life. However, the development of sophisticated techniques is costly. So is the limited supply of expertise and equipment required for their practice. The economics of medical specialization has increasingly shifted the emphasis from preventive to acute care. Consequently, people tend not to seek help until they are seriously ill. With the dilemma we are facing, the law of diminishing marginal return kicks in, as illustrated in Figure 14.2. While it is true that the more we spend, the longer we can expect to live, the incremental gain in life expectancy comes at increasingly higher cost. Thus, we can now keep grossly premature and drug-addicted infants on the brink of life; we can also tie the terminally ill to roomful of technology to prolong the agony

Figure 14.2 Diminishing Marginal Return on Medical Spending

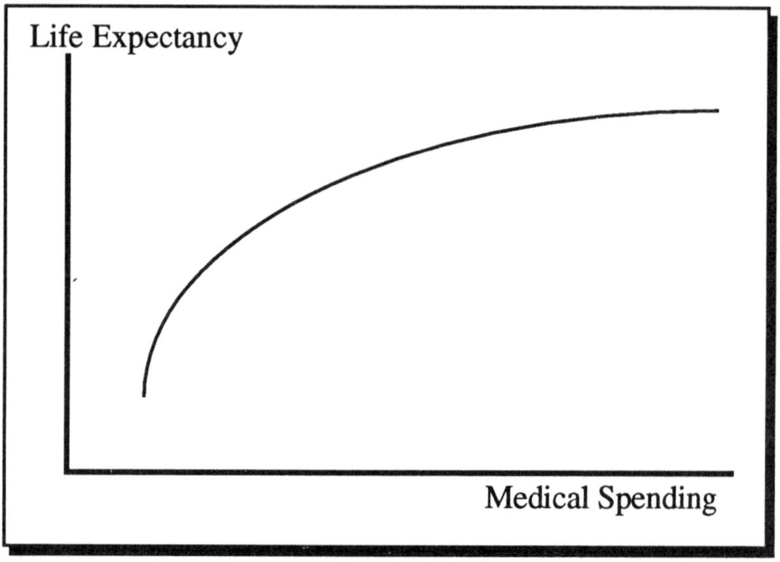

for a matter of days, weeks, or perhaps months—all at mind-boggling expenses. As it is unlikely that we can ever draw the line on how far we should go on ethical and legal grounds, society's outlay on health care is bound to increase. This root cause of escalating costs has led quickly to the situation where few individuals can afford to pay in full for the medical treatments that they may ever need.

THE CRISIS

The only way out is to pool resources and spread the risks among large enough a group, hence insurance. The latter can come in many guises, including business contracts and social entitlement programs such as Medicare and Medicaid. This buffer between the providers and customers of health care has grown to be a quagmire of the Financial Age. Since doctors and hospitals are paid by the insurers, they have little incentive to keep the cost or volume of their services down. To protect their own bottom lines, insurers (which may be insurance companies or government programs) get to regulate the service providers with myriad codes and formulas, and pay only for approved procedures. Some critics equate the system to a virtual usurpation of medical decisions from the professionals. The massive bureaucracy that ensued is also vulnerable to fraud, which drains as much as 10% of total expenditure ($84 billion in 1992) according to estimates by the Department of Commerce. To make matters worse, not knowing whom to trust, the only way the customers can protect themselves from incompetence or negligence is through the threat of lawsuits with dire financial consequences. To guard against such litigation, doctors and hospitals must carry malpractice insurance at exorbitant premiums. They may also resort to "defensive medicine" by ordering batteries of tests and procedures just to have all bases covered. Some even avoid high-risk specializations altogether. All of these measures raise medical costs further. In turn, the insurers seek to limit their own risks by "cherry-picking" whom they select to cover. The cost of health insurance for a family increased by over 70% from 1987 to 1991. As a result, some 37 million Americans are left without health insurance by 1989, according to the Census Bureau. In spite of spending almost twice the average of other developed nations (over $800 billion in 1992), the United States ranks 19th in infant mortality rates, 21st in life expectancy for men, and 16th in that for women. The whole industry is a classic example of management by the numbers, which has taken the care out of health care. For this reason alone, it is no exaggeration to call the situation a crisis.

THE ROLE OF INFORMATION TECHNOLOGY

As we alluded to in Chapter 12, short of fundamental reform to properly align the incentives for service providers and the customers, no amount of streamlining or cost cutting can put the care back in health care. However, since by 1990 we are already spending more on health care than on education and defense put together, any significant improvement in productivity can at least help extend services to more people who are in need. In this regard, IT has tremendous potential to make a difference, with or without genuine reform. Three kinds of opportunities can be identified: i) improving clinical and administrative transactions; ii) empowering providers as well as customers; and iii) enabling new practices that add value and reduce costs. These are not totally distinct categories. Rather, they represent the progressive realization of the potential of IT in health care. That is B.I.O Rhythm in our terminology. Since the industry is so information intensive, it is somewhat surprising that it has fallen so far behind in the productive use of IT. The lag is as much as two decades compared to other business and service sectors according to some experts. Resistance from the professionals is still cited as a major obstacle. As one observer pointed out, the status symbol for doctors is the luxury foreign car, not a high-end PC. As a consequence of the prevailing culture, the bulk of record keeping is still in the form of paper files. Bringing this function into the Information Age will be a big step forward. It is remarkable that in thirteen states, electronic data do not yet qualify as legal medical records. In the following, we describe a generic (and grossly simplified) integrated system for medical records. Examples of ongoing efforts to implement, at least in part, some of the

concepts involved are used to gauge progress in this direction. Extensions of the basic system that present further
B.I.O. Rhythmic opportunities are also discussed.

Figure 14.3 Integrated System for Medical Records

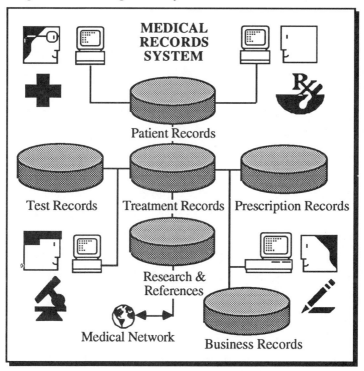

IMPROVING TRANSACTIONS

The schema for an integrated system of medical records
for a hospital or clinic is given in Figure 14.3. This can be
a client/server network of workstations connected to a
series of relational databases. (For a review of the technospeak, see Chapters 10 and 11.) From their workstations,
physicians access a patient's record, which is complete with
medical history, a log of previous visits, description of the

latest condition, and a list of treatment and medication pre-scribed. They can also order diagnostic tests from the labo-ratory and dispatch prescriptions to the pharmacy. In turn, the pharmacists can alert the physician about possible drug interactions or allergic reactions, record prescriptions filled, and manage the inventory of the pharmacy. The lab technicians report test results to the appropriate databases and may advise of follow-up procedures. Meanwhile, all the records can be pooled and tapped by administration for billing and accounting purposes.

The Harvard Community Health Plan, one of the nation's largest health management organizations (HMO) with 1,000 physicians serving over half a million patients at 14 medical centers, has a prototype system in operation since 1991. A dozen of doctors and nurses have been testing it out at the center in Burlington, MA, which serves over 7,000 patients. However, organizationwide implementation is not expected for at least several more years. The Mayo Clinic has announced a 3-year, $100 million plan for a medical records system for its entire clinical network that covers Rochester, MN, Jacksonville, FL, and Scottsdale, AZ. The Crozer-Keystone Health System in Delaware County, PA, with 4 hospitals and a network of clinics, recently entered into a $80 million, 10-year contract for an enterprisewide system. By contrast, the Duke University Medical Center has been using computerized medical records since 1968. It is taking B.I.O. Rhythmic steps to upgrade its TMR (The Medical Record) system by incorpo-rating advanced IT such as client/server architecture, graphical user interfaces (GUI), and object-oriented pro-gramming (OOP).

Since in most cases, health services are paid through insurers rather than by the customers, the transactions among all three groups constitute the major portion of the bureaucratic buffer. From 1983 to 1992, the number of health administrators grew 300%, over 16 times more than the 18% growth in the number of doctors, according to government statistics. Electronic data interchange (EDI), which has been used with increasing success in the business sector to reduce transaction costs and strengthen inter-organizational alliances among suppliers and buyers, can also be effective here. While many insurers have already mandated EDI, they adopted different proprietary standards that make it cumbersome for providers to comply. At the request of the Department of Health and Human Services, an industry task force, known as the Workgroup for EDI (WEDI) was formed in 1991. It is charged to set standards and guidelines for doctors, hospitals, insurers, and EDI vendors. Using EDI, four major HMOs in California have joined forces to launch the California Health Information Network to process claims and payments.

EMPOWERING THE PLAYERS

The players here are the payers, the providers and the patients. What is the game? It is called "Find the Customer." In the usual market situation, the provider of goods or services gets paid by the customer. The value of the transaction is in the quality-to-price ratio as judged by the customer. This is illustrated in Figure 14.4 for the purchase of a car, for instance. The better informed the customer, the better value the provider must deliver to do well. With health care, we do not have the same relationship. The situation is depicted in Figure 14.5. The provider is only indirectly paid by the recipient of services. So, who is the customer? How is value going to be judged? These are

Figure 14.4   Value is Judged by the Customer

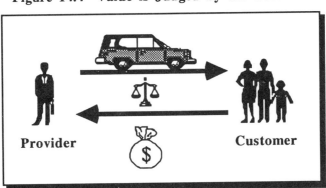

Provider   Customer

questions with no obvious answers. As long as this is the game, a rational solution is one in which no individual player can do better without at least one other player doing worse. This is known as an equilibrium. In such a situation, the level of care, the price of service, and the rate of premium are all stable in the following sense. Suppose the

Figure 14.5   Who is the Customer?

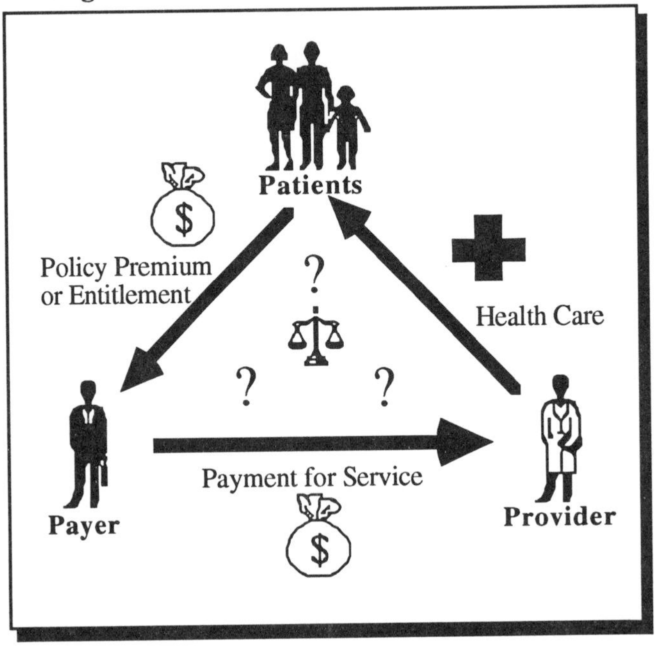

Patients

Policy Premium
or Entitlement   ?

Health Care

?   ?

Payer   Payment for Service   Provider

provider wishes to make more by delivering more care than needed in equilibrium. This will hurt the payer though the patients would probably not mind. If the payer attempts to increase its own profit by restricting care to below the proper lever, both the provider and the patients will suffer. Similarly, if the patients demand a given level of service at less than fair premium, the payer will have to take a loss. How does one get to a rational equilibrium? Not without market forces to push things in the right directions. The players must be empowered with choices, information, and mechanisms to adjust the parameters under their control.

The transaction between the payer and the provider is through a system of codes known as the Diagnostic Related Groups (DRGs). These are 5-digit numbers representing diagnostics and medical procedures. As its attempt to evaluate the service provided, the payer sets approved procedures for each diagnostic as well as their acceptable costs. In principle, what it has to guard against are mainly: i) fraudulent claims, which are billings for either unperformed or unnecessary procedures; and ii) erroneous claims that are incorrectly coded. In practice, the provider can, and apparently often does engage in "creative" billing for various reasons. Within the rigid system, it may find it impossible to justify unusual circumstances on behalf of the patients. Or it may simply be driven by its own profit motive. The practice is known as "code-gaming." For example, it is possible to "upcode" and charge more by switching primary and secondary diagnostics; or to "unbundle" by charging for grouped procedures separately at higher, itemized rates. Ironically, solution technology (Chapter 11) in the form of "code optimizers" has been exploited for this purpose.

With the proper incentives, the same logic can be

turned around to help the provider become more cost-effective. For example, a drug and test ordering system in use at the Wishard Memorial Hospital in Indianapolis offers physicians a menu of available options and their costs. It highlights the most cost-effective tests, cautions against expensive ones, recommends test intervals, and warns about drug interaction. It even bares the sales pitch of product vendors with "counter detailing" notes. In a study published in the Journal of the American Medical Association (JAMA), the system managed to cut 13% ($887) off the average patient charges.

For the payer, there is great need for IT assistance in auditing claims to keep "code gaming" in check. This will be essential when EDI becomes prevalent. As the basic problem has to do with the rigidity of the code system, there is tremendous opportunity to incorporate fuzzy logic and neural nets (Chapter 11) to capture expert judgment, especially on difficult cases.

How about the patients? Although they are obviously the ultimate customers, they do not seem to be in much of a commanding position in our scenario. Much of this is due to the fact that they do not quite know what to expect. The lack of useful information for the consumer of health care is astonishing compared to other products and services. We can easily find out everything there is to know about the performance of any car or mutual fund, or the quality of food in restaurants, but not about the health care that we are supposed to get. Granted, the data may be around but it is not part of the culture to treat it as an essential resource. This is where the information superhighway makes particularly good sense. Wonder what can possibly take up 500 channels? How about a few to educate us about health care?

ENABLING NEW PRACTICES

In the culture of B.I.O. Rhythm, technology is not used only to automate existing ways of doing things. The awareness of how work gets done and how technology can help is nurtured to open up new vistas. As introduced in Chapter 4, one major impact of IT is the liberation of professional knowledge. In the context of health care, this can lead to fundamental improvement in both preventive and primary care. Imagine a doctor who incorporates the experience and insight of every doctor and medical researcher who ever lived. No, not as your dream doctor, but rather as a round-the-clock consultant and mentor for the one you have. That wouldn't be such a bad idea, would it? This is what the convergence of IT can provide. It may take a while to deliver the full promise. It may take even longer for doctors to get over the fear that they are being second-guessed, if not displaced, by computers. Eventually though, anyone whose ego is so big as to forgo the assistance of such unprecedented resources would simply be unqualified to be a care provider. In that prospect, primary care physicians—your family doctor—can be better trained and empowered with liberated knowledge to reverse the trend of overspecialization. The latter has put the emphasis on acute treatment rather than preventive care. With a corresponding realignment of the prestige and financial incentives, there is hope to attract the proper share of talent that may help put the care back into health care. It should also make the entire industry more cost-effective.

In the generic example shown in Figure 14.3, we have made provisions for a connection to an external network. With this linkage, local data can feed national or even global research databases, and reference information can be piped in for local use. The ultimate connection of 7,000 hospitals and 550,000 physicians nationwide is perhaps decades away. A good start would be with regional networks, and they are beginning to appear. For example, eight hospitals in the Buffalo, NY area have planned a fiber-optic network with an on-line medical library supported by the State University of New York at Buffalo.

The application of workgroup technology also offers B.I.O. Rhythmic opportunities. With multimedia workflow systems, health-care professionals can consult with one another remotely in full view of all pertinent information, as depicted in Figure 14.6. This includes the digital storage and transmission of X-ray, CAT(Computerized Axial Tomography), and MRI (Magnetic Resonance Imaging) scans. Wireless personal digital assistants (PDAs) can be used to record and transmit data from patients' bedside. Finally, the digital infrastructure will enable "telecare" in various forms. These may include the remote sensing of vital signs, physician-patient teleconsultation, and even surgery performed with remotely controlled robots.

Figure 14.6   Teleconsultation in Health Care

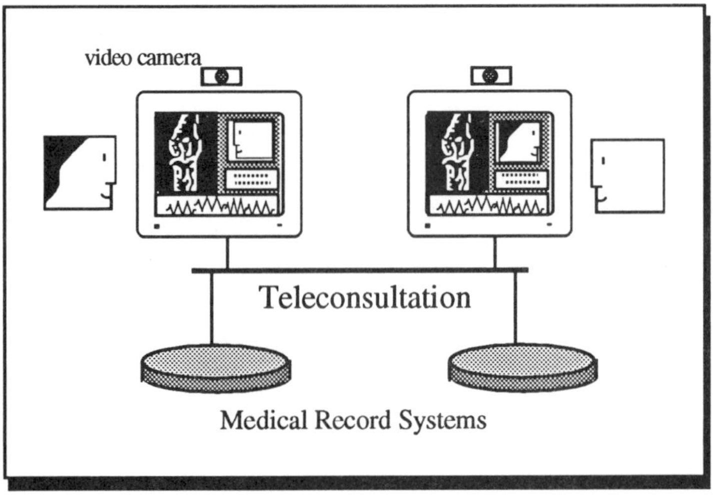

15

Reviving Education

Education is discussed in this last chapter because it is perhaps the most important link to our future. If the loss of job security, the fear for crime, and the spiraling cost of health care are society's open wounds, then the failure of our educational system would be a cancer that is killing it silently. While opinions on a prognosis vary, there is little dispute that the symptoms are worrisome. Raging indictments are plentiful. The National Commission on Excellence in Education published *A Nation at Risk* in 1983, a report that decried the state of American education as "an act of unthinking, unilateral educational disarmament." Myron Lieberman's *Public Education: an autopsy*; Lewis Perelman's *School's Out*; William Kilpatrick's *Why Johnny Can't Tell Right from Wrong*; Robert Tripp's *The Game of School*; Thomas Sowell's *Inside American Education: the decline, the deception, the dogmas*; and most recently, William Brock's panel report on *An American Imperative: higher expectations for higher education*—all expounded on the ills of the system. One would be hard pressed to find an apologist with nearly as much conviction. Financial woes are often cited as the culprit. However, a closer examination will show the root cause to be the fact that our way of teaching and learning never emerged from the Industrial Age. Without fundamental changes, no amount of financial infusion can extricate our educational system from its model of mass production based on the factories of the nineteenth century. Unlike business and industry, which are market driven, public education provided by government has a much harder time evolving with the times.

275

SCHOOL AS FACTORY

In the early factories, as well as subsequent industrial organizations through the Financial Age, management was from
the top down, and work was regimentally standardized and
supervised. There are exact parallels, as shown in Figure
15.1, in the two major factors in education: teaching and

Figure 15.1   Remnants of the Industrial Age

learning. (The symbolism in the figure is accurate historically, though it may be perceived as sexist today.) In our
system, teaching is analogous to managing. It is the driving
force and controlling component. Meanwhile, learning is
analogous to work in the factories of yesterday. Just as the
latter was well defined and regulated by time and motion
studies, learning in school is rigidly programmed and
scheduled. Teachers are the gatekeepers of knowledge.
They stand and deliver. As we have shown throughout this

book, the nature of work in business and industry is going through significant changes. The customer focus implies that it is the actual work, rather than the management of its process, that adds value. Empowered workgroups can be more responsive and flexible to customer needs. This is made feasible by the liberation of professional knowledge with the help of IT. Layers of middle management whose main function has been to funnel information are now redundant. New-age managers serve more as facilitators than as bosses. Education must change in the same way, not just to copy business, but because the need for it to shift emphasis from teaching back to learning is even more important. In an environment of constant and dynamic change, no one set of skills or knowledge could be sufficient to last through the working life of any individual in the future. One must be prepared for lifelong learning. The critical skill is then knowing how to learn. As workgroups of all different shapes and constitutions become the basic units for the creation of economic value, teamwork will outweigh individual achievement. Unfortunately, this is neither what we teach nor how we teach in our educational system, which was designed for a bygone era. The inadequacy of learning by rote and test-based credentials is becoming apparent as society's need shifted to knowledge workers and problem solvers capable of managing change. Still, we plod on stubbornly and complacently even though business leaders have remarked repeatedly that at best, our system is training the new generation for jobs that are no longer there. This is a clue that patchwork reforms, such as those aimed only at raising test scores, are missing the point. Can we count on educators to orchestrate a new theme? Not likely any time soon. Without market forces, what incentive is there for providers to change the tune?

WHAT DO CUSTOMERS HAVE TO SAY?

There are three different sets of customers of public education: students, parents, and employers. The students are in a peculiar situation. While they are "consumers" of education, they are also its product. The extent to which they should shape that product is a delicate balance. If none, they lose all prerogatives of a customer. If full, they become a self-shaping product. As it stands, this issue is of less concern in kindergarten through 12th grade (K-12), but has become significant in higher education.

Next, the parents are customers of the government that provides education as a public service. Since government is both the provider and arbiter of the merit of the product, the effectiveness of this second group of cus-

Figure 15.2   The Customers of Public Education

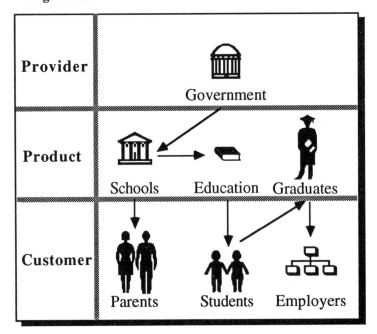

tomers in exerting market forces is limited. Moreover, only around 25% of American households are headed by parents with school-age children.

Finally, there are the employers who are the ultimate customers of the product of education: an educated work force. For them, market forces are real and unforgiving. As a result, they do speak up and vote with their actions. For example, until protectionist legislature clamped down on the practice, a large number of high-skill, high-pay jobs, especially in the technical fields of science and engineering, went to foreign students who graduated from American universities. While it is very much the American spirit that offers the opportunity for those who seek, the law of supply and demand was the true driving force behind this particular scenario. In recent years, U.S. employers have been spending upward of $30 billion annually on employee training. Apart from specific job skills, the significant need for training in "personal skills"—a euphemism for basic ability in speaking, reading, and writing—reflects poorly on our schools. The system is doomed if it turns a deaf ear to this group of customers. Corporate America has the incentive, resources as well as political clout to make a difference. Indeed, academic-corporate partnerships are in place for almost half the public schools in the country. While most are no more than routine arrangements for public relations, many islands of innovation can be identified. In any case, the impact so far has at best been localized and contingent on the continuing largess of the private sector.

Can the market system itself produce better schools? Some entrepreneurial pioneers think so, even though the issue is contentious politically. The Edison Project, a $2.5 billion plan to develop a national chain of 200 for-profit schools by 1996, was announced in May 1991 by Christopher Whittle, CEO of Whittle Communications. The significance of this venture is twofold. By starting from a clean slate, the project is clearly aimed to define education in the Information Age. Also, by budgeting costs to be no higher than those of public schools, the project is challenging the entire educational system to subject itself to the true test of the market and its customer focus. Whatever the outcome, it represents a bold vision—as opposed to myopic tinkering that is bound to be more costly and less effective in the long run.

LEARNING WITH TECHNOLOGY

In the top-down approach to education, the emphasis is naturally on teaching. As gatekeepers of knowledge, teachers hold the key to learning. The quality of learning is then necessarily geared toward the individual characteristics such as intellect, style, experience, commitment, and even charisma of the teacher. The analogy is the introduction to a foreign land through a travelogue. One's imagination is largely determined by how well the story is told. It is molded by what is in the script, which is usually in the form of a textbook. The traditional environment for learning in school is depicted in Figure 15.3. By contrast, IT has led to the liberation of knowledge. Learning with the help of IT is analogous to real travel. The perception of sights, sounds, and cultural encounter is individualized by the traveler. The role of the teacher becomes more like that of a guide. Textbooks are inadequate as the sole vehicle of knowledge not because they are printed on paper by a venerable technology, but because they cannot be individualized according to the needs of different learners. Using the

Figure 15.3 Yesterday's Learning Environment

Teacher
Textbook
Students

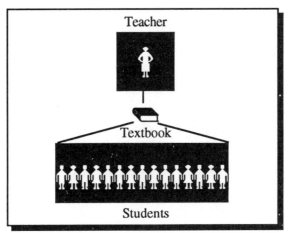

information superhighway, practically all of human knowledge can be accessed in multimedia. Special educational software tools allow individual students, with the guidance

Figure 15.4 Tomorrow's Learning Environment

Teacher as Mentor & Guide
Multimedia Link to Information Superhighway
Individualized Courseware
Workgroups for Cooperative Learning

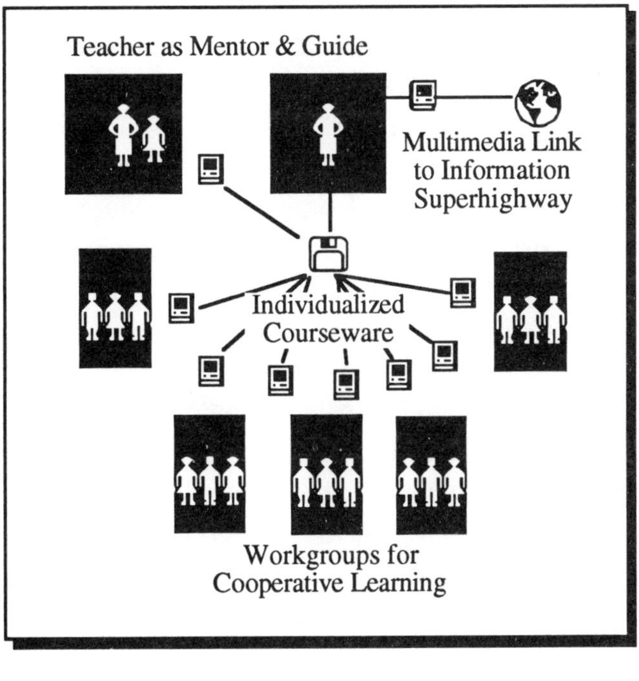

of teachers, to customize their own interactive courseware. This is the packaging of learning material endowed with advanced IT, probably based on fuzzy logic, neural networks and solution technology, that can closely monitor a student's work patterns. By detecting weaknesses and building on strengths, such self-adaptive courseware can anticipate the student's needs as learning progresses. Apart from self-paced sessions, students team up as workgroups to explore cooperative learning. They share the joy of discovery, and the delight to enlighten; they enjoy the power of pooling creative resources. This shift of emphasis from teaching to learning is critical to a B.I.O. Rhythmic approach to education (Figure 15.4). Without this improvement in how things get done—the O-step—putting IT in the classroom can only turn it into a videogame parlor.

TEACHING WITH TECHNOLOGY

There are two prerequisites to effective learning in the Information Age. The obvious one is IT. Annual spending on public schools is at the level of $300 billion. Yet, even in 1994, less than 0.67% is going into educational IT. With constantly lowering costs of hardware and stepped up contributions from a suitably motivated business sector, the outlook for gearing up the schools should improve. More critically, we must have teachers who are B.I.O. savvy. They have to recognize the liberating effect of IT and welcome their own changing role in matching technology to student needs that have long been overlooked. As we have seen, this is the same mind-set that people in any other profession will need to prosper in the workplace of tomorrow. It is all part of a culture of B.I.O. Rhythm. Particularly, the future of education will depend on whether teachers perceive themselves as adaptable knowledge workers, or simply as union labor of an industrial era.

PART OF A SOLUTION

It is important to distinguish between teaching with technology and the teaching of technology. Largely owing to the myth of computer programming that we tried to debunk in Chapter 1, there is a tendency to confound the two. This can lead to the belief that the introduction of IT in the classroom will accelerate society's transformation into a technocracy, with a corresponding erosion of humanism. It does not have to be so. It all depends on a balance between what we teach and how we teach. By enhancing learning in general, IT does not preclude the teaching of any particular principles. We must realize that, unless programmed otherwise, IT is by itself value-free. The ques-

Figure 15.5   Battle of Conflicting Dogmas

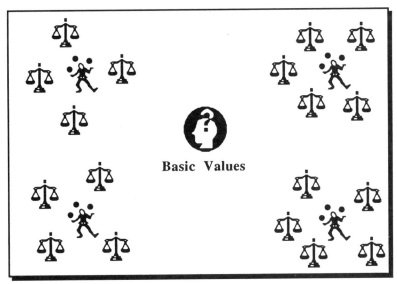

Basic Values

tions are then whether and which values should be taught. In the past, the answer seemed more straightforward, with values as wholesome as motherhood and apple pie. However, the contemporary preponderance of multiculturalism and political correctness is tipping the balance. Although cultures are presumably free of dogmas, what we are witnessing is no less than a power struggle among conflicting dogmas. This is illustrated in Figure 15.5. Our failure to face the tough choices and share basic values is going to turn us into a value-free society. In layman's terms, this simply means that there is an excuse for everything. The only way to survive in such a society is for everyone to retreat and cocoon into his or her special interests and beliefs. Unfortunately, IT can become a silent accomplice in this regression of civilization. With bandwidths that can accommodate thousands of channels of multimedia, and the unlimited capability to manipulate information, IT will be able to support "artificial truth" long before it finds artificial intelligence. This way, every dogma can be held as uncontested truth in its own domain in cyberspace. Can we prosper in such a virtual reality? I doubt it. If you agree, then we must not abandon our efforts to accept and maintain some basic values, and to see that they are taught to our children. In this sense, "B.I.O." can stand for the Basic Information and Operations of a society that can truly take advantage of technology to serve the needs of its people. The limit on resources and the randomness of their distribution mean that problems with conflicting human interests are always going to be with us. By nurturing the awareness of what should be done and how technology can help, the culture of B.I.O. Rhythm can empower all of us to be part of a solution. That is our best hope for prosperity in the Information Age.

Bibliography

PART I: Debunking the Myths

Allen, Thomas J. and Michael S. Scott Morton (eds.), *Information Technology and the Corporations of the 1990s: Research studies*. New York: Oxford University Press, 1994.

Arndt, Michael, "Rail workers feeling efficiency's sting." *Chicago Tribune*, February 27, 1994.

Baumol, William J., Sue Anne Batey Blackman and Edward N. Wolff, *Productivity and American Leadership: The long view*. Cambridge, MA: MIT Press, 1989.

Brynjolfsson, Erik and Lorin Hitt, "Is information systems spending productive? — New evidence and new results." *Proceedings of the International Conference on Information Systems*, Orlando, FL (December 1993): 47-63.

Dobrzynski, Judith H., "Relationship investing." *Business Week*, March 15, 1993.

Eames, Charles and Ray, *A Computer Perspective: Background to the computer age*. Cambridge, MA: Harvard University Press, 1990.

Eisner, Robert, *The Misunderstood Economy: What counts and how to count it*. Boston: Harvard Business School Press, 1994.

Gleckman, Howard, "The technology payoff." *Business Week*, June 14, 1993.

Larson, Richard W. and David J. Zimney, *The White-Collar Shuffle: Who does what in today's computerized workplace*. New York: AMACOM, 1990.

Lawlor, Julia, "Busters have work ethic all their own." *USA TODAY*, July 20, 1993.

Lee, Leonard, *The Day the Phones Stopped: The computer crises—the what and why of it, and how we can beat it*. New York: Donald I. Fine, 1991.

Levinson, Marc, "Can anyone spare a job? — why the world's jobless woes are getting worse." *Newsweek*, June 14, 1993.

Lewyn, Mark, "The information age isn't just for the elite." *Business Week*, January 10, 1994.

Longworth, R.C., "Job fears haunt growing economy: workers pay price of recovery." *Chicago Tribune*, January 2, 1994.

Maclean, John N., "Information highway traffic building." *Chicago Tribune*, November 12, 1993.

Makino, Noboru, *Decline and Prosperity: Corporate innovation in Japan*. Tokyo: Kodansha International, 1987.

Mandel, Michael J., "Jobs, jobs, jobs." *Business Week*, February 22, 1993.

Maney, Kevin, "A new superhighway: fiber optics to break open the data bank." *USA TODAY*, February 19, 1993.

Mateja, Jim, "Mustang galloped in: and the rest is history." *Chicago Tribune*, October 3, 1993.

Minkin, Barry H., *Econo-Quake: How to survive and prosper in the coming global depression*. Englewood Cliffs, NJ: Prentice Hall, 1993.

Newman, Katherine S., *Falling from Grace: The experience of downward mobility in the American middle class*. New York: The Free Press, 1988.

_____ , *Declining Fortunes: the withering of the American dream*. New York: BasicBooks, 1993.

Noble, David F., *Forces of Production: a social history of industrial automation*. New York: Alfred A. Knopf, 1984.

Panko, Raymond R., "Is office productivity stagnant?" *MIS Quarterly* (June 1991): 191-203.

Prokesch, Steven, "Service jobs fall as business gains: automation's impact shrinks employment in New York." *The New York Times*, April 18, 1993.

Ritchie, David, *The Computer Pioneers: The making of the modern computer*. New York: Simon & Schuster, 1986.

Roach, Steven S., in *Economic Perspective*. New York: Morgan Stanley & Co., July 1988 and January 1991.

_____ , "Services under siege: the restructuring imperative." *Harvard Business Review* (September/October 1991): 82-91.

Scott Morton, Michael S. (Ed.), *The Corporation of the 1990's: Information technology and organizational transformation*. New York: Oxford University Press, 1991.

Strassmann, Paul A., *Information Payoff: The transformation of work in the electronic age*. New York: The Free Press, 1985.

_____ , *The Business Value of Computers: An executive's guide*. New Canaan, CT: Information Economics Press, 1990.

Thurow, Lester C., *Head to Head: The coming economic battle among Japan, Europe, and America*. New York: William Morrow & Co., 1992.

Uchitelle, Louis (New York Times Service), "How Uncle Sam fumbled the job count—twice." *International Herald Tribune*, May 8-9, 1993.

Weizer, Norman et al., *The Arthur D. Little Forecast on Information Technology and Productivity: Making the integrated enterprise work*. New York: John Wiley & Sons, 1991.

Williams, Frederick, *The New Telecommunications: Infrastructure for the information age*. New York: The Free Press, 1991.

Wriston, Walter B., *The Twilight of Sovereignty: How the information revolution is transforming our world*. New York: Scribner's Sons/Macmillan, 1992.

Zinn, Laura, "Move over boomers." *Business Week*, December 14, 1992.

PART II: A New Driving Force

Barker, Joel A., *Future Edge: Discovering the new paradigms of success*. New York: William Morrow & Co., 1992.

Beer, Stafford, *Brain of the Firm: The managerial cybernetics of organization*. Chischester, UK: John Wiley & Sons, 1981.

Blasi, Joseph R. and Douglas L. Kruse, *The New Owners: The mass emergence of employee ownership in public companies and what it means to American business*. New York: HarperBusiness, 1991.

Bluestone, Barry and Irving Bluestone, *Negotiating the Future: A labor perspective on American business*. New York: BasicBooks, 1992.

Boyett, Joseph H. and Henry P. Conn, *Workplace 2000: The revolution reshaping American business*. New York: Plume, 1991.

Byrne, John A., *The Whiz Kids: Ten founding fathers of American business; and the legacy they left us*. New York: Doubleday, 1993.

_____ , "The virtual corporation." *Business Week*, February 8, 1993.

_____ , "The horizontal corporation." *Business Week*, December 20, 1993.

Calem, Robert E., "Working at home, for better or worse." *The New York Times*, April 18, 1993.

Cetron, Marvin and Owen Davies, *American Renaissance: Our life at the turn of the 21st century*. New York: St. Martin's Press, 1989.

Church, George J., "Jobs in an age of insecurity." *Time*, November 22, 1993.

Crawford, Richard, *In the Era of Human Capital: The emergence of talent, intelligence, and knowledge as the worldwide economic force and what it means to managers and investors.* New York: HarperBusiness, 1991.

Davidow, William H. and Michael S. Malone, *The Virtual Corporation: Structuring and revitalizing the corporation for the 21st century.* New York: Harper Business, 1992.

Davis, Stan and Bill Davidson, *2020 Vision: Transform your business today to succeed in tomorrow's economy.* New York: Simon & Schuster, 1991.

Eccles, R.G., "The performance measurement manifesto," *Harvard Business Review* (January/February 1991): 131-137.

Farrell, Larry C., *Searching for the Spirit of Enterprise: Dismantling the twentieth-century corporation—lessons from Asian, European, and American entrepreneurs.* New York: Dutton, 1993.

Galen, Michele, "Work and family." *Business Week*, June 28, 1993.

Garson, Barbara, *Electronic Workshop: How computers are transforming the office of the future into the factory of the past.* New York: Simon & Schuster, 1988.

Hackman, J. Richard (ed.), *Groups that Work (and those that don't): Creating conditions for effective teamwork.* San Francisco: Jossey-Bass, 1990.

Handy, Charles, *The Age of Unreason.* Boston: Harvard Business School Press, 1990.

_____ , *The Age of Paradox.* Boston: Harvard Business School Press, 1994.

Jacobs, Michael T., *Short-Term America: The causes and cures of our business myopia.* Boston: Harvard Business School Press, 1991.

Johnson, H. Thomas, *Relevance Regained: From top-down control to bottom-up empowerment.* New York: The Free Press, 1992.

Johnston, William B. and Arnold H. Packer, *Workforce 2000: Work and workers for the 21st century.* The Hudson Institute, 1987.

Katzenbach, Jon R. and Douglas K. Smith, *The Wisdom of Teams: Creating the high-performance organization.* Boston: Harvard Business School Press, 1993.

Kilborn, Peter T., "Wanted: those high-tech jobs for retrained workers." *The New York Times*, February 21, 1993.

Kuttner, Robert, "Talking marriage and thinking one-night stand." *Business Week*, October 18, 1993.

Levering, Robert, *A Great Place to Work: What makes some employers so good (and most so bad).* New York: Random House, 1988.

Levinson, Marc, "Playing with fire: empower workers? A small-town firm finds it tougher than it sounds." *Newsweek*, June 21, 1993.

Mathews, Jay, "The cost of quality." *Newsweek*, September 7, 1992.

McDermott, Lynda C., *Caught in the Middle: How to survive and thrive in today's management squeeze.* Englewood Cliffs, NJ: Prentice Hall, 1992.

Memmott, Mark, "Working in the '90s: the steady stream of job cuts." *USA TODAY*, October 20, 1993.

Murray, Chuck, "Robots roll from plant to kitchen." *Chicago Tribune*, October 17, 1993.

Neikirk, William, "Starting over—series of six articles on the fundamental restructuring of jobs, industry and institutions in post-Cold War America." *Chicago Tribune*, February 21-28, 1993.

Ohmae, Kenichi, *The Borderless World: Power and strategy in the interlinked economy.* New York: HarperBusiness, 1990.

Peters, Tom, *Liberation Management: Necessary disorganization for the nanosecond nineties.* New York: Alfred A. Knopf, 1992.

Primozic, Kenneth, Edward Primozic, and Joe Leben, *Strategic Choices: Supremacy, survival, or sayonara.* New York: McGraw-Hill, 1991.

Ray, Michael and Alan Rinzler (eds.), *The New Paradigm in Business: Emerging strategies for leadership and organizational change.* New York: J.P. Tarcher/Perigee, 1993.

Reich, Robert B., "Clinton's new jobs plan." *USA TODAY*, March 1, 1994.

Saltzman, Amy, *Down-Shifting: Reinventing success on a slower track.* New York: HarperCollins, 1991.

Simon, Paul, Senator, D-Ill., "Violence on TV." *USA TODAY*, October 19, 1993.

Stern, Aimee L., "Managing by team is not always as easy as it looks." *The New York Times*, July 18, 1993.

Tomasko, Robert M., *Downsizing: Reshaping the corporation of the future.* New York: AMACOM, 1987.

Wendt, Henry, *Global Embrace: Corporate challenges in a transnational world.* New York: HarperBusiness, 1993.

Wexley, Kenneth N. and Stanley B. Silverman, *Working Scared.* San Francisco: Jossey-Bass, 1993.

Womack, James P., Daniel T. Jones, and Daniel Roos, *The Machine that Changed the World.* New York: Rawson/Macmillan, 1990.

Yates, Ronald E., "Downsizing's bitter pill: CEOs plead survival, and workers cry betrayal as trust and commitment fade." *Chicago*

Tribune Magazine, November 21, 1993.

Zuboff, Shoshanna, *In the Age of the Smart Machine: The future of work and power*. New York: BasicBooks, 1988.

PART III: B.I.O. Rhythm—A Key to Prosperity for Workgroups of Tomorrow

Allman, William F., *Apprentices of Wonder: Inside the neural network revolution*. New York: Bantam Books, 1989.

Anthes, Gary H., "U.S. Post Office puts address changes on-line." *Computerworld*, December 21, 1992.

———— , "PC-based postal kiosk axed." *Computerworld*, October 4, 1993.

Bailin, Rebecca A., "What top executives don't know can hurt you." *Computerworld*, November 22, 1993.

Bermar, Amy, "TQM: CIOs are learning some hard lessons on the road to total quality management." *Computerworld*, November 1, 1993.

Cafasso, Rosemary, "Jean genies." *Computerworld*, June 14, 1993.

———— , "Rethinking reengineering." *Computerworld*, March 15, 1993.

Chaum, David, "Achieving electronic privacy." *Scientific American* (August 1992): 96-101.

Crawford, William B., Jr., "Globex system at turning point." *Chicago Tribune*, March 28, 1994.

Creech, William L., *The Five Pillars of TQM: How to make total quality management work for you*. New York: Truman Talley/ Dutton, 1994.

Crevier, Daniel, *AI: The tumultuous history of the search for artificial intelligence*. New York: BasicBooks, 1993.

Davenport, Thomas H., *Process Innovation: Reengineering work through information technology*. Boston: Harvard Business School Press, 1993.

De Jager, Peter, "Doomsday." *Computerworld*, September 6, 1993.

De Silva, D. Richard, "A confederacy of glitches." *Newsweek*, September 21, 1992.

Dyson, Esther, "The content challenge." *Computerworld*, August 2, 1993.

Elmer-Dewitt, Philip, "Who should keep the keys?" *Time*, March 14, 1994.

Gilder, George, *Microcosm: A prescient look inside the expanding universe of economic, social, and technological possibilities within the world of the silicon chip.* New York: Touchstone/Simon & Schuster, 1989.

Hammer, Michael and James Champy, *Reengineering the Corporation: A manifesto for business revolution.* New York: HarperBusiness, 1993.

Hoffman, Gerald M., *The Technology Payoff: How to profit with empowered workers in the Information Age.* Burr Ridge, IL: Irwin, 1994.

Hopper, Max D., "CIOs: time to move on or move out," *Computerworld*, July 12, 1993.

James, Barry, "Why this computerized chaos?" *International Herald Tribune*, July 14, 1993.

Johnson, Maryfran, "GIS popularity growing." *Computerworld*, March 22, 1993.

Jubak, Jim, *In the Image of the Brain: Breaking the barrier between the human mind and intelligent machines.* Boston: Little, Brown & Co., 1992.

Kallman, Ernest A. and Sanford Sherizen, "Private matters." *Computerworld*, November 23, 1992.

Keen, Peter G.W., *Shaping the Future: Business design through information technology.* Boston: Harvard Business School Press, 1991.

Khoshafian, Setrag, A. Brad Baker, Razmik Abnous, and Kevin Shepherd, *Intelligent Offices: Object-oriented multi-media information management in client/server architectures.* New York: John Wiley & Sons, 1992.

King, Julia, "Quality conscious." *Computerworld*, July 19, 1993.

Kosko, Bart, *Fuzzy Thinking: The new science of fuzzy logic.* New York: Hyperion, 1993.

Lucky, Robert W., *Silicon Dreams: Information, man, and machine.* New York: St. Martin's Press, 1989.

Margolis, Nell, "N.Y. Life moves back to the future." *Computerworld*, February 24, 1992.

_____ , "Imaging: It's a jungle in there." *Computerworld*, July 6, 1992.

Markoff, John, "Keeping things safe and orderly in the neighborhoods of cyberspace." *The New York Times*, October 24, 1993.

McNeill, Daniel and Paul Freiberger, *Fuzzy Logic: The discovery of a revolutionary computer technology; and how it is changing our world.* New York: Simon & Schuster, 1993.

Meyer, Christopher, *Fast Cycle Time: How to align purpose, strategy and structure for speed.* New York: The Free Press, 1993.

Naisbitt, John and Patricia Aburdene, *Reinventing the Corporation: Transforming your job and your company for the new information society.* New York: Warner Books, 1985.

Neikirk, William, "Worries about privacy arising as insurance goes electronic." *Chicago Tribune*, November 15, 1993.

Quarterman, John S., "What can business get out of the Internet." *Computerworld*, February 22, 1993.

Quinn, James Brian, *Intelligent Enterprise: A knowledge and service-based paradigm for industry.* New York: The Free Press, 1992.

Radding, Alan, "Groupware." *Computerworld*, December 13, 1993.

Radosevich, Lynda, "When overnight isn't good enough." *Computerworld*, May 31, 1993.

Ramstad, Evan, (Associated Press) "Computers keep Federal Express soaring." *San Francisco Examiner,* January 23, 1994.

Schrage, Michael, "Trying groupware on for (down)size." *Computerworld*, August 30, 1993.

Schwartz, Evan I., "Software valets that will do your bidding in cyberspace." *The New York Times*, January 9, 1994.

Senge, Peter M., *The Fifth Discipline: The art and practice of the learning organization.* New York: Double Day/Currency, 1990.

Tamarkin, Bob, *The MERC: The emergence of a global financial powerhouse.* New York: HarperBusiness, 1993.

Tapscott, Don and Art Gaston, *Paradigm Shift: The new promise of information technology.* New York: MaGraw-Hill, 1993.

Verity, John W., "Getting work to go with the flow." *Business Week*, June 21, 1993.

Wood, Lamont, "Office futz factor is a threat to PC productivity gains." *Chicago Tribune*, October 3, 1993.

Zellner, Wendy, "Portrait of a project as a total disaster." *Buiness Week*, January 17, 1994.

PART IV: Beyond Business—A New Culture

Armstrong, Larry, "The learning revolution: technology is reshaping education—at home and at school." *Business Week*, February 28, 1994.

Beach, Gary J., "Help upgrade the U.S. educational system." *Computerworld*, August 9, 1993.

Betts, Mitch, "Hospital proves IS can help cut health care costs." *Computerworld*, February 15, 1993.

_____, "States redefining public service." *Computerworld*, April 19,

1993.

Bogdanich, Walt, *The Great White Lie: How America's hospitals betray our trust and endanger our lives.* New York: Simon & Schuster, 1991.

Bowcott, Owen and Sally Hamilton, *Beating the System: Hackers, phreakers and electronic spies.* London: Bloomsbury, 1990.

Brimelow, Peter, "Are universities necessary?" *Forbes,* April 26, 1993.

Brock, William E. et al, *An American Imperative: Higher expectations for higher education.* Racine, WI: The Johnson Foundation, 1993.

Brody, Sam, "We have lost our humanity: a doctor ponders the effect of greed and technology on medicine." *Newsweek,* September 7, 1992.

de Lama, George, "Citizens plugging into computer government." *Chicago Tribune,* November 14, 1993.

Eckholm, Erik (ed.) and the Staff of the New York Times, *Solving America's Health-Care Crisis: A guide to understanding the greatest threat to your family's economic security.* New York: Times Books, 1993.

Education Today: Connecting—Computer age allows schools to become links in chain of information. *Chicago Tribune,* April 25, 1993.

Fox, Daniel M., *Power and Illness: The failure and future of American health policy.* Berkeley, CA: University of California Press, 1993.

Gifford, Bernard R., "The future of technology in education: transforming the way we learn." *Business Week,* November 15, 1993.

Gore, Al, Vice President, *The Gore Report on Reinventing Government: Creating a government that works better and costs less.* New York: Times Books, 1993.

Halvorson, George C., *Strong Medicine.* New York: Random House, 1993.

Hammonds, Keith H., "The hospital: an inside look at how one institution is struggling to remake itself." *Business Week,* January 17, 1994.

Henry, Tamara, "Computers serve as equalizers in schools." *USA TODAY,* December 15, 1993.

Jesilow, Paul, Henry N. Pontell, and Gilbert Geis, *Prescription for Profit: How doctors defraud Medicaid.* Berkeley, CA: University of California Press, 1993.

Johnson, Haynes, *Divided We Fall: Gambling with history in the nineties.* New York: W.W. Norton & Co., 1994.

Kilpatrick, William, *Why Johnny Can't Tell Right from Wrong: Moral illiteracy and the case for character education.* New York: Simon & Schuster, 1992.

Konner, Melvin, *Medicine at the Crossroads: The crisis in health care.* New York: Pantheon Books, 1993.

Lieberman, Myron, *Public Education: An autopsy,* Cambridge, MA: Harvard University Press, 1993.

Locin, Mitchell, "Imagine, a friendly, efficient bureaucracy." *Chicago Tribune,* June 27, 1993.

Mandel, Michael J. and Paul Magnusson, "The economics of crime." *Business Week,* December 13, 1993.

Mungo, Paul and Bryan Clough, *Approaching Zero: The extraordinary underworld of hackers, phreakers, virus writers, and keyboard criminals.* New York: Random House, 1992.

National Commission on Excellence in Education, *A Nation at Risk: The imperative for educational reform.* U.S. Department of Education, 1983.

Osborne, David and Ted Gaebler, *Reinventing Government: How the entrepreneurial spirit is transforming the public sector.* Reading, MA: Addison-Wesley, 1992.

Papert, Seymour, *The Children's Machine: Rethinking school in the age of the computer.* New York: BasicBooks, 1993.

Perelman, Lewis J., *School's Out: Hyperlearning, the new technology, and the end of education.* New York: William Morrow & Co., 1992.

Rifkin, Glenn, "New momentum for electronic patient records." *The New York Times,* May 2, 1993.

Rodwin, Marc A., *Medicine, Money, and Morals: Physicians' conflicts of interest.* New York: Oxford University Press, 1993.

Segal, Troy, "Saving our schools." *Business Week,* September 14, 1992.

Sowell, Thomas, *Inside American Education: The decline, the deception, the dogmas.* New York: The Free Press, 1993.

Toffler, Alvin, *Power Shift: Knowledge, wealth, and violence at the edge of the 21st century.* New York: Bantam Books, 1990.

Tripp, Robert L., *The Game of School: Observations of a long-haul teacher.* Reston, VA: Extended Vision Press, 1993.

Wachsman, Harvey F., *Lethal Medicine: The epidemic of medical malpractice in America.* New York: Henry Holt & Co., 1993.

White House Domestic Policy Council, *Health Security: The President's report to the American people.* New York: Touchstone Books, 1993.

Index

Appendix A: B.I.O. Rhythm Network

This book propounds B.I.O. Rhythm as a key to prosperity in the Information Age. Readers who are interested in following the development of this mind-set as a viable culture—both within the business environment and society at large—may wish to share further ideas, opinions, and experience. Please use the form on the next page to get on such a network. Depending on reader response, some appropriate medium, such as a newsletter or an electronic newsgroup, may be established to facilitate future exchange of information on this topic.

READER'S RESPONSE
TO
PROSPERITY IN THE INFORMATION AGE

☐ **B.I.O. Rhythm may indeed be useful for myself and my organization.**

☐ **I am interested in being posted on its future development.** Preferred medium: Print __ Electronic __

☐ **I may wish to contribute ideas, opinions, and first-hand experience.**

NAME: _____

TITLE: _____

ORGANIZATION: _____

NATURE OF BUSINESS: _____

ADDRESS: _____

_____

_____

PHONE: _____

FAX: _____

E-MAIL: _____

COMMENTS:

Permission to quote? ____ Signature: _____

Please return to J.K. Ho
c/o Infotomics, P. O. Box 8028, Wilmette, IL 60091
This form may be copied for its stated purpose.

Appendix B: Using this Book for Human Resource Development

Prosperity in the Information Age by J.K. Ho is distributed directly by the publisher. Information on bulk order and volume discount is given on the next page. Inquiries on adaptation of the material to suit specific organizational needs in human resource development are also welcome.

ORDER FORM
for
PROSPERITY IN THE INFORMATION AGE by J.K. Ho

Single copy $25.00 postpaid*

Volume Discount: Unit Price
5   - 9 $20.00
10   - 99 $18.00
100 - 999 $16.00
1000 - and more $14.00
                                   Plus 10% Shipping/Handling

Quantity	Amount

Plus 10% Shipping/Handling for Volume Orders _____
Illinois residents please add 8.5% sales tax _____

TOTAL: [   ]

Method of Payment:

☐ Check/Money Order (drawn on U.S. Funds only)

☐ VISA ☐ Mastercard   Name _____

Acct. # _____ Exp. Date _____

Signature _____

☐ Purchase Order # _____

Ship to:

NAME: _____
TITLE: _____
ORGANIZATION: _____
ADDRESS: _____
_____
_____

PHONE: _____
FAX: _____
E-MAIL: _____

[*U.S. only. $32.00 Foreign]

Please send order and payment to:
Infotomics, Inc., P. O. Box 8028, Wilmette, IL 60091
Phone/Fax (708) 251-6976

This form may be copied for its stated purpose. Prices subject to change without notice.

About the Author

James K. Ho is Professor and former Head of Information and Decision Sciences at the University of Illinois at Chicago, where he also serves as Director of Applied Research and Consulting Services for the College of Business Administration. He did his undergraduate work at Columbia University and obtained his Ph.D from Stanford University. Dr. Ho has published widely in professional journals and authored two previous books on software design and solution technology. He has extensive experience working with international organizations, major corporations as well as small businesses. *Prosperity in the Information Age* is the culmination of over two decades' insight into the application of information technology in the workplace.